OPEN SYSTEMS HANDBOOK

SECOND EDITION

ALAN R. SIMON / TOM WHEELER

OPEN SYSTEMS HANDBOOK

SECOND EDITION

ALAN R. SIMON / TOM WHEELER

AP PROFESSIONAL

Boston San Diego New York
London Sydney Tokyo Toronto

This book is printed on acid-free paper. ∞

AP PROFESSIONAL
955 Massachusetts Avenue, Cambridge, MA 02139

An Imprint of ACADEMIC PRESS, INC.
A Division of HARCOURT BRACE & COMPANY

United Kingdom Edition published by
ACADEMIC PRESS LIMITED
24–28 Oval Road, London NW1 7DX

ISBN 0-12-643870-6

Printed in the United States of America
94 95 96 97 98 IP 9 8 7 6 5 4 3 2 1

Contents

Preface

This second edition of *The Open Systems Handbook* builds on the work done for the original version by the late Tom Wheeler. To the greatest extent possible, I have tried to keep the form and content of his work intact, since that earlier volume was a landmark in taking open systems out of the worlds of marketing hype and "techno-babble" and providing an easy-to-read, thorough, management-oriented explanation of the promises, dangers, and realities of this important trend in information systems. The original edition was a companion volume to my own books *Enterprise Computing* and *Implementing the Enterprise.* Those two works have been combined into a single book—*Network Re-engineering: Foundations of Enterprise Computing,* which complements the managerial slant of this work with further discussion of how the various open systems technologies can be used to build a modern organizational communications infrastructure.

Where necessary, I have updated material that has changed significantly since the original edition was written in 1991. References to specific products and the various open systems consortia have been updated to reflect the events of the mid-1990s. Discussion of emerging open technologies that either didn't exist in 1991 or were in their infancy, such as client/server middleware, has also been added.

The timelessness of most of the material, though—particularly that dealing with architectural and managerial issues—is indicative of the foresight that Tom had with respect to computing in general and open systems in particular. With that, I pay tribute to him.

—Alan Simon
June 1994

1

Open Systems Computing

1.1 INTRODUCTION

Management of information technology (IT) represents a unique challenge to U.S. corporations, which spend over 50 percent of their new capital investments on IT (Kriebel, 1989). It is increasingly evident that the effective use of information technology is a major ingredient of a competitive company in the 1990s and has replaced traditional success factors in defining a competitive, well-leveraged company. Information technology is defined to consist of hardware, software, networks, workstations, robotics, and smart chips (Morton, 1991).

In its brief history, computing technology has passed through three major waves and is entering a fourth. Each wave changed the organization and culture as well as the uses of technology (Berstein, 1989). The companies that followed the advances were able to provide additional computational power at a continual reduction in prices. This increased power and reduced prices have helped to make the fourth wave of network computing a reality. This wave utilizes powerful desktop computers connected to servers on networks to create a new focal point of computing and spawn a new culture to manage it.

While computing has been changing, the business environment has also been shifting from an economy dominated by the United States to one in which there is global competition (Dertouzos et al., 1989). Windows of economic opportunity to introduce and succeed with very short product cycles can only be met by applying technology to the implementation of these products. Technology can also reduce the expected shelf life of products, as alternatives are brought to market more rapidly. Reverse-engineering is accelerated through technology assessments, which enable copies to be produced in a fraction of the time of the original product. Companies must learn to meet their competition with processes that effectively use information technology.

Throughout the world, there has been a shift toward lower-skilled individuals performing tasks with the assistance of computers. Computers are performing a larger share of the difficult tasks while masking their presence through easier user interfaces. At the same time, computer power has been shifting from mainframe processing to networks, which include desktop computers and servers. Additional compute power can be applied to solve challenging problems or to simplify user interfaces and permit easier access to information.

Computer managers and computer professionals have experienced a rapidly changing environment over the past three decades. The introduction of personal computers (PCs) in the 1980s accelerated change and created an environment that encouraged individual creativity. More importantly, the PC represented a revolution in the way computers were applied. It created challenges for organizations to learn to use distributed desktop processing. Companies were increasingly faced with the need to respond rapidly, as technology was introduced at an accelerated pace.

The PC demonstrated its value by empowering individual workers with the ability to complete more of their jobs through local control. It also introduced an era of rapid deployment of ideas with relatively low capital overhead and little management involvement. Personal computers represented the first wave of open systems. Different hardware vendors could access the operating code and provide a framework for unique application programs. The wide acceptance of open systems will take the PC revolution a step further by providing increased performance on the desktop and access to network capability. Open systems also increase the complexity of managing large numbers of computers connected to a network.

The PC also dramatically altered response to development requirements. Small teams could create immediate answers to solutions. These same teams could implement model solutions in a fraction of the normal development cycles.

Open systems expand the inventiveness of PCs and carry it to another stage. It is the creative next step of the well-designed network of desktop computers interacting with servers. The new networks challenge management to understand the new realm of computing and introduce steps to manage it. Open systems provide the opportunity for processing to occur across multiple layers of computing but also create unique design problems, unknown in single data processing environments.

Examples of client/server architecture abound in other technical environments besides computing. A good example is the telephone, which provides end users with powerful instruments at their fingertips. The telephone has many services that depend upon either the local branch office or the long-distance operations. Calls in the United States are routed through long-distance systems, for which the end user pays only for services used. An alternative paradigm to the centralized telephone system would be individual phone companies with autonomous switching systems. Existing systems charge end users only for the specific services needed and achieve an economy of scale from sharing, which is beneficial for all users.

Enterprise networks combine the functions of servers on local area networks (LANs) with the services accessible across wide area networks (WANs). These combinations introduce client/servers on a local level while retaining central computing facilities. Controversy has surrounded open systems, as the natural tendency to protect proprietary turf has driven computer companies to offer proprietary alternatives to open architectures. Specific architectures ensure repeat business and increase the difficulty of installing multiple vendors. Specific architectures protect product dominance.

1.2 OPEN SYSTEMS: DEFINITIONS AND HISTORY

Open systems are those hardware and software implementations that conform to the body of standards that permit free and easy access to multiple vendor solutions. The body of standards may be formally defined or simply de facto definitions adhered to by major vendors and users within a technology sphere. An open system is the opposite of a proprietary or vendor-specific implementation.

The goal of open systems is to provide application portability, scalability, and interoperability through the use of approved standards. Both vendors and users benefit from the adoption of open systems. The user achieves a flexibility of choice and an ability to respond rapidly to development needs.

Vendors gain access to a wider user community and also reduce their development costs.

Cooperative processing is the body of definitions that permits sharing of functions and data between processors in solving a common problem. Cooperative applications assume a knowledge of the architecture and data in the processors.

Distributed processing is processing that occurs on autonomous boxes connected together through networks. Distributed processors may or may not function cooperatively. Distributed processing applications reside on multiple computers, each with autonomous processing and data services. Each component in a distributed environment owns a data and an execution environment, which may or may not be shared. In the simplest form, distributed processing supports remote logons. In the more complex distributed data environments, data and functions reside in different processors or have a separate processor available to handle segments of information. Distributed systems can be distinguished from replicated systems that simply use the same application at many sites. Replication means duplication of resources and data; distribution means each element of the network has a portion of the total job to complete.

Distributed open systems refer to distributed solutions that conform to the body of standards that permit free and easy access to applications and data residing on multiple platforms. Distributed solutions refer to combinations of both data and processing, which can be spread across multiple processors.

Control points refer to the point within a system at which the events are monitored, controlled, and tracked. Control points affect the interaction between different nodes in a system and can help determine a system integration strategy.

Traditionally, the choice of enterprise computers was a selection of a vendor-specific system design that locked the company on a single computer manufacturer or those that emulated the manufacturer's design. During the past decade, the growing acceptance of industry standards has enabled an open environment. Standard software is replacing vendor-specific applications, and open systems design is replacing manufacturers' system designs. This conversion to open systems permits companies to determine the best solution based on their technology needs—not simply because open systems has a certain identifying logo.

Software has been pivotal to the success of computer hardware, but software advances have trailed hardware. The quantity of backlogged programs exceeds the ability of most organizations to respond to specific and immediate needs. Large numbers of software specialists are engaged in maintaining existing programs. Schedules have caused problems for many experienced companies, as they have been unable to meet the requirements of the users.

Open systems were introduced to solve engineering and scientific problems but have been extended to commercial problems. As the power of the chips continued to improve, it became natural to move central processing to the desktop. Engineers modified computer-aided design programs to use workstations and PCs. High-speed devices with large storage capacity served as repositories for completed design libraries, while interactive use with the engineer shifted to the desktop. Simple calculations and design programs could be run on the desktop and other features could be requested from network processors.

Software development followed the example of engineering. Tools enabled programmers to shift their development environment directly to desktops, using larger processors as repositories for program libraries and higher-speed processing. As the power of the chips used in desktop computers continued to grow, additional functions were shifted to the desktop. This included simulation of larger processor environments so the testing could actually be performed locally.

Manufacturing also adopted open systems solutions in conjunction with engineering. Driven by industry giants such as General Motors, manufacturing firms pushed for an open design that could use the best equipment available. There was a general shift and demand for industry standards to facilitate the communications between central manufacturers and suppliers. General Motors led the effort to define the Manufacturing Automation Protocol (MAP) to connect manufacturing systems. Large machines serviced distributed workstations that could request needed functions. Although manufacturing management systems remained on central processors, modern manufacturing lines used workstations that were networked across broadband networks.

The commercial environment was the last to use open systems solutions. Initial open solutions represented cumbersome implementations that many commercial enterprises were ill-equipped to use. As tools became simpler and easier to use, there was a shift of office applications, such as accounting, finance, and human resources, to open solutions. Viable new products adopted user interfaces that could compete with PCs.

Executive support systems (ESS)—also known as *executive information systems* (EIS)—which were originally located on central processors, have been shifted to open systems implementations. In the past, information was prepared especially for the ESS programs; but today, advanced uses of management systems can be built on data collected through normal operations. Extraction techniques have accelerated the identification of important information by mining data from existing databases. This data can be summarized and made available to the executives. Mining can be used to extract other important data for market modeling or other production applications.

The heart of the open system is software, which has provided a framework that can be built on top of most hardware definitions. The general recognition of UNIX for a wider span of user applications has led to its acceptance by multiple vendors. This acceptance on various-size computers has accelerated the support for open systems. It took IBM's introduction of their version of UNIX, along with the success of Sun Microsystems in the workstation marketplace, to crystallize this movement. The model called for source code portability along with widespread acceptance of common application models.

UNIX has become widely accepted for use on servers and desktop computers. The initial system design focused on multiple users, but the system has been extended as well to single-user systems. Other operating environments for the desktops include Microsoft's MS-DOS and Microsoft Windows, Microsoft Windows NT, OS/2, and Apple's Macintosh operating system.

By the end of the 1980s, it was accepted by many that the network had become the computer. This simply means the connected power of multiple computers across communications links assumed tasks once allocated to single processors. As a result, communications software has grown in importance through the decade. Implementors adopted a layered protocol, which can be matched symmetrically in connecting processors. At the lowest kernel, layers are the primary elements of a classical operating system. At its higher layers, protocols connect to symmetrical applications on other nodes of the network.

The user finds data manipulation at the heart of the open system. As a result, data handling code is fundamental in defining any system. Simple access to data files across the network helps to make the network stronger and more comprehensive to all end users. Elaborate database code built on top of UNIX provides significant power to servers connected across a network. Executive information systems have adopted a paradigm, which enables them to build on existing client/server models.

The power of the desktop has opened a new era in using graphical user interfaces for the end user. Known as GUI, they are a powerful tool in the hands of professionals and managers alike. Open user interfaces reduce the use of text and increase the reliance on graphics. Though initial implementations were available in the late 1970s, it was the 1984 introduction of the Apple Macintosh and the subsequent widespread acceptance of Microsoft Windows (particularly version 3.0, which was much better received in the marketplace than Windows Version 1.0) that made GUI technology the default standard interface paradigm for the desktop. Previously, the prevailing philosophy was that GUI technology was most appropriate for personal productivity desktop applications (e.g., spreadsheets and word processors) rather than "real" business applications.

A step function of implementation will retain existing applications, while at the same time justifying the building of new applications in the client/server model. Eventually, many applications will migrate from larger processors to the new environment, but this will take time. Companies have discovered it is simpler to justify the implementation of open systems on distributed processors.

During the past decade, industry applications have emerged that continue to have relevance in the new generation of computing. Applications from large software firms are being migrated to workstations and servers and rewritten to function well in a network. Various applications will be used as models throughout the book, and it will be shown how these applications can be modified for specific open environments. Tools will be investigated that support open systems using client/server models.

Open systems tools have neither the richness of function nor the numbers of alternatives found on mainframe computers. Many users are looking for a richer toolset before they commit to a shift from centralized computing to open systems. Fortunately, there are increasing numbers of new products that will alleviate this shortage, but the challenge of the decade is producing code that can be used to create client/server applications. Although existing development tools have become simplified, there remain many gaps in the overall support spectrum.

1.3 THE USERS

Different users will benefit from open systems solutions, but each set of users will require unique support capabilities. Figure 1.1 shows three categories of users of desktop systems who are candidates for open systems solutions. Each set can benefit from the use of open systems, but some will find more and greater value than others.

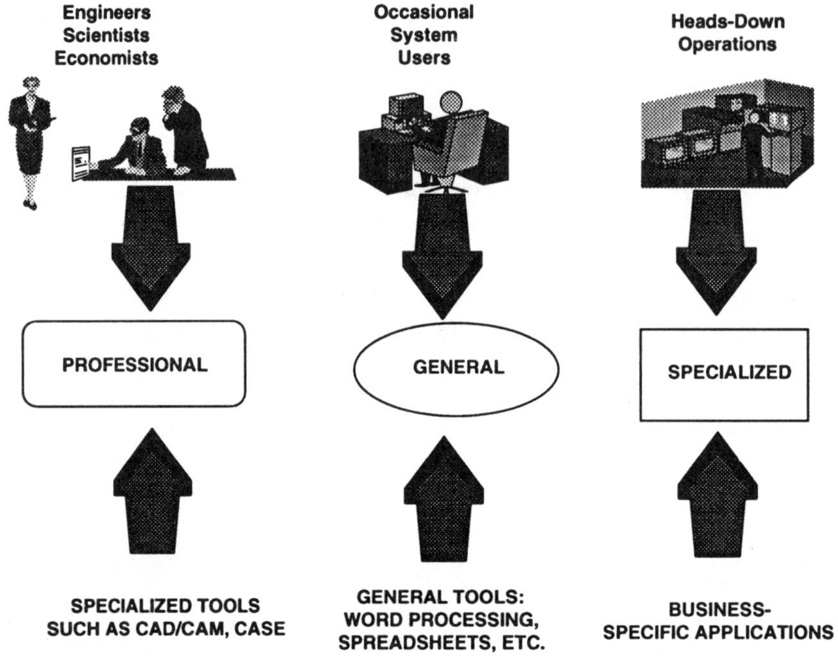

Figure 1.1 Open systems and user categories

Professional users have been the first to adopt open systems solutions. Professional users include engineers and scientists actively using computers as an extension of the design processes. Professionals also include experts in areas that use high-performance computing as an adjunct to their mental processes. Included in this category are economists, business modelers, forecasters, and Wall Street traders who can demonstrate an immediate benefit from the introduction of high-performance computing on their desktop or servers.

General users have adopted desktop computers to perform office tasks such as word processing, financial calculations, filing, and general applications. This group of users requires sufficient compute power to support general tasks but will not usually benefit from a major shift to open systems. As general users find the need to collaborate and work as a group, the application of open systems solutions will become more important. Increased need for business graphics will cause an influx in open systems solutions.

Specialized or vertical application users can benefit directly from the application of open systems. These users perform continual and routine tasks but must access computer databases for information. There are many examples of users who handle routine reservation services or telephone interaction with customers. Open systems enhance their ability to provide services by making immediate information available to them without the complexities of accessing databases. The increased power of desktop computers can be applied to provide additional compute power, which reduces the need for the users to remember details about connection protocols.

Each of the user categories has special needs from open systems and special benefits from the application of technology. Each user group requires different characteristics and interfaces to obtain optimal use of open systems. The professional users have been the first to adopt open systems, but specialized users can also gain a good deal of productivity from application of open systems.

1.4 BUSINESS TRENDS

Dramatic changes, which affect competition and the uses of technology, have been occurring in the global business environment. Accurately forecasting these radical changes seems impossible, but there are patterns that can be identified. Responding effectively to change is a measure of the success of a manager, and using information technology effectively often can provide the edge that contributes to that success.

Technology trends are simpler to predict because they are based on physical science and have a historical pattern that is often repeated. Although this pattern can be significantly altered through the creativity and actions of a single person or group of people, such change is the exception. Computer history is rich with discoveries that have altered the course of data processing in the workplace, but it is also rich with orphaned technologies that have had great promise but little real product value. There must be a natural combination of business forces and creative solutions to produce a viable product offering.

The use of information technology has been widespread in businesses, especially in large- and medium-size companies. Executives have recognized the value of computing in their businesses. At the same time, executives have become more knowledgeable about trends in computer technology. With this literacy comes a shift from total reliance on mainframes to acceptance of cost-saving workstations and servers. Central hubs with valuable corporate data are still based in central and secure processing centers. There is a shift to lower-cost computing, which can access the central data when needed, for local problems.

An example of these shifts can be seen in the U.S. banking industry, which spent $6.5 billion for information processing in 1990. The banks retained central data hubs that are reliable and secure from intrusion, but they also shifted to digital communications to move electronic data instead of money to complete many financial transactions. Financial institutions have relied upon mathematicians to project anomalies in money markets. These mathematicians are using open systems to model financial alternatives. Identification of unique market advantages can result in high automation payback in a relatively short time period for stock traders and economists (Pagels, 1989).

Equally important, local banks can achieve higher productivity through the use of open systems. Workstations have become familiar tools for many tellers, and these workstations can be connected through the network to active financial files. Local mortgage approval can be accelerated through the use of open systems processing at the local bank. The cost savings can be high and responsiveness to customers is even higher with this balanced open environment (Millison, 1991).

Some companies have adopted open systems as a competitive tool and have transformed their business goals to meet the new computing environment. Others have resisted change until it is too late for survival. Businesses are looking for measurable return from investments, but effective measurement of this return is different than in previous years. There is a need to focus on strategic roles of new technology.

Businesses are also searching for flexibility that permits solutions to be developed in specific work environments and then shifted into other appropriate environments. Equally important, the domination of a few vendors has been replaced by a search for solutions provided by many vendors. A cautious approach remains, as many executives have shown a reluctance to move into open systems until there is a stronger correlation between the business needs and the value of the new technology.

New demands within companies are refocusing skill requirements throughout the business. Information executives are being asked to help with the transition, since there is a similarity of problem areas. There is a strong desire to shift away from central processing for economy, but there is also a high degree of uneasiness about the potential problems with open systems (Bluestein, 1991). Each problem requires skills different from those used to manage large central systems.

At the user level, there is a widening base of unskilled people exposed to daily use of computers. Often, functionally illiterate users must use computers in their jobs. There is increasing emphasis on computer literacy in developing nations. The literacy scale is shifting to where it is possible to find trained individuals in undeveloped countries. Development of open solutions can become a global enterprise.

Work patterns are governed by the receptivity of society and the practical response to technical products. The reactions of a society are unpredictable but can govern their ability to compete in a world market. Cultural, religious, and ethnic beliefs affect the adoption of a given approach to business. Reactions of fear prevail when new solutions are introduced. Labor unions have been vocal about the introduction of open solutions, which may reduce the need for new members.

Governments reflect their society and dream of a place in the world competitive forces. The change in reaction to technology is an unpredictable factor that can modify business approaches to a problem. For instance, the long ban on shipping certain advanced technologies abroad affected the solutions that could be used by worldwide businesses. Geopolitical changes (such as wars) and government changes modify the desirability of data processing solutions. If a coup occurs, it may become necessary to shift processing to another country. Alternate processing centers may have to swing into action when there is a natural or manmade disaster. The high portability found in open systems facilitates this shift.

Changes in the specific workplaces are also driven by unpredictable forces. Educational changes, labor costs, and social practices affect the selected solution in any country. These changes are less predictable than technical trends, since they depend on the whims of individuals or the forces of nature. Distributed processing has the advantage of being able to select a workforce where the talent and abilities are located. Stability is achieved across a system architecture for an otherwise unstable world. Each new computer product introduction can provide opportunities to the alert organization.

The introduction of PCs has increased the individual autonomy and changed the roles of central information system (IS) staffs. The transition to open systems has again shifted the center of power and has reintroduced the need for experienced IS skilled workers. Solving network problems can be exceptionally complex and therefore requires skilled problem solvers.

Aggregate desktop compute power exceeded worldwide mainframe capacity by 1984. Since then, the separation between total desktop power and other computing has continued to widen, but desktop power has not been managed to the fullest. New programs are being introduced that treat the distributed processors as simply parallel computers that are connected through networks. The increased power predicted for the network extends the management challenge to effectively use the power.

For many years, the makers of equipment that interacted with unskilled end users recognized the value of ergonomics, the science of the workplace. With the growing use of computers by workers who assume simple interfaces, this science has grown in tandem with the use of computers. Products that are difficult to use will cost additional resources and create dissatisfied workers. Noise levels and keyboard alignment are regulated in many nations to improve the workplace. There is an increased awareness of the cumulative effects of workers' health problems—something that is a very real concern to both legislators and managers.

Managers are being asked to understand ways to shift from existing data processing environments to new solutions. The new technology solution must fit into a large and costly base. Older technologies being used to run the company today form a legacy system. The new introductions must work together with legacy systems to create an operational open system. Open systems assume a heterogeneous mix of hardware and software solutions. These solutions must be integrated with each other and with older solutions to present a comprehensive alternative.

The selection process has become both simpler and more complex. It is simple in that it requires vendors to conform to the open systems model. However, it is difficult to verify that they actually do conform. It was simpler to select a single vendor for all your solutions, but there is a conviction that no single vendor can provide all the correct answers for any business. Mixing vendors raises the complexity of your personal integration problems.

All levels of professionals have been introduced to personal computing. With the introduction of workgroups, they find themselves working in different environments. Collaboration, which was once limited to telephone or face-to-face meetings, can now be done through electronic mail. Workgroups, which were once geographically central, can now span continents or the world through electronic connections. With the power of standard interfaces, designers can use tools located in other nations.

Equally important, we find ourselves as members of different working groups. A technical manager will be part of a design team but also part of management. An engineer will work with other engineers in developing a design and with the manufacturing department in bringing the design to completion. Each brings a different group of people with which they must interact. Open systems provide tools for interacting with many groups at the same time.

Managing workers who span workgroups represents a unique challenge. New methods must be adopted to ensure there is an interaction with all the different groups. Technology can provide the capability of making this work. A number of studies are underway to investigate workgroup interaction. One such group is the Institute for the Future (IFTF) from Menlo Park, California (Johansen, 1988), which provides many insights into the interaction of working groups. Open systems provide common platform interfaces for managers trying to define international workgroups.

Calendar coordination and group interaction assume a new role in an age of electronics. Coordination occurs between managers on the open systems, and mail systems extend across this same system. Experiments have demonstrated that the best connection to executive information is by tapping into the normal reporting structure of the company. Executive information systems (EIS) have become a part of the open network. Functions once limited to central processing are now accomplished across an open network. Data are actively retrieved through mining processes and brought to the location of the decision makers.

Businesses around the world have recognized the need to adopt to the changing competitive environment. Individual productivity gained from PCs has strengthened the ability of small businesses to compete in markets dominated by larger companies. The business that adapts to new technology will achieve the highest payback.

1.5 MARKET FORCES

Computer market forces are constantly changing, reflecting the shifting interest in different solutions and increased dependency on financial cycles. Although open systems products have shown the strongest growth, the market remains very competitive. Most companies are still looking for solutions to their problems that will preserve the existing computer models but permit extension to new technology. Open systems solutions provide a base to retain existing computer models and permit extension to new technology.

The cultural changes within vendors have been as dramatic as those seen in the end-user community. Companies that did not respond to the PC found their market share erode, as people recognized the value of desktop computing. Open systems have caused the same erosion in the computer market.

Computer companies have turned to the workstation to improve their responsiveness to markets. Lessons learned from the automation process have extended to the need to use technology to create technology. Powerful servers located on the network can provide market models that will determine the requirements of the users and the ability of the company to meet these needs. Expert system analysis is replacing haphazard market studies. These expert systems will now reside in the network.

Alliances between former competitors represent another positive effect of open systems. Competitors are teaming up to demonstrate that their processors will interconnect with other heterogeneous processors. The alliances have gone further with well-published combinations to produce common products.

Another area of cooperation is the consortia created to develop and maintain industry standard approaches. This movement to consortia began in 1984 with the creation of the Open UNIX group, which became X/Open in 1987. Other important consortia followed, with the introduction of the Corporation for Open Systems in 1986. In 1988, the Open Software Foundation, MIT X Consortium, and UNIX International were founded. In 1994, a flurry of merger activity occurred among the consortia; this is discussed in Chapter 3.

Open systems are more complex to sell than PCs. The workstation and the operating system are each more complex than the simple hardware and software found in the PC. Integration has become an important factor in making a call in a large corporation. Integration of an LAN with the clients and servers is an important selling tool for small businesses. The market force must be more skilled and literate in open systems literature.

Standard architectures create a need to clearly differentiate products. This differentiation is based on added capability and function, which must be implemented within the framework of the standard. Complete solutions will include the hardware, operating system, applications, and integration into the existing code. The vendor must spend more time understanding the needs of the users and the existing network that is used.

Increased desktop power will challenge vendors to introduce new applications that can effectively consume the power of the workstation. Compute-intensive programs may be able to shift the success level for a business. Programs that effectively use the network will have more value than individual productivity programs.

Significant changes have altered the approach vendors will take to the business of selling open systems solutions. Traditional stores will be ill-equipped to introduce the technology. Value-added resellers will benefit from being able to bring experienced skills to focus on the problem.

1.6 COMPUTER CHANGES

Many changes found in open systems are generated from an ongoing evolution in computer hardware. The evolutionary rate accelerated with the acceptance of PCs as a fundamental part of corporate strategy. Dramatic shifts are continuing, as additional power becomes less expensive, and the half-life of a processor is reduced. At the same time, there has been a wide shift to introduce powerful software on the desktop and to standardize the interfaces.

The historical antecedent for change goes back to the original introduction of the computer in the 1950s. Original mainframes introduced computing, and although the prices were high and the software complex, they represented a significant gain to solving business problems. Initially, the computers were used by engineering and scientific groups, but their use eventually spread to the commercial community. Companies came to rely on centralized computers and developed professional teams to write software and handle the daily operations. Information systems matured with mainframe computers and became the primary focal point for decisions in the 1970s. Central computers met the requirements for enterprise control, and the computer became a natural adjunct to the business. Often the management of computers was assigned to financial departments, which used them as extensions of accounting.

Mainframes continue to have a vital but shrinking role in computing. Their central data protection makes them valuable for protecting important corporate data. Data for in-line operations still reside on mainframes in many companies. Archive information is usually accessible through these processors. Mainframes are finding a new role as central servers for secure operational and archive data in open systems.

Minicomputers were introduced in the mid-1960s to provide autonomy to engineering and scientific departments requiring local compute power. Central computing was shifted to the department so bottlenecks could be eliminated through distributed processing. It was during this era that the term, if not the reality, of distributed processing became widely used. Individual departments needed to find people who could write programs and run the minicomputers.

Minicomputers were widely used by engineering and manufacturing departments before they were accepted by commercial organizations. Companies that could not afford large mainframes adopted minicomputers as a low-cost way of computing. In larger companies, minicomputers augmented larger computers. Commercially, many of these computers used languages so simple that programmers with only a high school diploma could be hired. Minicomputers were used with PCs as servers, and, in an open systems environment, they still have the capability to support multiple clients.

The introduction of the PC in 1975 launched another era of computing. Low-cost computing became available to individual workers and the role of IS was threatened. Companies (particularly small businesses) that could not afford the minicomputers could afford PCs. More importantly, low-cost applications were introduced that turned PCs into desktop powerhouses. Simple electronic mail was possible with people who communicated on PC networks. Simple techniques connected the PCs together and eventually with designated servers. Local area networks were introduced to facilitate connection between these different boxes.

The PC prepared for the introduction of open systems. Both the hardware and software for the PC were generally open, except for a few proprietary architectures (and the open architecture of MS-DOS [and later Microsoft Windows] on top of the 80x86 family of processors became the dominant architecture in the marketplace). People became comfortable with data processing at their fingertips and enjoyed the freedom to establish their own levels of performance. Rapid success of the PC resulted in more performance on the desktops than in central processing locations. Scientists and engineers were the first users, but businesses followed rapidly. Robust applications made it a tool to be used across different departments. Many companies quickly moved to adopt the PC as a primary work tool for the corporation and designed programs to facilitate the connection between PCs and larger processors.

Not only did PCs affect the individual processing power, but they also established new levels of technology pricing, which changed corporate perspectives on computing. Additional features could be introduced on the PC for a relatively small expenditure. Many organizations adopted the PC as the vehicle to introduce new technology.

Open systems were built on the preceding technology, but by 1985 a new shift in computing was becoming apparent. Enhanced desktop computers combined with LANs to provide a technical environment for common protocols. At the same time, users became more vocal about the need to define commonalty and reduce proprietary systems. Neither the growth in desktop computing power nor the connection across networks were surprises, but the strong advocacy of the user community startled many observers. Up to this point, acceptance of proprietary architectures was common in most companies.

The heterogeneous environment, that is, open systems, assumed standards that could apply to all vendors. The standards evolved from vendor-specific definitions and provided the solutions users searched for. Standards helped to increase competition, as entry companies could participate in the industry solutions. Servers followed the same standards defined for desktop computers and became another node in the complete network.

Each subsequent generation of computers has built on the success of the previous generation. From the mainframe to the PC, a rich heritage has made each subsequent machine more powerful than its ancestor. By correcting problems of previous generations, powerful hardware and software that facilitates growth have been built. Connection between the different generations of computing assures a retention of the wealth of legacy code while creating new opportunities of computing.

The management of computers has depended on an adaptability to unique operations. We have moved from a strong central management to distribution of functions between mainframes and minicomputers. PCs created additional emphasis on individual productivity and shifted operation responsibility to the user.

Each form of computing has introduced new capabilities and new ceilings, which are the result of applying new technology. Limitations are driven by the needs of the organization as much as by the technology. System designs limit newer technologies, but creative imaginations will be able to drive systems to new limits of capabilities.

1.7 CONSIDERATIONS

Plans for open systems should consider a number of items important to assess technologies and their relationship to your business. Open systems provide unique options for large and small businesses to respond rapidly and compete in a global economy. Solutions, which once required large computers, can be run effectively on combinations of smaller processors.

Reduced-cost computers have become an agent of social change in individual workplaces and a tool that can permit developing countries to solve problems with technology.

Open systems introduce unique complexity into the information technology of a business. New paradigms of systems management will be required to integrate distributed functions in the existing business model and control complex open systems. Many paradigms will be derived from technology hitherto unused in computer management and probably will borrow from the management of many computers in a parallel processor. Open systems will derive lessons from other physical sciences that can be beneficial in managing the diversity of network components.

Businesses experienced a flexibility from the use of open systems that led to new business opportunities. Vendors can be selected for their ability to provide the best solution and not simply for their marketing prowess. Large businesses gain the most from scalability of their solutions, but small businesses gain from access to rapid information and reduced turnaround of data. As growth occurs, the number of users will increase and so can the data processing commitment. Open systems have the capability to expand and reflect the increased needs of more users and their expanded data requirements. Scalability is important in applying a solution across offices that differ in size and support capacity.

As additional users are added, the network and servers must have the capability to expand and adjust to meet the growing needs. Disk capacity must be able to be increased to support additional users. Equally important, the system must have the flexibility to increase the connection bandwidth without disrupting existing operations. Open systems permit a partitioning of the work, which is a natural opening for object systems. The use of object systems will further accelerate both the development and maintenance processes.

The implementation of open systems will create new challenges as they are merged with existing system code. New models of the system will be important in defining how the business will work. However, the real challenge of open systems is not technical but managerial. Since open systems are relatively young, the body of empirical knowledge is beginning to grow. This knowledge begins with an understanding of technology and rapidly moves into management questions. What are the characteristics that have made some companies successful in creating open systems and others fail to make the system work? Are there procedures that can be adopted to help management develop and install open systems? What techniques should be adopted to facilitate the introduction of predictable technology?

The remainder of this book examines foundations of open technology and describes how it has been adopted into unique processing models. The book will examine approaches used to connect open systems with legacy systems. More importantly, the book will examine transformations that become possible and seem necessary for success in benefiting from open systems.

1.8 REFERENCES

Berstein Research (written by Mark D. Stahlman). *The Desktop Computer Market.* New York: Stanford C. Berstein & Co., 1989.

Bluestein, William M. *Computing Strategy Report: The Politics of Technology.* Cambridge, MA: Forrester Research, 1991, p. 2.

Dertouzos, Michael L., Richard K. Lester, and Robert M. Solow. *Made in America: Regaining the Productive Edge.* Cambridge, MA: MIT Press, 1989.

Johansen, Robert, with contributions by Jeff Charles, Robert Mittman, and Paul Saffo. *Groupware: Computer Support for Business Teams.* New York: The Free Press, 1988.

Kriebel, C. H. "Understanding the Strategic Investment in Information Technology." In *Information Technology and Strategic Management,* edited by K. Laudon and J. Turner. Englewood Cliffs, NJ: Prentice Hall, 1989, pp. 106–118.

Millison, Doug. "Banking on UNIX." *CommUNIXations,* September 1991, pp. 15–22.

Morton, Michael S. Scott (editor). *The Corporation of the 1990's: Information Technology and Organizational Transformation.* New York: Oxford University Press, 1991, pp. 4–5.

Pagels, Heinz R. *The Dreams of Reason: The Computer and the Rise of the Sciences of Complexity.* New York: Bantam Books, 1989, p. 145.

2

Characteristics of Open Systems

Companies select computer systems to provide a capability which either cannot be performed manually or can be performed less expensively or more accurately using computers. Each implementation has characteristics that identify its strengths when measured against competing alternatives. As users, we are searching for the characteristics that make open systems unique and profitable for our businesses. This chapter will explore the qualities and characteristics users can expect from these systems.

Open systems have characteristics that can be measured across different installations. Each characteristic represents an advantage managers can expect in adopting the technology. As additional vendors support open systems, it is well to assess their implementations against objective criteria developed for all vendors. Characteristics can be used as a checklist to determine the value of open systems support. Benchmarks can be used to assess this value, but the benchmarks must be carefully built and used. Many will claim conformity with open systems, but not all can demonstrate their claims.

2.1 OPEN SYSTEMS COMPONENTS

An important element of open systems processing is *client/server computing*. Open systems are built around a processing model that assumes client/serv-

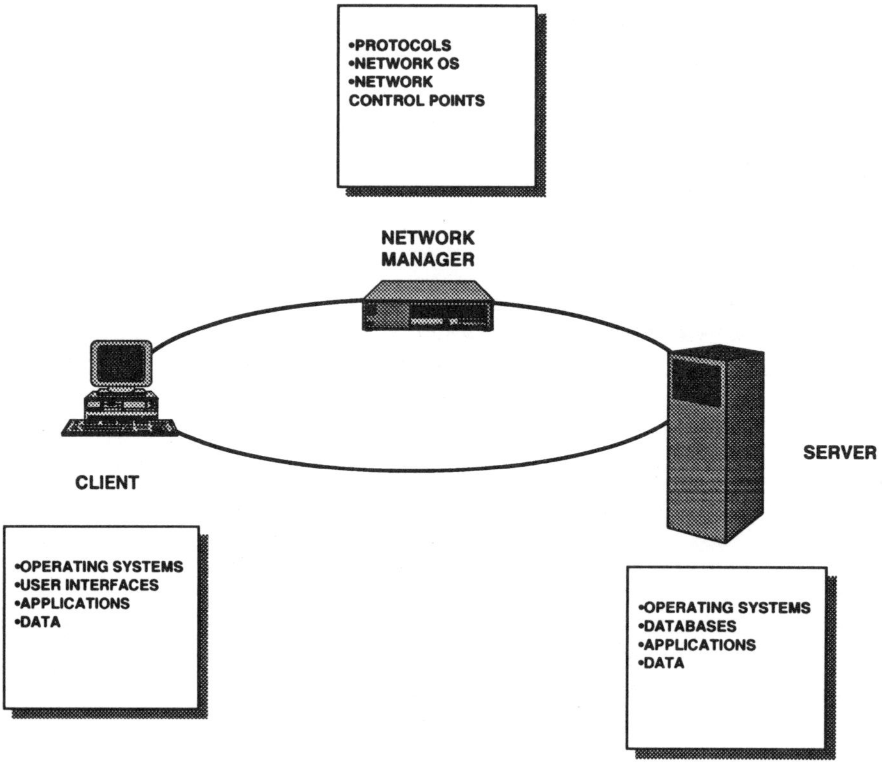

Figure 2.1 Client/server computing principles

er configurations, as shown in Figure 2.1. The four elements used to build most client/server systems include clients, servers, the network or networks, and the management network software. Both function and data are distributed across the active nodes of the network. Control elements reside in architected solutions that can effectively schedule different elements within the system.

Client/server computing can be used to partition work across different computers. Applications can reside in either the client on the desktop or be shared by multiple desktop computers on the servers. As a model, it represents a clear approach toward solving innumerable automation problems.

Clients are programs requesting services from another program, or they can be the computers requesting the service. Clients may reside in computers separate from the servers or even in the same processor. Both clients and servers will have variable degrees of processing capability. Engineering design computers will usually have richer capability in floating point and graphics than clients used in simple business applications. The introduction of advanced business graphics has increased the demand for floating point and special graphics engines in specialized business environments.

Typical early clients on desktops utilized PCs, which are still widely used. With the changes in technology, there has been a shift to more powerful workstations for complex applications. Lower-cost X terminals have been introduced, which require a high degree of management control, where there is little need for the more powerful workstation solutions. The increasing use of portable computers has created the remote client.

Servers are programs that respond to the request for shared service or they can be the computers that support those services. The server provides shared functions, such as database access for multiple clients. High-speed graphics, images, and special I/O features extend the range of capabilities for modern servers. A simple form of navigation to multiple data sources can be designed within the server, letting it access data in multiple operating modes. The server also houses the applications that are shared across multiple clients.

Servers traditionally began as enhanced PCs and migrated to more specialized processors. Larger-capacity servers have assumed the role once held by minicomputers. The mainframe works well as a server in installations where a large legacy code exists or where special requirements demand the capabilities of mainframes.

Servers rely on traditional building blocks to create an operating environment that supports specialized functions. The control functions found in operating systems combine with database management routines to provide data handling and security capability.

The network is the third element considered. The network consists of physical connections and software to support those connections. In its simplest form, a network will consist of wiring, switch boxes, adapters, and the software that facilitates connections between processors. Introduction of cellular connections has reduced the need for physical wiring, but it has created the need for communications capability within other components of the network. Network defines the transparent services available to the user interface. Logically, networks can be considered as residing between the different clients and servers.

The fourth element is network management, found in most networks. In the simplest networks, the management routines are relatively primitive. Production networks define capabilities that guarantee the operations of the network throughout the required operations cycle. Network management routines test the condition of the network and permit access to changes and modifications. The network management routines help ensure the integrity of the system and the seamless running of production. Network management routines determine the correctness of connections between the different processors and applications. The routines facilitate the movement of information between the processors by ensuring accuracy.

An examination of the different components will reveal that there are many common threads found in the different elements of open systems. Operating system or control code is basic to each element of the network. Although this control code will differ in complexity, it is required for a processor. Applications will also be developed for different components of the network. Later, we will examine the correct placement of different applications, but it should be understood that different portions of solutions can reside across the nodes of the network. Common application functions can operate on servers, and specific end-user applications can function on the client.

The modularity of open systems permits an effective partitioning for application development. Applications that interact closely with the user reside on clients, and those that can be shared across multiple users are coded for servers. Data control can also be partitioned between clients and servers, depending on the optimal residence location. Local data provide end users with a high degree of autonomy, while server data reduce local responsibility and service multiple users.

All user interfaces can reside on clients and be optimized to provide significant capability with increasing power in the processors and graphics devices. Full use of different functions found within the system can provide added capability to the end user. The user will seamlessly access any component within the network. Open systems interfaces enable any user to interact with systemwide applications in a transparent fashion, which will mask the location of specific applications or data. With increased desktop power, many clients have extensive computing capability and therefore provide extensive program execution environments. Storage capacity has continued to grow on client processors, and the amount of data retained at the desktop continues to increase.

The network manager can reside in one of the processing nodes of the network. Each network component will collect status information, which will provide the network manager with data to determine and correct different problems within the system. Synthesis of the data occurs in the network manager, which provides status information and automatically initiates correction actions.

Security is correctly assigned to all elements of the client/server system. It begins as a strategy for the company and defines the role of the different elements of the system. Since security is only as strong as the weakest link in the network, it begins in the kernel of the operating systems used in the client or server. There is a need to balance the different requirements of open systems in order to guarantee a freer and easier access to system components while providing a closed and secure system.

2.1.1 Clients

Clients are the natural focal point for user interfaces and local applications that require close user interaction. Increased processing power, coupled with low-cost and high-capacity memory, has made clients the natural support points for extensive local programming. The first candidate for residence on the client is the graphical user interface (GUI), which requires interaction with the end user. A key consideration is the substitution of graphics images for traditional textual information. Many studies have demonstrated that users can accomplish more work with GUI than workers using traditional textual commands. Wide acceptability of GUI interfaces has emphasized the client as a natural point to accomplish work.

The increased compute power found on desktop computers, and their adoption as clients, has resulted in a partition of work. Applications that depend on close interaction with the end user can be migrated to the desktop client. Off-the-shelf applications, such as word processors, spreadsheets, and local databases, are the first natural candidates for clients, but many business-specific applications benefit from placement on the client, since modern clients are powerful processors that can support extensive application programs such as simulation or rules-based processing.

PCs were quickly recognized as natural clients, since they combined easy-to-use interfaces with increasing desktop power. PCs supported special communications adapters that facilitated their connection to different network protocols. Extensive software support was introduced to make PC interfaces appear as natural human tools.

Continued improvements in desktop power led to the introduction of workstations and even more extensive user interface advances. Visualization applications have been introduced on the more powerful workstations. Visualization uses graphics capability to portray data as a 3-D image. Scientific visualization provides scientists and engineers with a three-dimensional view of traditionally numerical data. Visualization has shifted to the business community, as programs permit the analysis of numerical data and its portrayal in a three-dimensional format.

Clients are also beginning to have sufficient compute power for the migration of expert systems directly to the desktop. Knowledge assistants are possible on desktop computers to aid the individual worker in defining and understanding information. As an example, an engineering assistant is an expert system residing on a client containing guidelines about the local and general rules of engineering. The expert system can provide interactive support with the designer and can facilitate design and testing.

Increased power in portable computing has created an environment in which clients can be carried and used from any location. Portable computers are now available using most major architectures. It is possible for the client connected to the network to reside away from the geographic location of the server. Connection is through telephone lines connected to the system or, in some cases, through cellular connections using radio. Computing is possible anywhere with notebook, palmtop, and other portable computers.

2.1.2 Network Services

The client/server network depends on local connections of workstations. These connections are known as local area networks (LANs) and are supported through direct wire connections. Local connections can cascade into a wide area network, which can connect distant locations such as cities. Networks have many characteristics, which must be considered in creating a complete system.

One important characteristic is security, which extends beyond the typical boundaries of the computer hardware to include the entire network. Another important element is the ability to manage the network using software and hardware. In his keynote speech at the 1991 COMDEX, Andy Grove, the Chairman of Intel, pointed to the increasing power and diversity of networks (Grove, 1991). Growing from almost 2 million networks in 1991 to an estimated 10 million-plus by 1995, a new pressure is added to the support population. Each LAN requires a separate administrator today. Obviously, the answer lies in applying technology to manage the networks. A number of companies have provided products that have automated some portions of LAN administration, but a great deal more functionality is needed (particularly in the management of heterogeneous environments containing multiple LANs of different architectures).

The introduction of smartcards, which contain more extensive information than the typical passwords, provides added protection from experienced hackers. These intelligent cards can be used for more extensive security systems but can also eventually provide a high degree of data portability.

2.1.3 Servers

The computing industry is undergoing a shift from central mainframes to open systems. As this shift is occurring, new roles for servers are emerging to reflect the trend in compute power. Servers involved with storage once focused on textual information. Open systems applications include mixed forms of data, including text, image, video, and audio. Integration of these different storage techniques is leading servers to a knowledge server concept and eventually to knowledge repositories.

Output servers have shifted from simple printer support to complex printer and plotter devices. Media transformations have resulted in servers that can be used to produce animated films on video devices. There is a shift to multimedia servers that create unique forms of computer output.

Compute servers have also undergone a transformation from locations that provided specific compute algorithm for engineering tasks to full mathematical capability. Modern compute servers have extended beyond simple calculations to include decision algorithms using expert system routines or neural computing. The servers are shifting to full-solution devices, using embedded calls to more powerful processors when necessary. The speed of these shifts in function is determined by the availability of necessary hardware, software, and tools across the network. Full use of knowledge repositories, for instance, will require capabilities not yet available in the network.

Server hardware comes in a number of different performance configurations, as can be seen in Figure 2.2. Low-performance open servers use PCs with performance ranges supporting two to 30 transactions per second (TPS). Midrange servers introduce redundancy and fault tolerance and provide additional transaction rates up to 100 transactions per second. High-end servers use specialized processors with performances reaching 400 TPS.

The most powerful server hardware uses multiple parallel processors that can achieve performance in excess of 1,000 transactions per second. These

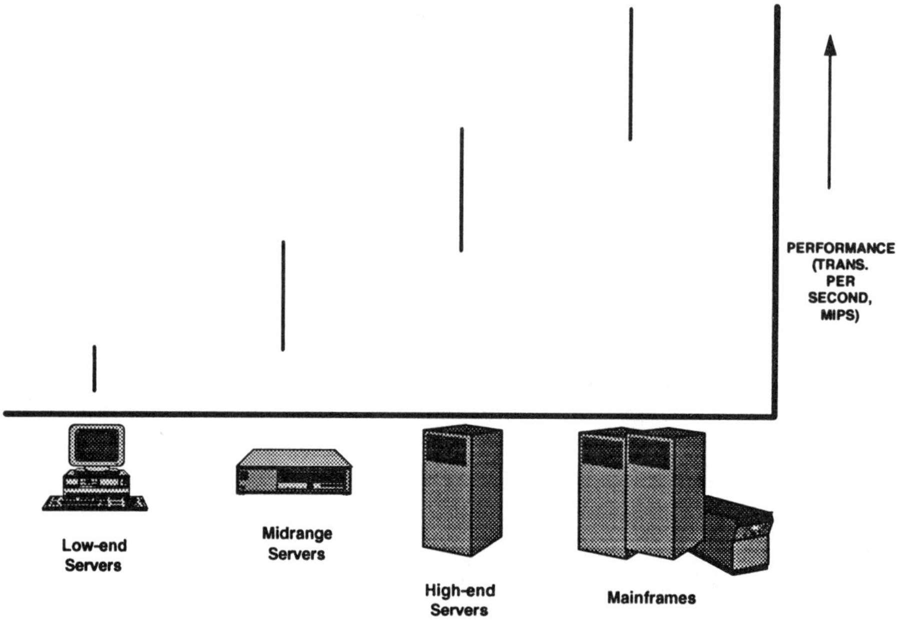

Figure 2.2 Relative performance of different classes of servers

processors service very large databases with rapid response capability. Since the larger processors are adopting open systems standards, it is possible to design a system that connects transparently to servers, based on performance requirements, without changing interfaces. This provides significant scalability for company applications.

Note that the raw numbers of transactions per second are not important, because the ever-increasing power in processors will constantly drive up the TPS performance in all classes. Rather, it's the performance of members of these different classes *relative* to each other. Different environments require different levels of power in servers, and *rightsizing* is just as important as *downsizing;* that is, it is just as objectionable to have too powerful of a processor in a particular environment (wasted capacity and wasted money) than it is to have insufficient power with the resulting delays in response time.

2.1.4 Considerations

There are advantages in the shift to standard interfaces. Clusters of minicomputers and mainframes developed during the past 30 years are especially

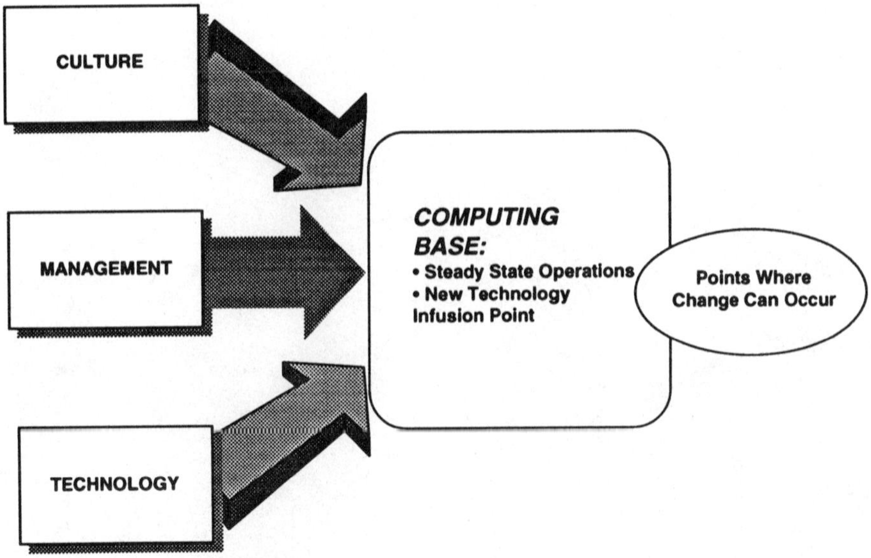

Figure 2.3 Considerations in technology evolution

rich in function. With the use of standard interfaces, these processors can now become an active participant in the open systems network. Large servers such as IBM mainframes, or very large database engines, serve as repositories for company-critical information.

Mainframes contain large amounts of legacy code and data that will remain critical to a company for many years. Legacy systems represent the body of code, data, and skills that has been developed over the years as the foundation for company data processing. They contain the primary processors, important data, backbone networks, skills, and the legacy languages used for development. Legacy code and data represent an important company resource, which must be considered in any new system plans. As illustrated in Figure 2.3, the culture, management, and technology of the legacy environments are all part of those considerations.

2.2 CHARACTERISTICS

Individual characteristics help to delineate between clients and servers. Some of these characteristics are shown in Figure 2.4. As can be seen from this figure, clients are operational computers, which traditionally reside on desktops. Usually they are PCs, workstations, or X terminals, but with the

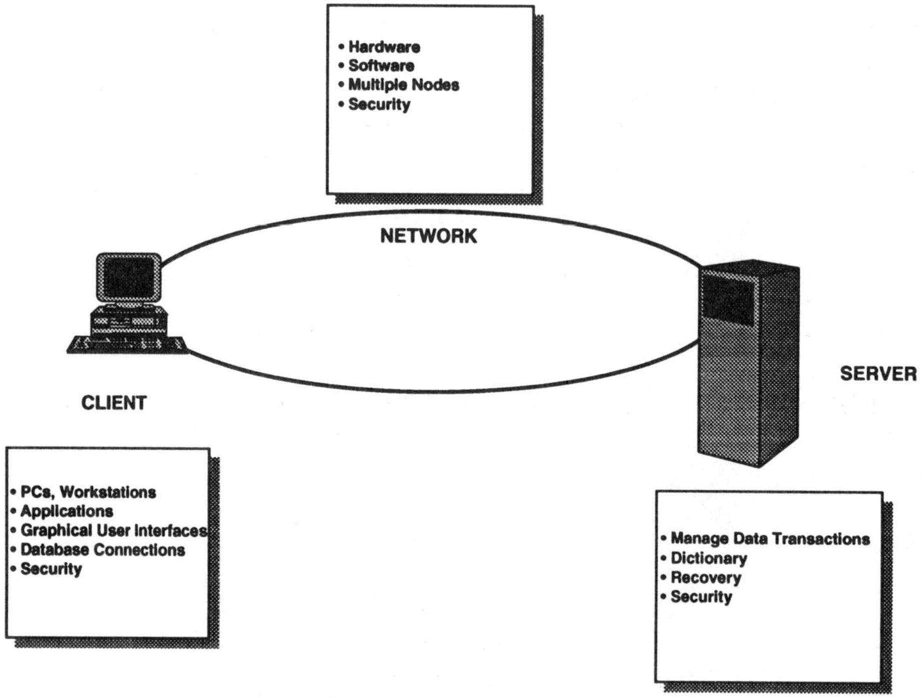

Figure 2.4 Characteristics of clients, servers, and the network

extensive use of portable technology, clients may actually be notebook, laptops, or even palmtop computers. Clients run applications that provide user interface support, contain portions of a distributed database, and provide the connections to the network. Security begins at the client but is an overall consideration for the network.

The network is comprised of communications hardware and software that connects different units of an open system together. As we explore the network, we will find it contains a mixture of functional processors as well as the wiring or other communications connectors. Increasingly, the network will be wireless, using either radio or infrared communications techniques. Networks usually consist of multiple nodes across either local or wide area connections.

Servers provide shared functions used by multiple clients. Servers may have functions that include input/output, storage, or special program execution. In a distributed network, special processors may perform the function of name servers to facilitate searches through the network. Although the majority of servers will work with single processors, many will require the robustness of fault tolerance.

Some characteristics are found in all the components of the network. Security, data integrity, and flexibility are characteristics that affect all the elements of an open system. Backup and recovery mechanisms are also located at all nodes of the network. More robust servers will have high availability requirements.

Three features of software typify the need to support different and distributed processors. Portability, scalability, and interoperability are characteristics of modern computing that must be found at each element of the open system.

Portable software can be moved across different nodes of the open systems topology without special sensitivity to hardware or operating system differences. Identical results are achieved on the software application—whether it resides on a PC, workstation, or more sophisticated server.

Scalability enables installations to shift application solutions to different environments. This entails a shift to different-size computers or different elements within the network. Common data can be accessed from the scalable solutions whether there is full access or not.

Interoperability enables the open systems solution to merge with the existing computing programs. Interoperability enables different processors to work with legacy code.

2.3 QUALITIES

Each network component should exhibit qualities that facilitate their intended use. Figure 2.5 illustrates the qualities that are important in open systems computing. Clients are usually intended for a single user, which provides a secure interface for multiple applications on the network. Clear and accurate graphics capability is included in modern clients. Most clients are programmable except for the X terminals.

Networks are constantly changing and must have flexibility for growth. As new attachments are made, it is expected the network will continue to function and accept the additional users without major perturbation. Since the network is a key link in security, connection linkages must be secure from interception either through direct or remote tap. Performance must be adequate to handle large numbers of connections in a transparent fashion.

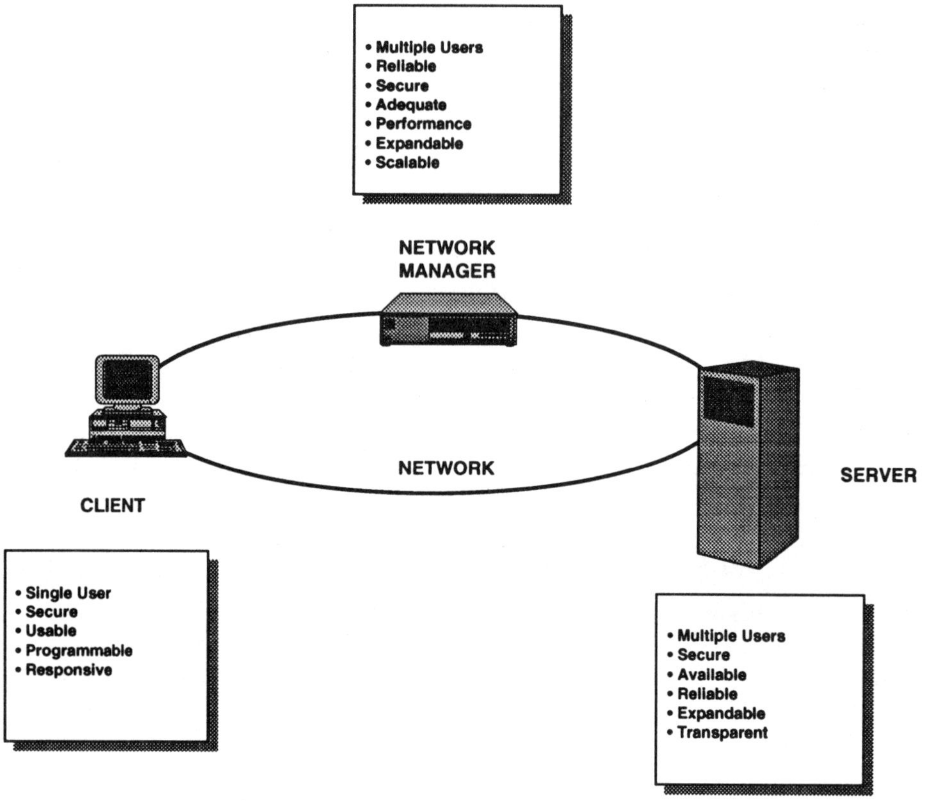

Figure 2.5 Qualities important to open systems

Since servers support many users, it is important that they are secure and provide high availability. Many servers have been expanded to include complete fault tolerance to improve system functions. Servers provide functions for multiple users, and they must be reliable. It is also true that the number of users is not usually predictable, so the server must be expandable and provide this expansion in a fashion transparent to the end users on the system.

2.4 SPECIAL CONSIDERATIONS

Open systems create new challenges in systems management. Simple processes such as security and data backup must be carefully designed across distributed processing nodes. Undesired penetration or destruction of data is easier in a client/server environment that is not designed for tightly protecting data and programs. Security spans the open systems network from individual clients to shared servers.

Professionals who have worked with open systems recognize the additional challenges involved in moving data from individual to department control. Certain data, such as financial records, must be retained for long periods of time and be accurate as soon as an update is completed. A good example is individual bank accounts, which must reflect deposits and withdrawals as soon as they are completed. If the local bank is using distributed processing, its records must be updated rapidly in the central database.

Archive storage must have a higher availability and protection for long periods. The periods of time differ based on data sensitivity and legal requirements from outside agencies. Design data, for instance, must be retained for the life of the product, and certain financial data must be retained for seven years.

Timing is an important consideration in selecting applications platforms. Open systems createsa different operational paradigm than central processing. Applications running on a client provide immediate response. Let us examine some special considerations of open systems.

2.4.1 Security

The challenge to protect data from destruction or intrusion becomes more difficult in open systems environments. We are all familiar with stories of hackers using core functions to penetrate the most secure systems. Disgruntled employees can damage a company's unprotected data files, and there are many cases in which vital company resources have been accessed and modified (Shaffer and Simon, 1993). Security represents a larger challenge in open distributed systems, since much processing power exists at the individual nodes.

Business places a value on data that varies with the sensitivity and age of the information. This year's design is more important to industrial espionage than historical products. As data are defined for protection, a number of characteristics of the network must be considered to ensure its protection. Traditionally, physical protection of a single central computer was relatively simple, but as data are distributed, a multiple unit security becomes a consideration (DoD, 1985).

Protecting data from accidental destruction can be as simple as insisting on a backup procedure at individual workstations or servers. More complex mechanisms, which provide an automatic backup and recovery mechanism, can be introduced. Traditionally called redundant systems, this automatic backup could be triggered normally through the servers. Many readers will have experienced the accidental erasure of a diskette on a PC. Backup is the only way to completely protect information from accidental or intentional destruction.

As long as a certain degree of backup is achieved, open systems have advantages over central systems. Physical protection is enhanced through copies of data residing in the network. Servers will require additional protection, since the work of many people can be lost through loss or penetration.

Security procedures for centralized computers are relatively simple in comparison with the procedures that must be introduced across communications linkages. Access to network functions is provided through entry ports to the system. These ports must be guarded through the use of passwords and other techniques for ensuring proper authorization of the inquirer.

A number of penetration techniques demonstrate that systems can be entered by either experts or novices. A simple approach to defend against is browsing, in which the skilled person searches for ways to enter different systems by simply scanning for easy access points. Elementary design flaws, such as failing to clear system memory between programs, help browsers find critical information to access data through the open system. Defense against browsing is strong access control, which logs constant attempts and alerts administrators.

A more persistent attempt to penetrate the system is the diligent attack. Diligent attack was made easier through the use of PCs that could repeatedly attempt to get information from the system. Workstations permit the skilled professional to program access to other systems. The 1983 movie *War Games* showed a persistent hacker who finally penetrated the supercomputer center that controlled the Strategic Air Command. Although disclaimers were made relative to the possibility, a number of penetrations have been well documented. A number of highly publicized security breaches are described in Shaffer and Simon (1993).

Unprotected data can be penetrated using eavesdropping across the open systems network. The Department of Defense has defined techniques such as cryptography to control eavesdropping, but this form of penetration points to the need to secure all portions of the network. In cryptography, encryption occurs at the sender node, and decryption occurs at the receiving node. Inexpensive cryptographic boards using board- or chip-level Data Encryption Standard (DES) have aided network security. Using this technique, a special key gives authorized parties access to the encrypted data.

Developers can use a Trojan-horse approach, which embeds code that activates on a given signal such as a date. When the signal is given, the code becomes active and either ferrets out information or begins to destroy code, as in the case of a virus. Detailed inspections of critical code are a good defense against Trojan horses. Although Trojan horses can be placed at any control point in the client/server environment, servers are particularly susceptible to this form of penetration.

Special access to the system to permit effective servicing has resulted in system designers coding a trapdoor entrance. Often this code is needed by system debuggers to enable diagnosis and repair of complex system problems. Since the code is a good way for an attacker to enter a system, it should be deactivated before the system is shipped.

A time bomb is used by disgruntled employees to destroy major portions of the system or databases. The code appears innocent until a time or an event triggers the destructive routines. Time bombs have been used by dismissed employees to cause severe havoc. Since it can take only a few instructions to alter system processes, this type of security penetration can cause real problems in design automation. A first step to protect against time bombs is to remove dismissed employees' passwords from the system immediately. Inspection also represents a defense against the time bomb.

The virus is another problem placed in the system for mischief. Much like its medical counterpart, the virus attaches to one program in a system and eventually infects other portions. Often, a virus expands beyond the goals of the implementor and moves uncontrolled through many computers. A famous virus was introduced to the Internet network in 1988 (Shaffer and Simon, 1993). After entering the network, it propagated itself through the system and disrupted large numbers of UNIX computers. Some computers were inactive for a day and a half as a result of this virus.

Michelangelo and Jerusalem viruses are well known. Triggered by a change of date, the viruses access and destroy data throughout the hard disk. Scan programs, which can detect and eliminate most common viruses, are available.

In the world of massive parallel processing, good viruses can have a beneficial effect of propagating data and code through multiple processors. In the worse case, unprotected computers can become the targets for destruction. Viruses can be stopped using virus examination programs, but there is no foolproof technique.

Open systems have made the security task more complex, as individual workstations have an autonomy of action that can crash the system (Murray, 1984). Workstation users must adopt a discipline to perform regular physical backup on files and programs. Server and mainframe hub data are usually stored in vaults located away from the physical computer location.

Although open systems represent unique challenges, solutions do exist that can help secure a client/server network. Project Athena at MIT identified techniques to protect open systems. The security system was named Kerberos and has been adopted by companies searching for stronger techniques for protecting open systems. The simple combination of physical and system protection will work in most cases. Simply placing a physical lock on each workstation is a step toward security. This is enhanced through the use of software locks, which regulate the users of the hardware.

2.4.2 Recovery

If you have experienced the frustration of destroyed data, it is easy to imagine scenarios that could have major consequences on business. Imagine an engineer who has created a key part for an important new product. The engineer leaves on a Friday without backing up critical design files. Over the weekend, an electrical failure ruins the files, and there is no recovery. These simple problems of destroyed disks occur frequently.

Managing data in open systems is more complex than in a direct central processing environment. Automatic backup of enterprise data is an alternative selected by some companies. Data recovery plans are necessary, even when they depend on participation by the end users. Failures can result from hardware, system, application, or user problems, and recovery plans must address them all.

Backup is the first line of defense when coupled with recovery. Workstation users discover that periodic data backup is valuable to avoid the loss of important data. Site backup avoids complete destruction of essential information. Site backup preserves all major data elements within the system. A management plan defines basic recovery and the retention period for backed-up files. Inexperienced users are looking for reasonable guidelines. Protected vaults could be used for server hubs containing critical operational data. The primary purpose of all these steps is to ensure that the department and company can recover from a disaster in sufficient time to avoid business losses.

Recovery uses backed-up information to reintroduce operations. Backup data will bring mainstream applications into a full production state and will be synchronized with actions that occurred after the backup was taken.

2.4.3 Usability

An important reason for the acceptance of PCs has been their usability. Although many users have encountered initial problems with complex interfaces, the movement to autonomous computing has been driven by the comfort level in using PCs. This requirement remains foremost, as open systems include new levels of untrained users. Every effort must be made to extend the usability of PCs across the client/server network.

Human factors experts have defined usability techniques for accessing complex machines. The controls of aircraft, nuclear reactors, and automobiles have required simplification defined by these specialists. Increasingly, specialists are asked to simplify machine design to avoid failure by the end users. Studies have demonstrated that computer users are looking for simpler ways to access complex data information across the network.

Computer usability can be a managed occurrence, as guidelines are established for effective usability. Evaluation of planned installations in light of usability helps define a user strategy for the company. Equally important is an awareness of ergonomics, which is the science of the workplace. Increasingly, ergonomic findings have resulted in legislation governing the use of computer devices. These laws reflect studies conducted in the workplace and the effects of use of computer devices for prolonged periods of time.

In addition to these laws, researchers have identified many factors that can affect the health of desktop users. These factors must be considered in designing and selecting desktop computers and the environment in which they are placed. Since the flow of data can affect usability, even server performance can modify the interaction people have with open systems. The most obvious problem arises in the constant use of display screens, which can provide a source of discomfort or result in physical problems. Noisy desktop computers can distract the end users and lead to production problems. Guidelines have identified techniques to use in placing, lighting, and positioning display units for maximum comfort. Using information from ergonomics, managers can select equipment that provides the maximum level of safety and comfort.

Each new technology presents challenges when it is introduced to the people who will be the ultimate end users. Return to our analogy about sailboats. Novices introduced to sailing are nervous about the complexity of guiding the craft using the different sails. Increasingly, sailboat design has made sailboats easier to operate for weekend sailors. But the yachts that race in the America's Cup are manned by experienced sailors, who can use the design and technology to win. These yachts are carefully designed to achieve the highest leverage against competition.

Workstations must appeal to the novice users and provide sufficient power for the expert to win against competition. Working modes in an automated environment seem to be constantly shifting, and workers are asked to adjust to the shifts. Productivity tools bring with them unique features, which must be learned and mastered for continued success in the business. Initially, desktop computers required more skill than many people needed to perform their job. With the introduction of new features, the workstations have become easier to use.

We have long known that usability begins with the design of the system to be used (Gould and Lewis, 1985). This has been true in such consumer items as appliances and automobiles. It is also true for computer networks. The increasing use of personal workstations connected to a network has shifted the usability focus from central processing software to the workstation software. Extensive use of icons and graphics has simplified usability and reduced the demands on human memory.

Advances in desktop computing, coupled with advanced I/O devices, have provided new horizons for usability. Conversion of data into animated pictures increases the capability of untrained users. Rules can be embedded into the language to increase the capability of supporting the unskilled at the desktop. Open systems have become platforms that facilitate advanced 3-D interfaces for users. Gains in applications can also lead to long-term productivity gains.

2.4.4 Reliability, Availability, and Serviceability

Reliability, availability, and serviceability are often grouped together to define access to individual computers.

Reliability is a measure of the time components will run without failure. With advances in electronic technology, the reliability of individual components has continued to improve, but in open systems, reliability measurement is applied to the entire system. Reliability of an open system is the summation of the hardware and software reliability for both clients and servers. Path reliability refers to the expected error-proneness of the total system.

Availability is a measure of production systems' readiness to respond to the demands of the business. Availability determines the percentage of production time that can be expected on the network. Clients can have lower availability than servers, which must be ready to provide service to multiple clients.

Serviceability represents the system tools and connections that facilitate access to units or the whole to troubleshoot and correct problems. Individual processors within the system will have a level of serviceability, but the entire network will also demonstrate characteristics that support service access. Detecting problem sources in a complex network represents a challenge.

Diagnostic programs were once used by professionals operating on local computers. Error information for correction was delivered through the mail or express messenger to expert teams in the laboratories. Corrections were distributed in the same manner and usually took long periods of time to be completed and delivered to the users. Using the same techniques with networked computers could only cause confusion and delay in producing well-balanced, running systems. Improved diagnostics, which can travel through the system, pinpoint the source of the problem, and transmit the correction across the communications media, are necessary. Interactive diagnostics enable expert teams, whether in the customer or vendor location, to see the problem and correct it rapidly. Often, different workers or machine domain owners will look to other places for the source of errors. Good serviceability tools permit the accurate debugging of different elements of the open system.

Vendors have directed their attention to specific open systems components. Recent additions to open systems standards can expand the scope of these improvements.

2.4.5 Timing Characteristics

Timing has been important in the design and acceptance of computer systems since their introduction. Initially, the effects of automation were measured in terms of being able to perform tasks that either people could not perform well or that were simply very slow in meeting the needs of the business. Eventually, the computer has been viewed as an adjunct device or assistant to the people performing some task, and the need for rapid response time has increased.

Service businesses rely on their ability to handle large numbers of transactions. *On-line transaction processing* (OLTP) involves rapid response to inquiries in businesses as diverse as airlines and banks. Often, these inquiries involve access to large amounts of data spread across multiple databases.

The airline reservations system, which responds in a short time to the flight and seating needs of the flying public, is an example. These systems are pivotal to the airline operations and are viewed as more valuable than the equipment.

OLTP requires accurate information to be delivered reliably and with a high degree of security to the end users. The most successful transaction monitor is CICS, which was developed by IBM in the 1960s. There has not been a wide adoption of open systems for OLTP, but there is a growing acceptance of the use of servers attached across an open systems network to perform these functions. Various approaches have been taken in open systems definitions to describe OLTP. Specifically, TUXEDO was introduced from AT&T to handle Regional Bell Operating Company OLTP applications. Encina, which provides OLTP facilities for Distributed Computing Environment (DCE)-based systems, is a product from Transarc Corporation (DCE is discussed in Chapter 3.)

Real-time characteristics have also been important in industrial processes with critical process requirements. Real-time operations in the chemical, nuclear, and oil industries are well known to most people. In these cases, the system, whether it is a person or a computer, must be geared to respond rapidly. Often, a delayed response in these sensitive cases can seriously affect the entire process.

Another time characteristic is the actual time required to get a process operational within a company or division. Computer system installation occurs over time and is affected by the duration of the effort. As in life, computer systems are installed in a forward direction but understood backwards (Pagels, 1989). As we define new system architectures, they are usually created with a clear understanding of the past.

Time can be viewed from many perspectives in open systems. Executives view time as the period in which the project becomes functional and begins to produce the required results for the organization. The implementation manager will view the arrow of time from the perspective of immediate schedules. The definition of a completed task will vary with the observers.

Another way to review the time period of open systems is to consider the history of computing within a company. The arrow of time (Figure 2.6) begins in the past with legacy systems, which help form the environment in which open systems must function. The information repository has grown since the first introduction of computing and continually grows as new systems are introduced. Additional information technology is introduced to meet specific application requirements, and the system has continued to grow with complexity and age.

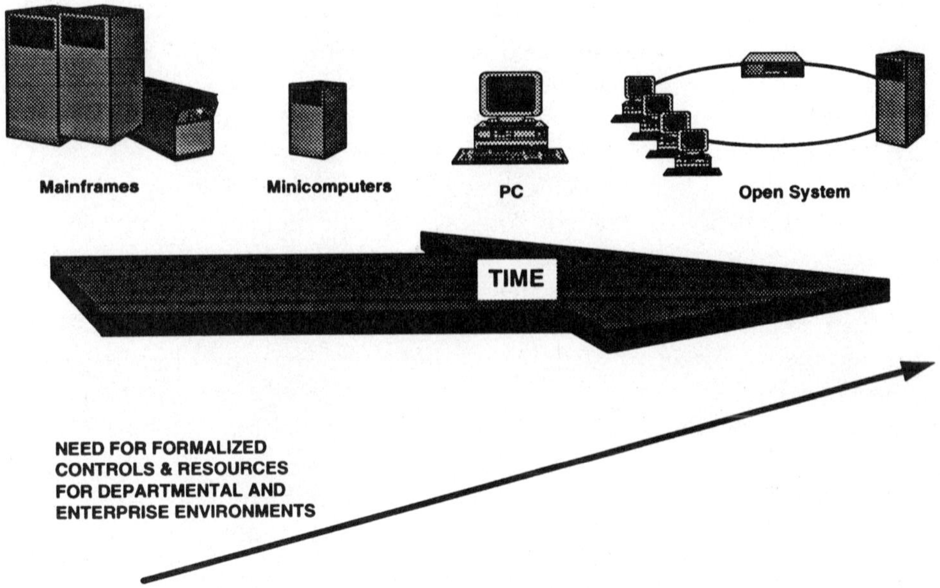

Figure 2.6 Computer history's arrow of time

Systems also progress in time from the point where a decision is made until implementation is complete. The active time of building the system may find the hardware and software passing through a number of changes. Since technology is changing very rapidly, there is a need for flexibility in plans to permit a response to this change.

Time is an important characteristic, which is improved by using open distributed systems. Since the system has moved closer to the needs of the end user, there is a much faster response time. Systems are subject to predictable change, but they must also contend with changes that are not predictable. Standards help the predictable; flexibility is needed to adjust to the unpredictable.

In considering open systems, it is clear that performance testing will vary with so much capability focused on the local processors. Additional tools will help in measuring individual parts of the network.

2.5 CONSIDERATIONS

Open systems are in the early stages of development, and their unique characteristics and qualities are still developing. Client/server configurations reduce the complexity of application development by partitioning applications and data, but the partitioning raises a new challenge of coordinating the different parts of a network.

Client/servers also can provide centralized control of shared data. Although the data may reside on shared resources, each data element is protected from changes in the rest of the open systems.

Although open systems provide new challenges to security design, techniques exist to ensure the security and integrity of data in complex networks. Scanning techniques can be used to detect viruses, but complete system diligence must be observed in protecting all open systems components.

Security systems require the full commitment of company management. Techniques for protecting all levels of computer systems enhance overall system integrity.

Reliability, availability, and serviceability create unique challenges for open systems designers. Conventional approaches to these designs have been changed as a result of the distributed nature of the network. Additional requirements for system managers have also been created by the distributed nature of open systems components.

Although technology is important, it can be effective only if the end users can access it. Computer usability is vital to systems that depend on less-skilled workers to perform tasks on the network. Interfaces to the network must reflect the different requirements and skill levels of the users.

Although open systems are largely based around UNIX, an increasing number of applications will reside on different system protocols, as long as they can comply with the interfaces defined by standards groups. An open systems architecture can reside on different hardware and software bases.

2.5.1 Note

The term *language* is used frequently in computer literature to refer to specific cryptic languages that produce series of commands. Natural language refers to the ability to use traditional language to access computer information.

2.6 REFERENCES

Department of Defense. *Department of Defense Trusted Computer System Evaluation Criteria.* Washington, DC: Department of Defense, 1985.

Gould, J. D., and C. Lewis. "Designing for Usability: Key Principles and What Designers Think." *Communications of the ACM,* March 1985, pp. 300–312.

Grove, Andrew S. Comments made during his keynote speech at 1991 COMDEX in Las Vegas, October 22, 1991.

Murray, William H. "Security Considerations for Personal Computers." *IBM Systems Journal,* vol. 23, no. 3, 1984, pp. 297–304.

Pagels, Heinz R. *The Dreams of Reason: The Computer and the Rise of the Sciences of Complexity.* New York: Bantam Books, 1989.

Shaffer, Steven, and Alan Simon. *Network Security.* Boston: AP Professional, 1993.

3

Foundations of Open Systems: Hardware, Software, and Standards

Technology developments contributed to the introduction of open systems in the 1980s and continue to affect its wide adoption. In 1991, the technology available exceeded the expectations of forecasters in 1980 but in many areas followed predictable trends established earlier. Both positive and negative surprises have affected computer installations. We can expect the decade of the 1990s to follow this pattern.

The four foundation areas that determine solution alternatives used for open systems are shown in Figure 3.1. The primary foundation is hardware technology, which has been improving at exponential rates since the 1960s. Changes have affected computer chips as well as supporting technologies that enable low-cost solutions on desktops. Modern hardware systems, designed using advanced technologies, are more powerful and have a wider address spectrum than early mainframes. These systems have demonstrated unique power when packaged directly into new solutions.

The second foundation is software, which is used to mold hardware in performing complex tasks. Operating systems are combined with modern development tools to provide a framework to support networked applications. Increasing emphasis on network tools will further enhance group productivity and add value to the completed systems. Without software, the entire set of hardware becomes relatively worthless.

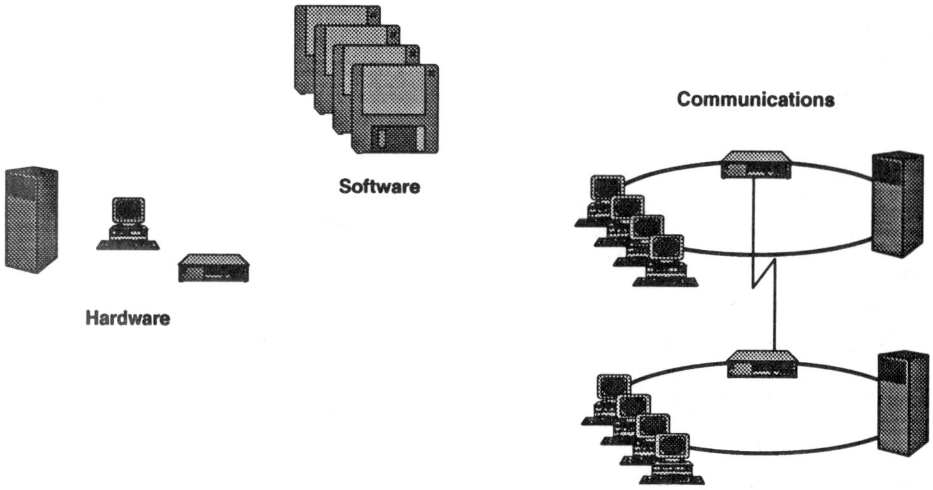

Figure 3.1 Foundation areas that determine solution alternatives for open systems

The third foundation is the growing body of industry standards, which is shown in the figure as the glue that connects the different pieces together. Worldwide cooperation between users and vendors has resulted in international standards, which permit different vendor solutions to be used together. The cooperation has been further stimulated by strong involvement of world governments. The U.S. government, in particular, has been pressing for the adoption of standards in many agencies. This provides the users with a higher selectivity and enables application developers to profit from selling their products on multiple processors. Continued development of de jure or de facto standards will accelerate the acceptance of open systems.

The fourth foundation is the open communications support, which provides the connections between different hardware and software systems. This topic will be explored in depth in Chapter 8 and will not be examined in this chapter. Communications is vital to the linkage between different components of the open system and is an important ingredient in network computing.

In examining foundations, it is well to understand that all pieces, when placed in a network, provide a system that must run the business or the department. Each foundation will require a quality of completion that guarantees the smooth operation of a modern competitive business.

3.1 HARDWARE TECHNOLOGY

Hardware technology advances have contributed to the acceptance of open systems solutions and have enabled open computers to replace functions traditionally allocated to large computer complexes. The matrix of potential hardware solutions is shown graphically in Figure 3.2. Four important, separate types of technology are shown in this figure. The first is processors, which have shown price and function improvements every 18 months. The second is large storage, which is used by servers. The third is secondary storage, which supports both clients and servers. The fourth is media, which includes the various input and output devices.

Central to the wide acceptance of open systems have been the revolutionary advances in hardware technologies. Electronics has been the pacing element for the entire industry. As an example, individual circuit design has continually advanced since the introduction of computers. When it was introduced in the 1950s, the transistor replaced the vacuum tube and launched a search for further miniaturization in electronic components.

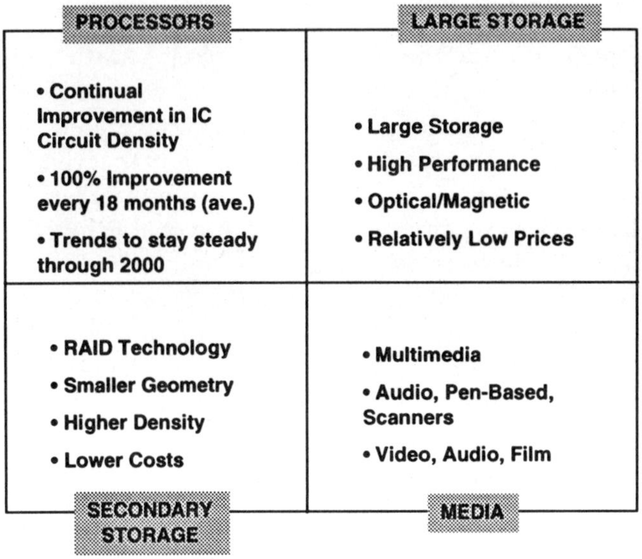

Figure 3.2 Matrix of potential hardware solutions

Work by Jack Kilby of Texas Instruments and Robert Noyce of Intel helped introduce concepts that are fundamental to the continued growth of electronic solutions. Their search was to combine transistors with capacitors and resistors on a single circuit and eventually on a single chip. Expansion of this work has led to dense chips, which contain many circuits on a single superchip.

The reliability of hardware built from integrated circuits is an important factor in these advances. Early reliability was observed in the chips designed for larger computers (Pugh et al., 1991) but has been exceeded by each subsequent release of processor chips. Modern electronic components are so reliable that they can be considered safe for use in many life-critical or production environments. Critical applications can use new technology with little anticipation of failure under reasonable operating conditions.

Design tools have facilitated the continual refinement and improvement of the integrated circuit designs, so many transistor equivalents can be included on a simple silicon chip. Design techniques refined development processes to use computers as tools to improve quality and accelerate the time for introduction of functions. These advances have led to over 1 million transistors on a single chip in 1991, with projections of over 100 million by 2000.

The introduction of Application Specific Integrated Circuits (ASICs) has enabled the creation of special designer chips within a very short time. Advances in automation tools for chip design have greatly accelerated the introduction of these special chips. The result will be computers that can be tailored for relatively low cost to the individual needs of the installation. Custom chips will meet the needs of specific applications and enable individual departments or companies to have an advantage over competition.

At the center of each computer hardware system is the processing unit located on the microcomputer. The microprocessor unit contains the central electronic complex and is augmented by power supplies, special processing features, and attachments to input and output devices to create the desktop computer. Since desktop units are so important to open systems, it is well to understand the composition of the processing units and how they have been affected by microprocessor developments.

Complexity of the instruction sets in computers has grown over the years. In the 1980s, there was a return to simpler instructions that could be completed in single machine cycles. The older designs have been called Complex Instruction Set Computing (CISC). CISC computers rely on hardware design to provide performance and functionality. These instructions are widely used in minicomputers and PCs and therefore will be found in many open systems configurations.

Continued advances in design have helped produce processor chips that use reduced instructions. Studies demonstrated that only a small portion of the program instructions were used in most programs. As a result, Reduced Instruction Set Computing (RISC) was born (Patterson, 1985). Initial RISC chips were designed for supercomputers, but by the 1980s they were incorporated into major new processor chips. Many workstation and server vendors have adopted RISC chips for their products.

Instructions determine a processor's performance and functions. Conventional processors have used single instruction and data streams to run programs, but advances have permitted the introduction of multiprocessing on units as small as workstations. Parallel instruction and data streams are valuable for servers for higher performance or fault tolerance.

Open systems solutions require additional compute power beyond scalar functions. Floating-point functions are used in engineering and commercial accounts for calculating large numerical models and supporting imaging on the desktop. With the introduction of graphical user interfaces, it is important to consider graphics engines and their contributions to the ability to effectively use images. Graphics engines use separate processors to enhance screen images.

Another design area of importance is the computer bus. Buses are electrical data highways between processors and other devices, including local memory. They provide connection protocols to different devices. Their efficiency determines the interaction rate between different processors and supporting devices. Although there are dedicated memory buses, system buses can provide general-purpose connections for memory, peripherals, and system components. Dedicated peripheral buses provide special connections for disks, tapes, or printers. These devices are usually attached through adapter boards inserted on an attachment bus.

Since buses regulate traffic flow, it is important to understand their techniques for arbitrating conflicts between signals. The signals and protocols are a major part of the system design and should be examined for conformity to industry standards, performance, connectivity, and extensibility. In modern systems, there is a trend to minimal 32-bit bus connections with a strong trend in larger network units to 64-bit designs. These bus sizes are important to determine overall performance on the open systems network.

Microprocessors have consistently outperformed other computer designs for performance and function. The acceleration of performance and function while prices have fallen has made workstation technology unique. Advances have occurred so rapidly that modern designs are dependent on language compilers to reach their full potential.

In addition to the power of the central processor, memory prices have tumbled while the amount of addressable storage in a unit has continued to climb. Desktop computers are being shipped with millions of characters of memory and the system designs permit virtual memory exceeding terabytes (trillions of characters). Virtual memory uses secondary storage devices as an extension of local memory, giving the userly near limitless addressing capability.

The chips that comprise the heart of the microprocessors have been shifting in their addressing. Design has shifted from simple 16-bit-wide instructions and data to a 32-bit level. This not only provides extended addressing but also increases the performance of normal operations. More recent introductions have included 64-bit offerings, with some high-end servers using 128-bit processing chips.

The fact that a relatively quiet desktop unit can reside in the office is partially attributable to developments in power supply units that have eliminated the need for high-speed fans. Advances in disk drives and high-performance, low-noise input/output devices have also improved the environment at individual desktop computers.

Modern systems use basic building blocks to create different capacity processors. Scalability is achieved through the use of microprocessor units to build different nodes in open systems. As an example, SPARC (Scalable Processor Architecture) chips are widely accepted for multiple system designs. Designers have used the chips in products ranging from low-end portable computers to massive parallel processors that outperform mainframe computers. Support products are widely available for the popular chip.

SPARC was originally developed by Sun Microsystems and defined as an open chip design. It is maintained and distributed by the SPARC International consortium, which makes the design available to companies seeking to build products using the architecture. A number of different chip manufacturers have adopted the chip and made it available to product developers.

Chips that were introduced with the PC have continued to have an acceptance within open systems products. Most notably, the Intel 80X86 chips have been adopted by multiple vendors for use in workstations and servers. The 8088, used for IBM's first PC, was a derivative of the 8086 chip, which permitted low-cost I/O device attachments. The success of the PC made the Intel chip line popular for desktop processors (Strauss, 1986).

Intel's more advanced chips provide significant new features over the originals used in the PCs. Many features that required special support chips have been embedded in the main processors. The extension to 32-bit-wide processors and improved instructions has made modern processors using these chips superior for many applications. Some companies have used multiple chips to achieve high performance for servers. The use of these chips has been popular, since there is a widespread development environment in place that can be tailored to new products. In addition, many companies can benefit from existing PC software that provides a rich customer support base.

For open systems solutions, scalability is a requirement for fixed and removable storage units. Disks are the major fixed storage units, and these devices are available in 3.5- or 5.25-inch configurations. The wide acceptance of these units has made them usable in desktop computers and larger-scale processors. A composite design of all these technologies is the desktop and tower units, which are so popular in many different working environments. Complex devices are molded into the system through easy-to-connect attachments.

An important new storage technology, RAID (Redundant Arrays of Inexpensive Disks) was developed at the University of California at Berkeley and has had growing use in open systems solutions. RAID connects multiple low-cost disks together in a redundant array. These devices group standard 3.5- or 5.25-inch disk units into redundant banks that provide fault-tolerant storage. This solution splits data across multiple disks, speeding both the read and write process. Since large numbers of small disks are used, the configuration significantly reduces the footprint in machine rooms or where servers are used.

Many of the hardware components are found across multiple open systems solutions. Their application to large servers, as well as the large numbers of desktop computers, helps to increase the production runs on the parts and reduce their costs. As advances continue in hardware technology, there will be a greater use of modular solutions applied across different devices. The result will be higher quality and continued reduction in costs.

Although this discussion has focused on subproducts shared across multiple hardware vendors, open systems applications are not confined to open hardware definitions. Interfaces are architected across multiple vendors, which shifts the primary levels of support into software.

3.2 SOFTWARE FOUNDATIONS

Eventually, the value of any computer system is measured in the effectiveness of applications built on the system. Applications are based on software foundations that help define open systems. Unlike hardware, which follows the symmetrical laws of physics (Penrose, 1990), software is asymmetrical and must be tailored to meet the specific needs of the user. This lack of symmetry led to the definition of control points in the operating systems.

Software was introduced in the 1950s to reduce the complexity of cumbersome rewiring. It has been over 30 years since the first computer operating systems were introduced to simplify transitions between different programming steps. Since then, increasing functions have been added to the operating environment—languages to simplify programming, databases to facilitate rapid access to information, and subsystems to make systems simpler for end users. Network support systems make the system available across multiple processors.

The operating system enabled users to support multiple jobs on a single machine. Since then, operating system functions have grown to support hardware designs, complex application software, and simplified end-user interfaces. In the 1950s, individual programs managed the hardware resources used, and operators managed the transitions between jobs. As complexity increased, the difficulty of each task also increased, and additional software was introduced to simplify the process. Complexity was evident early in the development of the Semi Automatic Ground Environment (SAGE) for U.S. air defense. Operating system models were developed for SAGE and later influenced commercial developments during the early 1960s. SAGE and the commercial experience led to the development of large operating systems for commercial computers (Watson, 1990).

By today's measure, early operating systems were relatively simple (Lorin and Deitel, 1981). The introduction of IBM System/360 in 1965 represented a significant breakthrough in comprehensive programming packages that still affects open systems designs today (Pugh et al., 1991). Job and memory management were introduced, which simplified the application programmer's task of allocating storage. Smooth transitions were possible between programs without operator intervention. Terminals replaced card devices, and the entire process of running software advanced.

By 1972, advances in operating systems were introduced that affected open systems. IBM extended OS/360 with the introduction of virtual capability and, in 1975, introduced OS/MVS (Operating System Multiple Virtual

Systems). OS/MVS remains an important element in open systems support and will be the base of many interoperability problems. MVS introduced programming concepts that can prove valuable in defining distributed system support.

The characteristics of distributed systems began evolving in the 1970s, as minicomputer vendors announced new products. It was recognized early that communications should be embedded in a distributed kernel. Data flow became an important element in the definition of an open systems operating system, since it regulated the movement of data between different nodes of the system. Calls issued in a program refer to data or applications resident in either the local node or some distributed node. Refinements on distributed operating systems continued, as early PCs were introduced in the 1980s.

By the mid-1980s, IBM had defined many concepts used in cooperative processing. Cooperative processing assumed systems cooperating with applications residing in mainframes. Interfaces could be tightly defined, permitting autonomy in both processors and cooperation between the applications residing in the different processing elements of a distributed system. Transaction routers were defined in the remote nodes to interact with comparable code residing on mainframes. Much of the cooperative processing definition was folded into the *System Application Architecture* (SAA) work, IBM's ambitious enterprise computing architecture introduced in 1987.

Control points are critical in understanding open systems design, since they affect system design and integration. A control point provides the domain management for data, program, and hardware interaction. Each computer requires control code for its local domain, which includes hardware and software scheduling and resources. Network nodes contain routines that handle physical- and link-level connections. Sophisticated store-and-forward systems provide primitive database elements, which have been proposed as separate standards. Synchronization of the information flow between organizations has also been handled by these software control points.

Figure 3.3 describes four different control point designs. The first is the individual control point found on workstations and PCs. The second is the LAN control point, which affects multiple workstations and servers. The third is the mainframe control point, which controls actions of the devices that attach to a mainframe. The fourth control point is the enterprise control point, which spans workstations, LANs, and mainframes.

Early computer designers spent a good deal of time identifying how to control the various functions included within a network. This is also true for

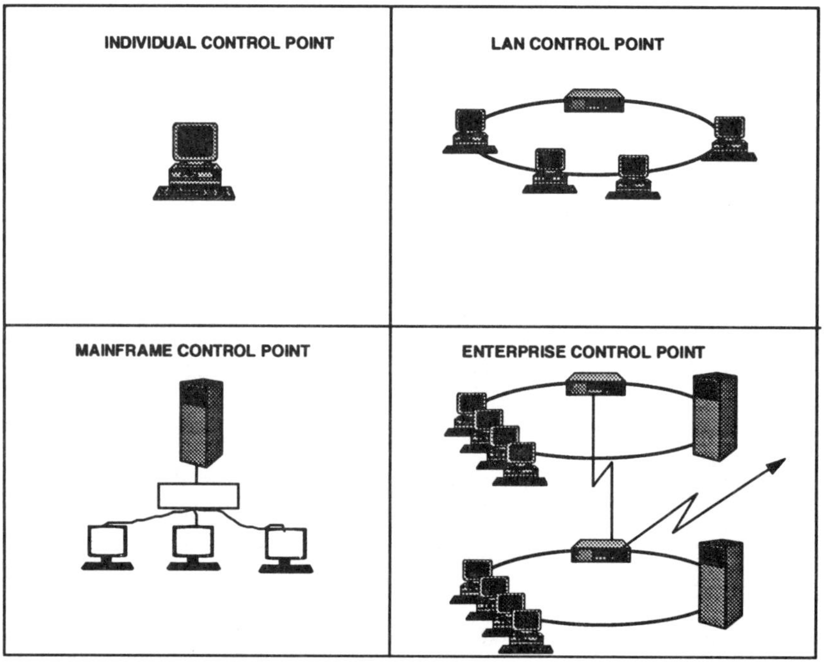

Figure 3.3 Control point designs

distributed systems, but since the system is heterogeneous, there is not a single system control point. The distributed system continues to grow in processing power and memory capacity in a system similar to physical systems.

A PC is an individual productivity tool controlled by the end user. The same PC connected to an LAN for a vertical application is controlled by a network control computer for shared tasks. A mainframe is similar to a PC and controls terminals attached to its applications. In defining the network control programs, careful consideration was devoted to the control points. As terminals were replaced by workstations, control shifted from single points in the mainframe to shared control points between the workstations and mainframes.

A control point for workstations connected to an LAN will reside in the LAN. In an enterprise, the control point may shift to a larger computer. In a supersystem, it is possible to define a virtual point that does not reside on any single processor.

The enterprise control point (Figure 3.4) provides the logical functions normally found in a single operating system or within the operating system

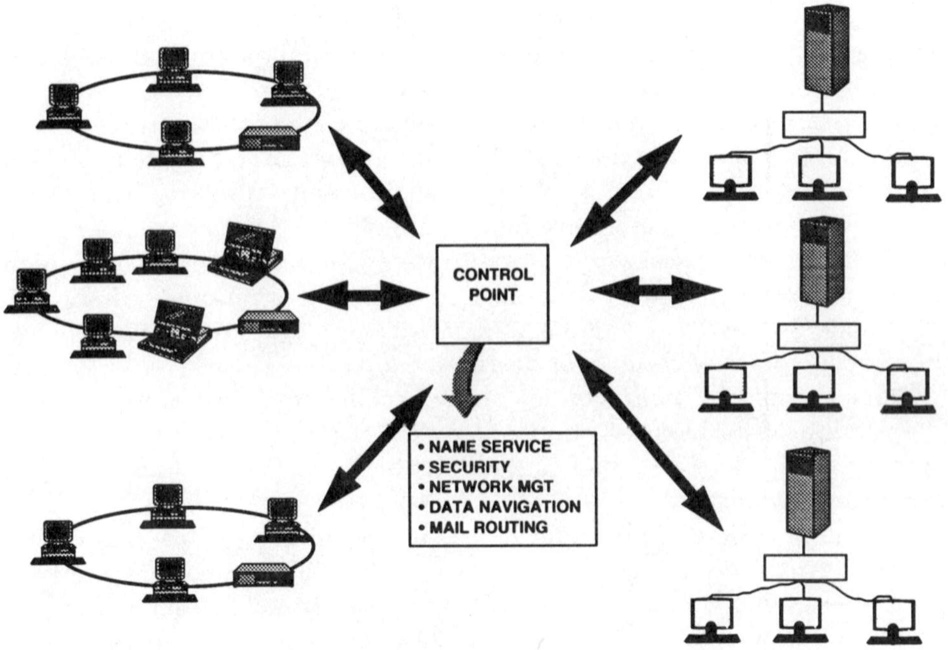

Figure 3.4 The enterprise control point

and communications code. This sort of system represents a well-ordered and predictable system. Open distributed systems can be considered indeterminate, and thus the interactions are often difficult to predict and control. The enterprise control point has functions such as name service, security, network management, data navigation, and mail routing.

Penrose gives an example of system regularity by using a billiard ball (Penrose, 1990). If the system is regular with one or two balls, the results can be predictable. When multiple balls are introduced, the results can become more difficult and potentially chaotic. Different techniques must be adopted to predict the results from these different systems. When a single or a few computer systems interact, the results can be more predictable than a system with hundreds or thousands of peers.

An indication of the complexity can be further understood by investigating the interactions between gas particles in a closed space. There is a high degree of similarity of the growing entropy of a closed gas system with the constant growth of the distributed system. An alternative approach to network management in an unbalanced environment can utilize knowledge of balancing between elements in a neural network. Three separate computing technologies, which require virtual control points, are converging. These are massive parallel computing, discussed in the server section of this book, distributed computing, and neural computing. It is probable there will be a high similarity between the solutions applied to each of these problems.

The control point that does not reside on a single processor is, in effect, a virtual point. It is defined by the architecture and standards, which now comprise many of the functions traditionally allocated to operating systems. Early design for such a system was introduced in SNA with LU 6.2, which could be viewed as a virtual operating system. The importance of network operating systems has extended to modern open systems. Standards have become the point of control for distributed systems.

Since the control point resides in the architecture, the conformity and monitoring of the control point will reside in the adherence of network software to standards. Self-policing will disable code that does not meet the connection requirements.

Operating code was introduced early in the history of PCs. Many early systems focused on the simple utility tasks which, in many cases, resembled early mainframe systems. These operating systems controlled such functions as input/output connections and the flow between different programs. Functions enabled the users to code, compile, and eventually run single-stream programs. Some memory management was performed, but there was little to be done in single-stream systems. As PCs matured, users sought extensions in the operating systems to support multiple tasks and even multiple jobs running on the same processor.

Microsoft Disk Operating System (MS-DOS) was introduced with the IBM personal computer in 1981 and has been the most successful operating system in history. The system was built as a personal system, which used some modern techniques but remained difficult for many people to learn in detail. The operating system has served as the base for much early client code. Advances in presentation services helped to make the system an important desktop computer, and the release of Windows has provided additional capability to run multiple programs. The popularity of the system and the subsequent adoption by large numbers of application vendors have made the system very important for desktop support. The addition of the Microsoft Windows operating environment gave MS-DOS what might be termed a "midlife kicker" and made Windows the dominant desktop environment in the PC world.

In 1987, Microsoft and IBM combined to produce Operating System/2 (OS/2). The system was originally introduced as a 16-bit system in a world dominated by 32-bit processors and received only hesitant acceptance. By 1992, IBM had adopted the system as its offering and raised the system to a 32-bit architecture. OS/2 combined many of the lessons learned with MS-DOS and UNIX and produced a universal client/server system. OS/2 has many positive features, which make it superior to other alternatives. The client communications' extended edition is superior to other alternatives, since it was adopted from mainframe transaction processor technology.

Another popular operating system on PCs is the Macintosh operating system developed by Apple Computers. The operating system uses an advanced object design for the user interfaces, which has been appealing to end users, whether skilled or unskilled. The user interfaces, coupled with a synchronization of data across multiple applications, have contributed to a wide popularity among end users. The Macintosh operating system has not been strong in open connectivity, but its ease of use has made it an appealing alternative for many users. Increased connectivity and additional computing power on the individual Macintosh computers will enhance the system's popularity as a client that can be modified to meet standards of open systems.

The operating system that is most important in support plans for open systems is UNIX (Norton and Hahn, 1991), which was originally developed at Bell Laboratories by Kernighan and Ritchie (Bach, 1986) in 1972. The original UNIX is a derivative of the MULTICS work performed at MIT in the 1960s. The system was widely used earlier at AT&T locations and released to the academic community, which enhanced the system as they expanded support to other processors. Wide academic acceptance helped to popularize the system.

At the heart of UNIX is the kernel, which balances system resources across multiple requesters and provides resource sharing for other programs. UNIX provides scheduling between specific jobs in a multiple-user environment with multitasking, which was inherent in the design even in the single-user environment. UNIX spans open systems alternatives from the PC to multiple parallel processors. Extensions have been made to the kernel that enhance support for parallel processing, distributed processing, and real-time environments. All these extensions have increased the use of these systems within the network.

Building blocks of UNIX include processes, which are execution instances of programs and are comparable to tasks in other operating systems. Forks are calls that initiate processes within the system. Pipes are conduits for interprocessor communications. The primary interface to UNIX functions is through shells, which provide simple access to system functions. The user communicates to the kernel using one of the available shells or creates a unique shell. Newer shells permit users to define asynchronous commands, which reduces wait times. Although many shells are available, a number of tools are merging, which will facilitate building new ones. Many versions of UNIX provide shell support for MS-DOS applications.

After considering the shell, the next level of importance is the UNIX tree-structure hierarchy using directories and files. Although other data structures have been built on top of the basic file system, it remains the most widely supported file base. Some companies have introduced object file systems, supplementing the UNIX linear byte representations. Peripherals are treated as extensions to the file system, which simplifies their program access.

The high level of activity to expand UNIX has resulted in advances on all levels of the system. Windowing, GUIs, and communications protocols have been defined. For example, Motif provides 3-D PC-like appearances on multiple platforms. Coupled with modern tools, it is possible to identify widgets that define text and graphical storage space, pushbuttons, and sliders. Modern aids facilitate screen creation and connection across the network.

UNIX was originally created for an old minicomputer with teletype terminals. It has become the software backbone of open systems, as it has been extended to operate on PCs and workstations. UNIX has been transformed by the efforts of companies and standards units to create an operating system that can compete for a slice of the advanced system revenue. UNIX used TCP/IP protocols for network support and contributed to the wide acceptance of the protocol. Subsequent to UNIX's adoption of the support, other systems have been using the protocols, and the network has become important for all open systems networks.

The multiple implementations of UNIX on different platforms helped spur its wide acceptance. The ease of transporting code between different systems is driven in part by the acceptance of C language on multiple processors. Applications can be recompiled across many machines using the common compiler. Consistent interfaces, clearly defined, also helped to make the transition easy.

Extensions to UNIX are planned by standards groups and vendors, which will further enhance its use in open systems. Modern operating systems provide a wide range of functions to connect the user with the computing environment. The operating systems support the power of the hardware in a usable manner for end users. Multiple systems will be found in the complex networks that typify open operating environments. In addition to appearing on desktop computers, operating system code will be found in servers and attached computers. The range of function will vary across the different desktop computers and mainframes connected to the network.

Open systems have provided new challenges for operating system designers. For instance, an early problem for all operating systems is to determine when binding is established between the program and data the program will access. In a distributed system, which includes heterogeneous hardware implementations, the problem is even more complex. If allocation of tasks occurs during the request, the binding process may force the loading of code from a library specially designed for the specific system.

Increased requirements for open interfaces have resulted in extensions of traditional operating systems. Capabilities such as multitasking, networking, and usability are assumed and provide the base for newer functions such as object and data flow. The increased power of input/output devices has increased the support of multimedia applications heterogeneous computers. Balancing work in a distributed system will require a repository of information about the capability of different systems. Traditional multiuser code remains important to server implementors, but increasing demand for groupware support will force the definition of cooperative scheduling routines. Advanced networking protocols will replace TCP/IP over time, but the need will be for tools to provide management of the network and the individual local systems.

The selection of operating system code for open systems is an important decision, since it will prove to be the foundation of the open systems direction for some time. There is intense competition between the existing and projected systems for a place in the open configuration. It is important to assess the value of each system for a given range and to select a system that meets the long-term needs of the company. Further discussion of selection criteria will be found in the chapters about clients and servers. The operating system and its support code will remain important as a foundation point for open systems.

3.3 STANDARDS AND OPEN SYSTEMS

Standards form the fundamental underpinnings of open systems. To achieve common access to multiple vendors, common interfaces are essential. Many efforts to define standards were underway by the late 1980s, and the 1990s have brought about reorganization and consolidation among the various consortia. The development of standards for computing maps closely to the development of standards for rail transportation. In the early decades of rail development, each developer created unique tracks and coupling techniques. It was not possible to move from one railroad to another very easily. Eventually, standards were accepted for train gauge and coupling protocols. It is now possible to travel on many railroads in a trip across the country.

For many years, each computer company created an architecture that served as their blueprint for developers and users. These blueprints were used to implement both hardware and software solutions and were extended to include the parameters of use across multiple proprietary boxes. These vendor-specific architectures provided the computer company with a significant leverage over competition, since the using departments developed a large investment in specific applications. Many of these architectures became de facto industry standards, as multiple companies adhered to the rules for using the different processors.

Computer designers recognized the value in defining clean layers between discrete functions. These clean layers could be extended, as hardware or software improvements permitted. More importantly, layers were easy to understand, as new generations of implementors were introduced to architectures about which they had little knowledge of the original reasons behind the decisions. The concept of simple, focused interfaces has helped architectures endure.

Initially, hardware was accepted as an architecture, or standard, level by many different companies. Early in the stage of developing computers, three different standards groups were directly involved in the creation and maintenance of new standards. Now, there are over 100 different groups directly involved with standards.

As an example, the chips that became prevalent in PCs were based on Intel 80X86 architecture. This became a standard of the industry, as many hardware companies adopted the chip for inclusion in multiple boxes. Equally important were the different levels of hardware connection protocols. Input/output attachment protocols became popular and were accepted, as different vendors gained from the commonalty of hardware attachment. The IBM PC AT Bus became widespread, as the number of duplicate boxes increased. Hardware standards were formalized through direct documentation of de facto standards or through general adoption of existing protocols.

The threshold of standard acceptance has continually shifted higher in the development spectrum. After common chips were adopted, it was possible to adopt common software protocols. Operating systems could be run across many hardware vendors. Programming languages had been standardized by committee since the 1960s. Recent efforts have focused on the definition of standard user interface languages.

For communications, a number of protocols were accepted across many companies. De facto standards emerged from the larger computer vendors, such as IBM and Digital Equipment. Companies wishing to connect to vendor systems had to comply to the specific architecture of the company. IBM's Systems Network Architecture (SNA) became a standard for many corporations, and thus many companies have developed code that supports SNA on separate units. Digital Equipment's DECnet received wide acceptance in manufacturing and engineering communities and was adopted by a wide range of companies that connected their devices to those in the commercial and scientific community. Documentation enabled vendors to implement to either vendor architecture.

With increasing acceleration of the technology cycle, it was recognized that reliance on a few vendors not only provided them with a unique competitive advantage but also meant they were critical to the implementation of modern technology. In addition, vendor architectures were often inadequate to support the rapidly emerging technology. Apart from the technology bottleneck, competitors and users were searching for a level playing field, which provided them with competitive options.

Users benefit from industry standards by reaching a higher degree of flexibility to adopt different vendor implementations. Alternatives can be chosen from a much wider repertoire of alternatives, making the selection less costly and more flexible to the needs of the individual companies. Standards provide a clear-cut management direction for the company's technical implementations.

Some users have succeeded in defining their own protocols through standard documents and purchasing agreements. This is an expensive option, since it requires a staff sufficiently skilled in different protocols to define and monitor the standard. Most companies choose to let industry groups define and police the standards.

Industry groups are involved in defining and verifying standards across a number of commercial fields. For instance, railroad trains can move across the country because there is a standard that defines the track separation.

The United States has a large body of standards governing many different commercial enterprises.

Since data processing is international, there is a direct need for coordinated effort across many countries. As you can imagine, there would be a great deal of difficulty in moving data across international borders without the efforts of these groups. The International Standards Organization (ISO) has access to the work of thousands of engineers and scientists from countries around the world to define standards for data processing and telecommunications. Vendors and users are represented on standards committees in the international and the national levels.

Within the United States, the primary standards groups are the American National Standards Institute (ANSI) and the Institute of Electrical and Electronic Engineers (IEEE). IEEE especially has defined many standards for open systems, such as the Portable Operating System Interface for Computer Environments (POSIX) (IEEE #1003.1). POSIX has been committed for existing systems, which will enable these systems to interface directly into an open system. Although operating systems have been the nucleus of open systems, related standards in user interface and languages have proven important in open systems environments. Communications groups have been working separately on refining these important connection protocols.

By the middle of the 1980s, UNIX was recognized as an acceptable operating system that could be used on many different hardware platforms. Many versions developed, as each vendor added a small amount of uniqueness. Popularity of the system has led to the extension of functions to include windowing and GUIs in the definitions. Many vendor participants sought to improve and build on the basic UNIX definitions. Potential buyers were attracted by the code portability and functional richness of the system, which led to an increasing acceptance. The various implementations were creating a good deal of confusion on the part of the users who clamored for a single UNIX. To straighten out the growing chaos, two important industrial consortia emerged in the late 1980s.

The first of these consortia is UNIX International (UI). UI was founded by AT&T and other major UNIX vendors to lead in standardizing future releases of the system. The original charter was expanded beyond the limits of the operating system, as additional support areas were recognized. Definition of user interfaces was an early addition to the charter as more users complained about the complexity of the UNIX interfaces.

UI defined a detailed roadmap of technology growth within the standard, called the System V Roadmap (UNIX International, 1991). The roadmap defined additional networking support areas of distributed processing and graphical user interfaces. Transaction processing permits the operating system user to handle multiple transactions across different boxes. International capabilities extend to include support for languages and currency considerations. System management standardizes the system control processes.

The second consortium, Open Systems Foundation (OSF), was created by vendors who recognized the importance of UNIX as an established system and wished to move beyond the definitions then included in UNIX. They defined a system that extended support capability in an equitable fashion, which could then be met by a variety of vendors. Such major companies as IBM, DEC, and Hewlett-Packard (H-P) created OSF in May 1988 and developed its charter to plan new directions based on the original UNIX foundations but with modern alternatives.

OSF recognized the need to move beyond basic systems definitions and provide support for emerging technologies. After searching for an appropriate kernel to couple UNIX support with modern technology, the consortium adopted Carnegie Mellon's Mach as an operating system kernel in 1989. The group also recognized the need to define a user interface and defined Motif as its primary interface. Expanded frameworks include object support, distributed management environment (DME), and distributed computing environment (DCE). Innovative designs are being built on the existing definitions to further enhance OSF's role as a leader in defining modern operating environments.

In 1993, another organization—the Common Open Software Environment (COSE)—was announced, its goal being to develop common UNIX specifications for use in open systems (sound like a familiar goal by now?). A major COSE effort was the production of the Common Desktop Environment (CDE).

By mid-1994, many of the standards consortia had undergone consolidation and/or reorganization, and the turmoil continues at press time. For example, OSF reorganized and created *Org94*, under which the sponsorship processes for various projects were changed (Lytton, 1994; Wong, 1994).

The turmoil and controversy in the standards community is nothing new, though. Early contention between the different bodies of vendors resulted in a group of European users meeting to define a charter for a third definitional group. Although this group consisted primarily of users, invitations were extended to vendors. The X/Open Consortium Ltd. was chartered to focus on pragmatic guidelines that permit applications to run across the operating systems defined by the two vendor groups. A primary goal became application portability across different UNIX systems. Their definitions extended to other elements of software that affect portability, such as languages, databases, GUIs, and networking protocols. X/Open adopted IEEE POSIX UNIX definition and defined measurement criteria to judge the different versions of UNIX. It has also provided a seal of approval in the form of branding, which identifies the capability of each implementation.

In early 1994, X/Open made several announcements indicating they planned to broaden their universe of interest beyond the UNIX realm into other areas of open computing; the results of this strategy will be seen in upcoming years.

Worldwide standards groups have been in existence for years. Communications standards were quickly recognized as being important to international cooperation. The International Telegraph Union was founded in May 1865. By 1932, the title was changed to the International Telecommunication Union (ITU). By 1947, the group was affiliated with the United Nations to maintain and extend international cooperation in telecommunications. The International Telephone and Telegraph Consultative Committee (CCITT) was established by ITU in 1956 to recommend changes in technical or operating standards for telecommunications. The CCITT has focused on telecommunications questions relevant to network computing, such as data communications networks, network operations, and integrated services digital network (ISDN). CCITT uses worldwide experts to provide the complex definition of standards applied to the variety of communications networks. Much of their work has been adopted for use throughout the world.

The International Organization for Standardization (ISO) began functioning in February 1947 as a collaborative group of national standards bodies focused on standardization in all areas except electrical and electronic engineering. Those are handled by the International Electrotechnical Committee (IEC). In 1987, recognizing increasing areas of overlap, the ISO and IEC created a Joint Technical Committee to work on standardization in information technology. The joint committee has also worked with the CCITT in defining such important open systems work as remote operations service, systems management, directories, and open distributed processing.

An important definition provided by the joint committee is the *Open System Interconnect* (OSI) reference model, which defines information interchange ground rules across multiple heterogeneous systems and networks. The standard uses symmetrical layers, located in each processor, to provide clear but simple implementation levels in supporting computers. The standards have been extended from the international levels through the application of ground rules for locally connected computers. These standards can be applied to the interconnection between different computers, whether they reside on a desktop or larger processors.

Existing network protocols, such as Digital Equipment Company's Digital Network Architecture (DNA) and IBM's SNA, have been mapped to OSI standards. This mapping effort provides a migration path for users of vendor-specific architectures to standard open systems support. Most computer companies have developed programs to assist the migration, but the shift to OSI is still expected to take a significant amount of time.

The rich OSI standard has provided many alternative ways to conform, especially to the higher layers of the definition. General Motors defined a manufacturing subset of the OSI protocol for manufacturing. The Manufacturing Automation Protocol (MAP) was defined to meet the needs of General Motors, but it is extendible to other manufacturing companies suppling parts. Vendors were asked to conform to this definition, and many companies supplied MAP versions to GM.

Many parts of OSI are supported in the industry. Connection-level protocols are moving rapidly for implementation across multiple implementations. Even higher-level applications protocols have been adopted, such as the X.400 electronic mail protocol. The directory X.500 standard is also being implemented by growing numbers of companies.

In addition to operating environment and communications standards, some basic standards have proven fundamental in support for client/server environments. Implementors must understand a broad range of hardware and software standards, which provide definitions for cross-vendor implementations. A good example is the graphics standards (Bono, 1985).

A fundamental standard originating from the 1980s work of the German Standards Group is Graphics Kernel System (GKS), which defines two-dimensional interfaces for graphical support on desktop devices (such as personal computers). Computer Graphics Metafile (CGM) was introduced by ANSI in 1985 to simplify transmission of 2-D images. Computer Graphics Virtual Device Interface (CG-VDI) extended GKS to provide three-dimensional support, and Programmer's Hierarchical Interactive Graphics System (PHIGS) provided programmer interfaces for 3-D graphics, including lines, polygons, and arrays. Later standards additions defined application protocols for lighting and shading, which are important to modern graphics systems.

Service Area	Representative Standards
Operating System/ Services	POSIX SPEC 1170 WIN32 XPG
Graphics/ UI	COSE, CDE MOTIF X Windows
Communications	ATM FCS OSI TCP/IP X.25 X.400 X.500
Distributed Computing	CICS CORBA DCE
Systems/ Network Management	DME SNMP CMIP
Data Management	SQL IRDS ODMG-93

Figure 3.5 Relationship between proprietary and industry standards

Each standard provides a framework to develop applications that appear common across dissimilar processors. The operating environments provide a definition of software protocols that can give commonalty to applications developed on different hardware. Hardware standards or combinations, such as the graphics standards, provide a common look and feel, which is important as users move across multiple desktop computers.

Activity levels vary across different support levels within the standards body. At the hardware level, there is a good deal of activity to define standards that permit input or output devices to attach to the workstation or server. Activity is less in defining a common chip, although only a small number of chips are used in actual implementations.

There has been and continues to be a high level of activity to define standard communications protocols that can be accepted across multiple processors. Communications standards work has a long and successful history, which has helped to make it an example for other standards groups.

Figure 3.5 shows the relationship between standards defined by a single vendor (proprietary), and industry standards. Standards may be strictly proprietary or vendor-controlled. They may be accepted because of such common usage as TCP/IP or MS-DOS. Standards can have their origin in a consortia of vendors, such as X-Windows and Motif, working together to reach agreement. Standards reach their highest form of acceptance when they are adopted de jure by many countries or organizations. Examples of de jure standards include POSIX and SQL.

In the software area, there is increasing activity to define additional standards. Activity continues for operating systems but has expanded to focus on user interfaces and control languages. Databases are increasingly important, especially in the languages used to access the databases. Work is also underway to define a standard program development environment. There is increasing activity in defining standards to reflect advances in software technology. Work is underway for object support, network management, and distributed computing. Although these areas are important, they are also complex.

3.4 CONSIDERATIONS

Technological advances have been important in reducing the price for desktop computing and providing an environment for open systems support. The low costs, coupled with increasing function and performance, make desktop computers attractive alternatives to open systems solutions. The enhanced reliability of the new hardware makes it a reasonable choice for production operations. It is anticipated that advances will continue in technology, which will further enhance the appeal of open solutions. As systems are planned, they should be built on an open architecture that permits an easy upgrade to advances in many technology areas.

Modern workstations couple advanced design techniques for components from the simple processor chips to the attachment devices. Components introduced to provide advantages for workstations have been extended into servers. These components provide better capability and performance than mainframe computers and provide the basic building blocks for even the fastest computers.

Operating systems have been changed since their introduction in the late 1950s. The transitions have resulted in increased functional capability and ease of use. This growing capability has aided the move to open systems, as new processing capability could be applied at the desktop and server levels. Five major operating systems are found on clients in open systems. These are MS-DOS, MS-DOS with Windows, OS/2, Macintosh Operating System, and UNIX. OS/2 and UNIX are also server systems, but there is a wider acceptance of proprietary operating systems for servers. Modern versions of these operating systems are being designed to match emerging technologies and reflect changes in system technology. Further advances will enhance the usability of the systems and improve client use.

Originally, having the same operating system helped installations achieve a work balance across many machines. Different operating systems were deterrents to work balancing. Open systems standards aid work balancing by permitting binary-compatible applications to run on different hardware and operating systems that conform to the standards.

International standards are an important force in the wide acceptance of open systems. Experts from throughout the world have worked together to define the specific nature of acceptable standards. Although there are many standards groups, the final arbiter of acceptance is the market, which determines the use of specific standards. Heterogeneous computers conforming to standards can be connected in a network that gives the user an option to select the best processor to meet specific needs.

3.5 REFERENCES

Bach, Maurice J. *The Design of the UNIX Operating System.* Englewood Cliffs, NJ: Prentice Hall, 1986.

Bono, Peter R. "A Survey of Graphics Standards and Their Role in Information Interchange." *IEEE Computer,* October 1985, pp. 63–75.

Lorin, Harold, and Harvey M. Deitel. *Operating Systems: The Systems Programming Series.* Reading, MA: Addison-Wesley, 1981.

Lytton, Nina. "The Restructuring of OSF Promises a Bright Future and the Right Direction for UNIX." *Open Systems Today,* March 28, 1994, p. 27.

Norton, Peter, and Harley Hahn. *Peter Norton's Guide to UNIX.* New York: Bantam Books, 1991. (This is an easy-to-read treatment of UNIX with a good description of the history and major features supported in the operating system.)

Patterson, David A. "Reduced Instruction Set Computers." *Communications of the ACM,* January 1985, pp. 8–21.

Penrose, Roger. *The Emperor's New Mind.* New York: Penguin Books, 1990, pp. 168–169, 302–303.

Pugh, Emerson W., Lyle R. Johnson, and John H. Palmer. *IBM's 360 and Early 370 Systems.* Cambridge, MA: MIT Press, 1991, pp. 39, 109, 291–365.

Strauss, Edmund. *Inside the 80286.* New York: Prentice Hall Press (A Brady Book), 1986.

UNIX International. *1991 System V Roadmap.* Parsippany, NJ: UNIX International, 1991.

Watson, Thomas J. Jr., with Peter Petre. *Father, Son & Co.* New York: Bantam Books, 1990, p. 231.

Wong, Carolyn C. "Yet Another New Era for the OSF?" *Open Computing,* June 1994, pp. 27–28.

4

Clients

The client is a desktop computer that provides user interfaces to a total system, including multiple processors. The client performs local applications as appropriate and cooperates with other processors in completing an entire job scenario. It serves as the host for screen control and the user interfaces that facilitate access to data, either locally or remotely. The interfaces simplify and personalize tasks used in the network. Embedded in the client are hardware and software functions that simplify linkages to communications devices and database access. It is anticipated that increasing processing capability will further simplify operations for end users.

With continual improvement in function, clients can be modified to meet the interface requirements end users demand. Special interfaces that meet the needs of a specific business or national requirement can be defined in the design. The interfaces to the users can be tailored to match the skill levels of users and can be improved as the end user shifts from novice to a more experienced level.

There is a cost consideration when selecting clients. Figure 4.1 shows the differences between different types of client costs. X terminals and diskless workstations can provide significant capability with relatively low cost.

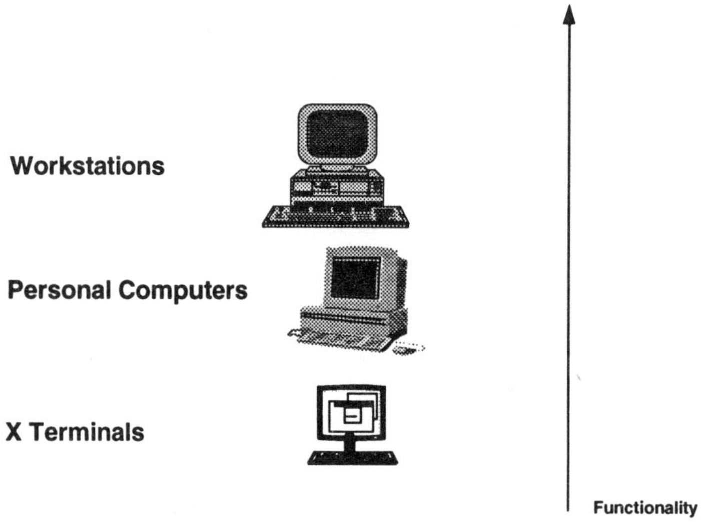

Figure 4.1 Different types of client costs

4.1 DESKTOP PLATFORMS

Desktop platforms can be found in many different shapes, but they fall into three categories as clients. The categories reflect the hardware differences and software systems that run on the different platforms. The most popular platforms are the PCs, which were originally introduced as individual productivity products. Over a third of all PCs are used on LANs as parts of a client/server configuration.

The most powerful desktop computers are workstations. The differences between workstations and large PCs are difficult to project accurately. Workstations usually have higher-performing processing chips for normal computation and floating point. Workstations have special graphics capability for high-performance screen processing. They also run many of the traditional software packages found on PCs, but the primary operating system is UNIX.

The lowest-cost desktop computers used as clients are the X terminals, which have reduced computing capability but provide significant user processing over traditional terminals. These stations incorporate user interfaces, which follow open systems definitions but share applications across common servers. The graphics in the stations are powerful enough to support user interfaces but lack the power traditionally found on either PCs or workstations.

Each platform has characteristics that make it acceptable for specific applications. The platform benefits from improvements in technology, but translation of the benefit is affected by the supported job mix. Each provides unique and powerful functions in an open systems environment; therefore, each of the alternatives represents a real choice for those configuring an open system.

4.2 END USER INTERACTION POINTS

The client is the first point of contact between the end user and open systems. Most input/output devices that communicate directly with end users are connected to the client. Input devices convey user-generated information to the computer system, and output devices bring the information contained in the computer to the end users.

Advances in these devices have simplified interaction between people and computers but have also made design tasks more complex, as the interaction between different output modes must be balanced to achieve the best potential presentation. Summary access to the computer begins with something as simple as a text or as complicated as an image signal from a frame grabber. Figure 4.2 shows some important input/output devices that are available on clients.

Interface characteristics have continually changed over the history of computing. Figure 4.3 shows the growth from early user interfaces to the new wave of interfaces available on modern workstations. The advances from simple card devices to the advanced screen and icon use available today are partially driven by advances in workstation technology. Since typical user I/O devices reside at the client, it represents the focal point for end user interaction with the computing systems. It becomes a complete working environment that interacts with the user.

The client determines the acceptability of the total system to the end user. The user interacts with the client and judges system completeness by the interactions found at this point of contact. User comfort with the system stems from client interaction.

4.2.1 Input Processing

If you use your imagination, you can mentally visualize different devices that could provide input to computers. Electronic keyboards can connect to an open network and produce the equivalent of a symphony orchestra when

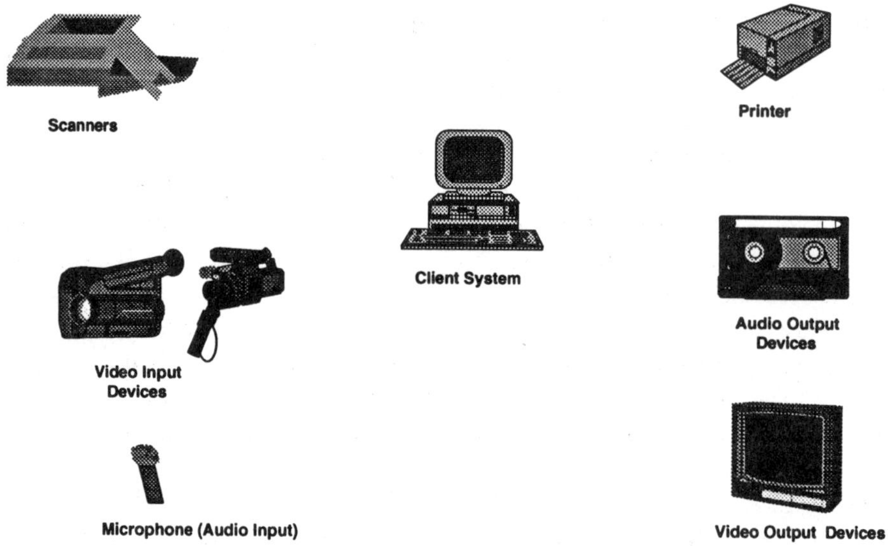

Figure 4.2 Input/output devices available on clients

	SOFTWARE	HARDWARE
EMERGING INTERFACES	Visualization	Multimedia
PC/WORKSTATION INTERFACES	GUI Components: Windows, Menus, Icons	Desktop Computers Graphics Cards Mouse/Other Pointing Devices
MAINFRAME/ MINICOMPUTER INTERFACES	Programming Languages Operating System Commands Utilities, Tools	Cards Terminals
EARLY INTERFACES	Card Entry Toggle Switches Wiring Changes	Cards Toggle Switches

Figure 4.3 Interfaces—early to emerging

the music is synthesized on a supercomputer. Early input devices for computer systems included card readers, which have been replaced by electronic keyboards. Nearly any device that can digitize data can serve as an input device for open systems.

Traditional input devices, such as keyboards or drawing pens, have been augmented by voice, scanner, and video input devices. Existing recognition devices can scan written Japanese and convert the characters into digital input. Voice input is captured using comparable technology to translate the words directly into digital format.

The most important input device remains the keyboard. Although increasing use of graphics has expanded the use of pointing devices, such as the tablet and mouse, the keyboard is the main device used to enter textual information. Initial time-sharing devices used modified typewriters as an input device. The computer keyboard descended directly from the typewriter alphanumeric standard, called QWERTY, for the first six letters on the top alphabetical line. A person trained in the touch-type system can easily use the computer keyboard. Extensions were made to the typewriter keyboard to improve the use of special commands. Eventually, too many function keys were added to some keyboards, making them difficult to learn and use.

Extensive studies by ergonomists demonstrated features that needed to be altered in modern keyboards. Function keys were moved from different locations to a single placement at the top. The function keys were limited by people's ability to retain large numbers of options. The introduction of the 101-key variation became popular with many users, since it could be used across different desktop alternatives.

The wide use of computer keyboards focused attention on physical disorders that might be caused by continued use of keyboards (Mallory and Bradford, 1988). These cumulative trauma disorders arise from long exposure to constant wrist or hand motion and also can be found in other professions. Carpal tunnel syndrome in particular has received wide attention, since it has appeared in those using keyboards for long periods of time. It derives its name from the swelling in the tunnel formed by the carpal bones and ligaments.

The author was introduced to extensive studies performed in universities in Europe. These studies have focused on the physical effects of the workplace. Electrical sensors detect changes in the use of muscles. Keyboard use affects not only the arms and fingers but has shown measured effects on back, shoulder, and even neck muscles.

Many studies resulted in changes in keyboard designs to simplify the physical task of typing. The slope and angle of the keyboard and shape of the keys can affect the usability of the devices. Audibility, or the creation of a sound when a key is depressed, provides feedback indicating key contact. Designs have also had to reflect the span between different keys, as the users must use them all day. Good desktop computers assume quality keyboards. Testing mechanisms can be introduced to ensure the quality of the keyboard.

Most workstations combine a keyboard with a mouse to handle input. The computer mouse provides the ability to point to data on a screen, drag, pick, and click on various characters. As the mouse moves across the desktop or special pad, highlighted figures move across the screen. Through these processes, it is possible to modify icons on the screen or change text input. The mouse can be used to increase or decrease the size of figures through very simple manipulation. An increasing number of programs respond well to mouse interactions. The mouse, although a small item in the consideration of equipment, has become a large item to end users.

Innovative input devices are being connected to desktop computers. Simple hand-held scanners have been replaced by those that can read whole sheets of paper. Engineers can scan old design drawings and then modify them in modern databases. Interactive programs using fuzzy logic correct errors in these images and improve the scanned image. Japanese companies such as Toshiba and Nippon Electric have introduced devices that can read handwritten Kanjii and decipher a vocabulary of over 3,000 characters.

Modern desktops have introduced devices that permit the advanced use of multimedia. Advanced devices create objects to be used across the network. For example, video cameras facilitate the introduction of active data across the network to other workstations and servers. A remote camera can be connected to the network to demonstrate a procedure or to have the procedure introduced on other workstations.

The use of speech is increasing for both annotation and commands. Simple microphones are now part of the standard package for some PCs. Microphones can pick up quality input and then annotate it or broadcast it across the network. These same devices will be used for expanded support for audio commands. The increasing performance on clients has resulted in units that accept dictation. Dictation quality permits the creation of documents. Advances in devices promise new characteristics on networks, but keyboards will continue to be the most important single support item on a workstation for the foreseeable future.

4.2.2 Output Processing

Two special output devices are used with workstations. The first of these is the video display. Each client will have a display device that must meet the criterion of performing well during the desired connection periods. Displays have been used in computers for some time, but increasing use of bit mapping has provided graphics capabilities to business and scientific users alike. The second important device at the client is the directly connected local printer. Special design considerations have made these printers function well as silent partners to processors and displays.

Displays

Improved performance on display screens has made interactive graphics and visualization a reality for end users. Visualization enables the end user to view typically flat data as 3-D images. Predictive applications can make use of the enhanced information and enable agents to make better decisions. Screens that exceed the quality of even the best graphics devices from a few years ago are used extensively in the business and professional environment. New applications are already challenging the design of the best screens, as interactive graphics and video place new design considerations on them.

Two factors are important in selecting desktop display units. The first is the quality of the images; the second is the performance in painting and creating images on the screen. A measure of display effectiveness is the frequency of the repaint operation. A third factor is the ergonomic qualities of the screens (DataSaab, 1981). The third factor affects the continued working environment for the user and has generated legislation relative to use and installation of workstations.

Display hardware uses technology developed for televisions. The cathode ray tube (CRT), which is the most widely used technology for clients, relies on an electron gun firing on phosphor-coated screens. A number of factors determine the quality of the image, including the durability of the phosphor image. Picture refresh rate depends on the decay rate of the specific phosphor.

Many desktop displays provide quality color support on CRTs. Separate electron guns activate primary colors of red, green, or blue, which are mixed to form a wide spectrum of alternatives on the screen. Very large palettes of colors provided on modern display screens can be selected through simple programming techniques. There are fewer differences between business displays and engineering displays. Nineteen-inch screens with large numbers of picture elements are popular for business graphics as well as for engineering. Although smaller screens are used, frequent users select the larger units.

The portable computer has introduced quality flat screens with backlighting. These units are relatively thin and light and have appealing characteristics. Originally limited to monochrome operations, there are increasing numbers of color displays provided with portable computers. Flat panel displays have been extended to desktop computers. It is expected that this trend will continue as the display requires less space and provides unique alternatives for office design. It is believed flat screens will continue, to proliferate beyond portable units. In defining open systems applications, a number of screen factors will help select the client.

Color is an early selection criterion for many users. Rich palettes of colors are available for workstations. Many applications benefit from color technology, but it is important to remember that there must be alternative approaches for people with color deficiencies. Color can be used effectively to designate special attention areas.

After color, screen size is the next determining factor considered by people selecting desktop processors. The size of the screen will determine the amount of information that can be viewed on the screen at one time. Size can also affect the viewing angle, which may cause muscle problems. Neck, back, and head muscles can be affected by incorrect positioning. Correct screen sizes can eliminate problems encountered in frequent use.

Picture elements or pels determine the accuracy of representation of graphics data. The more pels, the higher the resolution and clarity of the characters portrayed on the screens. Drawings that require a high degree of precision will benefit from increased numbers of picture elements.

Intensity and resolution are important in the selection of a display that is to be in constant use. Resolution defines the character detail. It is a key factor in defining the quality of presentation, since accuracy is determined by resolution. As mentioned before, refresh rate also contributes to the overall quality of the screen.

Graphics, whether for business or professional purposes, have benefited from advances in computer technology. Many of the basics described by earlier authors (Foley and Van Dam, 1982) remain the same, but technology advances provide new options for graphics implementors. Once-specialized applications can now be implemented well on PCs. The adoption of standards has permitted the porting of applications across multiple platforms, which has helped build a repertoire of powerful applications.

A number of studies on the effects of continued use of visual display terminals have been conducted. Throughout Europe and in some counties in the United States, stringent laws have been enacted about the use and effects of continued screen use. Groups using screens extensively have contended that displays have been responsible for everything from miscarriages to eye disorders caused by screen flicker.

Detailed studies have demonstrated that careful attention to screen design and placement can affect the long-term usability of the products. Vendors have produced manuals reflecting these studies. Focus has been on reduction of glare and creating an atmosphere conducive to extensive screen use.

Early solutions included adding glare shields to existing screens or simply changing the placement of the screen in the room or on the desk. Modern screen designs have been able to correct many problems through a change of the screen or phosphors. For instance, flicker problems can be repaired through internal adjustment to phosphor and by adjusting the refresh rate for screen painting. Adjustment dials help make screen brightness acceptable to end users. Different working environments contribute to the overall usefulness of these solutions. Maximum flexibility is achieved through finely tuned brightness and contrast adjustments.

Another ergonomic consideration affecting the workplace is exposure to noise or unwanted sound. Scandinavian countries have focused on this problem in university studies, but the problem is far-reaching. Sharp, loud, or constant noises adversely affect the workplace. A hospital executive demonstrated this to the author in Stockholm when he placed an oscillator tuned at 45 decibels on the conference table. The disruption of my concentration caused me to turn it off after a brief period of time. Office workers are constantly exposed to this level of noise from their workstations.

There are a number of ergonomic problems in the individual workplace. Some of these problems are discussed in this chapter; however, as technology changes so do the challenges of these new problems. Legislation is forcing a focus on some of the problems, but other problems are occurring with the introduction of faster technology. For instance, studies have demonstrated that a person can deal with 1 billion bits of information per second from a graphic device. We are currently at that threshold, and some researchers doubt we will be able to drive the number higher. This raises the question of the value of faster processors.

In a comparable manner, the results of high-speed computing may produce results too fast for the average person to grasp. Usability functions included in the system design have assisted the complexities of the speed problem. The display is the center for system usability functions. Users want simple accesses to complex system facilities. Once-popular mainframe interfaces have been displaced by approaches that use GUIs to portray data in unique approaches.

Much of the interface usability can be tracked to work performed at Xerox Corporation's Palo Alto Research Center (PARC). PARC designed uniquely usable interfaces around windows, icons, and menus. Windows are screen sections assigned to individual program tasks. Icons are picture representations of tasks processed on a computer. Menus are lists of program alternatives selected interactively through keyboards or mouses. The company introduced their 8010 Star Information System, which incorporated many of these features but was not successful in the market (Johnson et al., 1989).

Many ideas developed by PARC in their work on Star were later incorporated into Apple's Macintosh. Using this technology, the Macintosh has established a strong reputation for powerful ease of use. Leebaert and Dickinson believe the Macintosh's reputation is enhanced by the lack of fatigue experienced by end users (Leebaert and Dickinson, 1991). Fatigue can be caused by the mental shifts the user makes as different alternatives are selected.

Modern window support uses extensive bit-mapped graphics found on modern display screens. Expanded numbers of pixel elements have enabled the reproduction of complex graphics and images. Recent designs have supported video and animation in full color. Advances in display technology, whether based on flat panel designs or the advances in high-definition television (HDTV), promise to affect the quality of these important desktop devices.

The advances in displays have challenged printer designers to match the precision of the display devices.

Printers

Desktop printers augment display output and enable the user to create immediate hard copies of the output. Printer advances have enabled designers to create relatively low-cost units that produce quality output on the desktop. Nonimpact, or laser printers, have replaced noisy hammer printers for the production of images and characters. Laser printers support all-points-addressable (APA) technology, which enables the user to produce images or complex graphics. The four separate printer types that provide quality images are the wire dot matrix, laser, electro, and thermal printers. Precision drawings can be produced with detail on these lower-cost printers.

There continue to be higher-priced printers that can best be shared on a print server. These printers usually require a separate operator, or they function at such performance that they should be shared. Printer servers will also manipulate the contents of a page and provide functions still too expensive for individual use. Very high speed laser printers can consume large amounts of paper in a very short time.

Printers use computer chips to provide logical processing once consigned to the computer. Features such as font processing, page formatting, and color are handled directly with additional logic. More importantly, the same processing capability is used to support connections to standard protocols, which transmit the page layout information. Linkage to databases and communications is provided directly by onboard chips.

Color printers are available even in portable configurations. Information created on color displays can be transmitted to color printers and retained, or it can be used in presentations. Since quality color printers are expensive, most of them are attached to servers; however, low-cost color printers with good-quality output are available for desktops.

Since printed output remains important for most businesses, the selection and placement of printers will often determine the quality image your company creates. As advances continue in both the printer technology and connection protocols, we can expect to find more quality devices available on desktops and portable units.

4.3 PERSONAL COMPUTERS

Personal computers were first introduced in 1975. Eventually, they provided a desktop capability that compared favorably with advanced graphics workstations. With the success of the PC in the early 1980s, expectations were raised as each subsequent processor provided increasing power for computation and user interfaces. Individual productivity applications were fundamental to the success of the PCs and have endured for the modern desktop client. Open systems have created an environment in which personal applications have to be augmented through the introduction of group software.

During the 1980s, a shift away from terminals used for shared systems occurred. PCs were adapted to link to larger computers and assume the appearance of standard terminal interfaces. Eventually, tasks once performed on mainframes and minicomputers migrated to the PC, as applications were either shifted entirely to the desktop or were split between the desktop and larger computers. By the end of the decade, many software packages could be transported on portable computers and connected to work locations through embedded modems connected to analog telephone lines. Professionals and managers began to carry work across the country using battery-powered PCs.

New network designs were introduced using the PC as a substitute for terminals. Recognizing the power of coupled desktop computing, LANs were introduced to multiple computers. Using the PCs as terminals provided connections to applications in larger processors. When the terminal concept was introduced, the PCs used simple terminal emulation devices on adapter cards to attach to systems. Connection as a single terminal was referred to as a single-tail or single-stack connection. Using additional attachment cards, the PC could be made to look like many different types of terminals. Software was designed that connected the PC to different hardware programs. The connection to multiple processors was referred to as multiple-tail or multiple-stack processing.

Leading-edge companies discovered significant productivity gains by using PCs on desktops. More importantly, by the end of the decade, collaboration projects used the desktops to facilitate group interaction. The term groupware was introduced to mean software that facilitated group interactions. Communications was at the heart of this new software, which was based on extensive communications between individuals in the working group.

The PC power enabled applications depending on graphics and objects to be shifted to desktops. Often, applications would be split—with database handling routines residing in larger computers and user interfaces migrating outward to the desktop computer. The PC became an excellent corporate productivity tool.

The PC has significantly shifted the culture of computing and changed the professional working environment. Traditional daily tasks, such as report writing, estimating costs, and communications between peers, now occur at the PC. Company- or profession-specific tasks can be performed on the same PC attached to the network. Whether the task is writing a support document or completing a design, interaction can be shifted to an intelligent electronic interface. The PC's open design challenged the industry to look further and identify standards that meet the needs of customers and vendors alike. It has been the entry vehicle of client/server computers and will remain important on the desktop. PCs have achieved a dominance on the desktop that will be difficult to match with other architectures.

From the beginning of Apple II, the Apple Computer Company has had a unique vision, which brought an ease of use and operation to the desktop. The original design for Apple II flourishes in many school districts, but, by the mid-1980s, Apple recognized the need for a more powerful computer for business use that combined the best user interfaces with a simple file access capability.

The result was the introduction of the Macintosh computers in 1984. These computers provided an ease of use for personal productivity unsurpassed by other alternatives. Simple icon manipulation could be used to handle the most complex problems. Although their initial design attracted many engineers, memory and screen limitations restricted their wide adaptability as a network computer.

The Macintosh has been very successful as a special productivity tool, but the introduction of modular design in subsequent versions made it more powerful and provided a potential base for open computing. Although there was an early LAN support, this support focused on special Macintosh protocols. The company did expand connections to other protocols, but these features did not function as well as their own internal networks. AppleTalk was developed for connecting Apple processors and servers. Continued development of protocols has enabled the company to attach to other LANs such as Ethernet or Token Ring. It is expected that agreements between Apple and IBM will enhance the connection to networks.

Since the Macintosh embodies the power possible on a desktop with increasing capability to connect to the network, it will continue to be a major alternative for clients.

The IBM Personal Computer and its clones are the most widely supported clients. The original PC was announced in August 1981. The design was based on an Intel chip set with support products matched to the same architecture. Early models were designed to facilitate connection to communications protocols. Open slots were designed into the computer to facilitate the addition of communications connections. Early support was provided to make the desktop computer appear as though it were a standard terminal.

The original PC design provided an architecture that supported many different hardware and software connections. This openness made the development of hardware copies simple and enabled many companies to announce competitive products shortly after the real product was announced. Clone announcements appeared so rapidly that users could easily wait for lower-cost alternatives.

Additional power and storage made the IBM Personal Computer AT (advanced technology) a very strong candidate for network computing. Introduced in 1984, these computers provided real capability to the end users but also provided acceptable levels of performance to drive networks. Since these computers used more powerful Intel chips, they could also become servers. The first microprocessor-based servers were built on PC AT computers. Successive generations of Intel-based systems (up to today's Pentium systems) have brought increasing amounts of power to the PC desktop.

IBM's commitment to System Network Architecture created a strong internal pressure for the PCs to support it early. Corporate management information system (MIS) groups, which were heavily dependent on SNA, were also interested in a strong commitment. As a result, SNA was the first protocol to be supported on PC architecture.

4.4 PROFESSIONAL WORKSTATIONS

It has become more difficult to distinguish between workstations and PCs. More powerful microchips have permitted the high end of the PC to compete actively with workstations. A good distinction is to note that the workstation usually contains added power for handling normal compute operations. It also has extended floating-point instructions to handle calculations for engineering and scientific applications. Graphics performance has also been enhanced in workstations. Workstations have tended to require UNIX as the operating system, since the system is best designed to handle multiple tasks and some of the complexity of graphics. Price was a factor in distinguishing between the two desktop units.

The distinctions between workstations and PCs have grown more difficult, as the prices for workstations have become lower than some PCs. PCs have enhanced their performance for regular compute operations. The vendors have also added floating-point functions and graphics capability nearly equivalent to that found on workstations.

Workstations were introduced for engineering and scientific applications using architectures with 16-bit addressing. By the middle of the 1980s, most vendors were offering expanded addressing in the form of 32-bit processors.

Current workstations, such as those based on Digital Equipment's Alpha processor, are shifting to 64-bit capability, which provides a richness of applications alternatives.

Professional applications written for workstations seemed to consume all the power designed into the processors. Graphics performance was devoted to advances in kinematics for engineering design. Workstations also became good tools to use for animation. Floating-point power enabled many engineers to perform tasks once allocated to dedicated numerical processors.

Continued improvement in workstation performance, along with reduced prices, makes workstations the best alternative for certain critical applications. Even where low cost is a requirement, the additional power of the workstation can be devoted to simplifying the end-user involvement with computing. Scientific visualization was introduced to facilitate the understanding of complex engineering and scientific equations. The same visualization is being applied to the financial world to model changes in econometric models.

When the workstation power is applied to group applications, it can have a high payback. Engineering applications for electronic design were the first to benefit from this power, but it was not long before mechanical counterparts also began to shift to the workstation as a primary tool for design applications.

Productivity gains will find users shifting from the PCs to workstations, particularly as the distinctions between the two classes of desktop computers continue to blur.

Multiple levels of performance alternatives have resulted in an entire spectrum of professional workstations. From stations priced less than some PCs to workstations many times the lowest price, desktop units span an entire spectrum of price and function difference. Superworkstations serve as ideal units for animation projects. This continual improvement of workstations will result in high-powered workstations being available for very low prices.

Introduced in the early 1980s, professional workstations were initially intended for design engineers and scientists. Eventually, their applicability to other markets, such as financial modeling, became obvious, and, by 1989, workstations had become the fastest-growing segment of the computer industry. The major vendors have contributed to the acceptance of open systems.

The industry movement to open systems, aided by Sun Microsystems from Mountain View, California, has helped lead the industry to open systems.

Their approach of providing and supporting early systems, which were open on a physical as well as a software level, helped to make them the leader in workstations. Sun adopted an openness in their early products in 1982. The company demonstrated early leadership in the development and propagation of UNIX support.

Originally, their workstations were built using Motorola M680x0 processors, but, by 1989, the company had shifted to its popular 32-bit Scalable Processor Architecture (SPARC) chips as the basis for their workstations and servers. The units based on these architectures provide a range of price/performance alternatives which compete with PCs. Since the SPARC chips are widely used by other vendors, there is an advantage in supporting Sun software.

Sun's support couples the performance power of SPARC with innovative industrial design to make it a significant workstation offering. The introduction of SPARCstations using gate-array technology and a flat profile package helped popularize the support. The desktop graphics, coupled with dual high-capacity disk units and an energy consumption less than a 100-watt light bulb, helped to make the units successful. Higher-performance products have shifted the company into a spectrum of products that supports workstations and servers.

Sun is responsible for many innovative introductions in open systems. Most important: their support for heterogeneous connections across LANs using their Open Network Computing (ONC), which provided an intersystem command structure; Network File System (NFS), which provided portability for data; and the Remote Procedure Call (RPC), which enabled clients and servers to communicate across the network. These functions have been adopted either in part or totally by other open systems vendors.

The continued growth of the company resulted in a major refocus to provide additional emphasis on the software portion of the business. Separate companies have been created to focus on software, compilers, and the integration process, as predictions for growth in open systems stress these portions of the business.

Digital Equipment Company (DEC) introduced its first 32-bit workstations in 1984 using its minicomputer architecture (Levy and Eckhouse, 1980) and its proprietary operating system. Although DEC embraced elements of open architecture earlier, it made a significant move toward full support by establishing an open systems group in 1985 in Palo Alto, California. The group established DEC's presence in the open systems with workstation offerings based on RISC architecture and UNIX. In 1989, the company introduced chips from MIPS to serve as the base for their workstation and server product lines. The introduction of the high-performance workstations was coupled with the adoption of high-performance turbochannels to support the necessary I/O devices. DEC has committed its architectures through the product line to use open standards. The company was a founding member of OSF, and it has provided leadership in defining X Windows through its close affiliation with MIT. By the early 1990s, the Alpha processor had been announced, and DEC was fervently trying to shift its focus from VAX- and MIPS-based systems to those based on the Alpha.

IBM has more directly embraced open systems in their workstation offerings. Although the company has been active in the UNIX workstation market since 1984, their announcement in February 1990 of the RISC System/6000 family placed them in direct competition for a piece of the client market. Further efforts, such as the PowerPC joint development with Apple Computer, have brought about another candidate platform for powerful desktop clients.

4.5 X TERMINALS

A number of jobs within an enterprise do not require the full power of a desktop computer. Other jobs require a tight control from supervisory groups. End users are often limited from accessing full compute power based on the nature of their responsibilities. As servers emerged, it became apparent that a new form of desktop processor could provide additional intelligence but not the full capability of a PC. The X terminal grew from the desire to have a certain amount of shared code but still use computer power to produce a simpler user interface to multiple computing resources.

These cost-effective desktop platforms were introduced through lower-cost stations that conformed with standards for user interfaces to UNIX servers. X terminals couple high-quality window support with minimal code to service special application requests across an LAN. Through the network, the user can access applications in one or many servers. X terminals represent low-cost alternatives to other client alternatives.

The user interfaces for X terminals grew from work performed on Project Athena at MIT. This work was initiated in the early 1980s to install a campuswide network of thousands of stations. As a part of the Athena project, a user interface known as X Windows was developed to define window systems for multiple forms of hardware. In addition, the work provided vendor-independent mechanisms to connect to the network. Beginning in 1984, X has passed through a number of developmental transitions, which have enhanced its appeal to the industry. By 1988, an MIT X consortium was formed that could police what had been accepted as a standard for the industry and provide additional versions of the standard to the many users.

Toolkits made available to X implementors have facilitated the creation of user interfaces, which conform to the protocols defined in the standards. Features included in the toolkits support menus, buttons, scroll bars, text windows, and user preferences. There are three types of toolkits that have emerged from X. These include X-based toolkits, Xlib based, and intrinsics based. Multiple implementations exist for all these different types.

Carnegie Mellon and Texas Instruments have defined X-based toolkits. CMU, Stanford, the University of Illinois, and Sun Microsystems have all built Xlib-based toolkits. MIT built their own version of intrinsics for Athena. Motif has been adopted by the OSF as the standard for toolkits and is widely used in the UNIX desktop world.

Since applications are actually run on servers running the UNIX operating system, the number of workstations per server will vary. The user interface and the communications protocols reside on the X station. A single X station can have multiple tails or connections to multiple UNIX servers.

Eventually, the Athena work was adopted by industry as commercial products including not only user interfaces but work-flow definitions also. The work-flow protocols permit the X terminal to connect to a heterogeneous environment, including workstations. UNIX servers provide the connection protocols to the rest of the system. Synchronization takes place across the network with multiple stations sharing the same network.

A number of vendors provide products that conform with the X terminal definitions. These include the leader, Network Computing Devices (NCD), which only provides X terminal products. Major workstation vendors such as DEC, Hewlett-Packard, and IBM provide products that conform to these standards. Since this is a growing market, additional vendors will be able to produce simple X terminals conforming to the standards.

X terminals were originally introduced for CAD/CAM applications. Engineers could access common design and manufacturing information that had been generated in minicomputer design packages. These packages were shifted to servers and accessed through the enhanced capability of the standard. Application of X terminals is natural in those applications that require access to data and small amounts of local calculations. Thus, reservation agents and other commercial users could apply the terminals to their problems.

The continual acceptance of X terminals for shared applications demonstrates the versatility of the open systems architecture. Mixtures of X terminals, PCs, and workstations can reside effectively on the same network. Each has a place in solutions that develop open systems approaches for large corporations. Coupled with portable computers, it is possible to reach anywhere computing (see Section 4.6).

4.6 MOBILE COMPUTING

Low-cost chips and lightweight design have helped introduce the concept of anywhere computing within open systems. Sufficient power resides in briefcase computers or even in computers that fit in the palm of the hand to support work across the network from any location. The network can be accessed via cellular radio from moving vehicles or directly from a hotel room through communications lines. Since most portable units are still character-only, the user interfaces are different from the workstations. The extent of portability is determined by many design characteristics of the specific units, but if the unit follows standard workstation design, it can become a client in the network.

User interaction with a remote client is similar to the local alternatives, but often there is some additional connection work required. When the salesperson arrives in the hotel room, he or she has the capability to connect to the remote network and access the servers in the network. The designer can access design computers and make changes as long as there is an identification possibility.

Modern portable computers are fully compatible with desktop versions in the office. Whether the design is a PC or the more popular professional workstations, it is possible to find devices that meet the design of the stationary devices. Notebook and subnotebook computers that are very light, yet rugged, can meet the needs of field personnel to communicate with the active system and interact with their different groups.

Portable computers support standard operating systems and their interfaces. The tools, which are used to create applications programs for desktops, can be used to create portable applications.

Connectability requirements from the system point of view grow more complex when remote connections are permitted. Additional consideration for security validation is required. Portable computers have become extensions of the local workplace and provide mobile compute capability unimagined only a short time ago.

4.7 CONSIDERATIONS

Open systems have been driven in part by the wide acceptance of the client/server models. I/O considerations can help determine which client is acceptable. This begins with ergonomic considerations for both keyboards and displays. The checklist for client acceptability includes the ability of the screens to clearly support advanced graphics. Clients are attached to desktop laser printers, which provide quality and silent output.

Sun Microsystems' effective use of open technology to achieve rapid growth in the market has served as a model for their success in the past decade. Active support and participation by the different desktop products have given a strong impetus to the entire open systems effort.

During the past decade, there has been a marked improvement in the performance and function of desktop platforms. Beginning with the PC, performance has improved on the desktop. Eventually, companies have shifted to more interaction across the network using these processors.

The IBM Personal Computer and its clones were used at an early stage to connect to the mainframe and eventually to servers. Continued microprocessor power increases have extended the function and made these processors effective desktop clients. The expected change in processing performance will result in enhanced desktop processors.

The Apple Macintosh will have a growing role in client computing as support for UNIX expands. The ease of use that characterizes the Macintosh has made it very popular as an individual productivity tool, and as the products shift from proprietary to open architectures, they will be widely adopted on the network. Implementation of standard connectivity designs will enhance their acceptance by business applications.

The PC was the first client in a historical sense, but it has been followed by the workstation, which provides more performance and even better price performance in certain cases. The X terminal is a low-cost alternative for installations looking for ways to use open systems without paying a high per-seat price.

Clients determine the system characteristics seen by the end users. GUI support is centered in these desktop units, and there will be continuing simplification of the interfaces found on these processors.

Security begins with secure clients. Access to a client can often provide access to the rest of the network. There are a number of viable techniques for securing the client from intrusion and from being used as a vehicle to break into the rest of the open system.

In determining the correct client, it is well to remember that the client works in close interaction with the entire open system. Selection of clients that meet only the goals of end users will miss the need for the client to interact effectively with the rest of the system. Changes will often come from the system administrator to reflect modifications in operating procedures. Synchronization of fixes across multiple processors remains a requirement in many operational systems. Equally important are synchronized hardware and software updates, which must be reflected throughout the network.

4.8 REFERENCES

DataSaab. *Ergonomics, The Third Factor.* DataSaab Corporation, 1981, #IN 5000272-923.

Foley, James D., and Andries Van Dam. *Fundamentals of Interactive Computer Graphics: The Systems Programming Series.* Reading, MA: Addison-Wesley, 1982, pp. 93–136.

Johnson, Jeff, Teresa L. Roberts, William Verplank, David C. Smith, Charles H. Irby, Marian Beard, and Kevin Mackey. "The Xerox Star: A Retrospective." *Computer,* vol. 22, no. 9, September 1989, pp. 11–26.

Leebaert, Derek, and Timothy Dickinson. "A World to Understand: Technology and the Awakening of Human Possibility." *Technology 2001,* edited by Derek Leebaert, Cambridge, MA: MIT Press, 1991, p. 309.

Levy, Henry M., and Richard H. Eckhouse, Jr. *Computer Programming and Architecture, The Vax-11.* Bedford, MA: Digital Press, 1980.

Mallory, M., and H. Bradford. "An Invisible Workplace Hazard That's Harder to Ignore." *Business Week,* January 20, 1988, pp. 92–93.

5

Client Software

Most users are first introduced to network computing through software residing on clients. Although this software may be connected to other systems, applications seem to run locally. The software may reside on other processors in the network with only the communications front end residing on the client. This chapter examines client software with an emphasis on individual productivity tools that enhance end-user computing.

Like other computers, the client has a resident operating system with support tools that service local requests as well as interact with larger computers. On top of the operating system code, there are service routines that provide local housekeeping. Most important is the communication and user code, which defines the characteristic of clients and provides connections to other attached processors. Many applications have been shifted to clients and work in conjunction with other software in the network.

Many personal productivity packages have been shipped on PCs. Each of these packages was intended to improve individual productivity but has been extended to include group processing. Group processing software has been defined that facilitates the interaction of individuals working toward common objectives. Group processing packages extend productivity from the individual working alone to a team of professionals working together.

Many companies have introduced vertical applications focusing on the roles of individuals. These applications may be specialized to the goals of the specific business or may be packages that apply across a profession. An example of professional packages is the many computer-aided design (CAD) packages available on most clients. Simple drawing packages are available on PCs, and more complex design tools have migrated from shared processors to desktop computers. Comparable general software is available for other professions.

With the increased compute power on specific clients, it is now possible to migrate expert system technology, in the form of resident assistants, to the desktop. Desktop expert systems can automate rules handling, providing the end user with additional capability. For example, an engineering assistant program can aid professional engineers in assessing designs against known design rules. Financial expert systems include packages such as traders' assistants, which can aid commodity and stock trades.

Increasingly, there is a body of open systems software targeted at management. Initially, this software expanded on decision support systems and executive information systems, which were originally programmed for mainframe computers. More recently, there has been an emergence of distributed executive systems, which downsize the software prepared for mainframe systems and place it on workstations. More importantly, normal input data are collected and provided to management information systems.

The large numbers of clients introduces management challenges unique to an environment rich in capability at individual desktops. Synchronizing releases across very large numbers of desktop processors forces new solutions, which affect the client and the supporting servers. Support for a single desktop computer is relatively straightforward, but when the number is multiplied, the problem becomes large and complex. Geographic dispersion makes the problem even more complex, as update and modification processes must be synchronized across multiple locations.

Balancing results across multiple distributed processors forces the introduction of new software. Although groupware will be discussed later, the synchronization of output and the control of the data flow will cause the addition of code on desktop computers. Each processor has autonomy, but in many companies it is assumed the code must have some control.

5.1 ELEMENTS OF OPEN SYSTEMS SOFTWARE

The rapid emergence of workstations has changed our perspective on the expected level of software support at each node of the system. The richness of packages available has raised expectations for subsequent generations and created a challenge to open systems vendors. Software applications are often partitioned between the client and multiple servers located on the network.

The network attachment creates communications requirements on the client software. As the compute power on the desktop has continued to grow, the aggregate compute power on networks has exceeded the collective power found in central processing complexes. Recently, companies have discovered techniques for using this new power, but software remains pivotal to fully exercising the power of the network.

Heterogeneous environments have become important in exercising the options of open systems, but practical considerations have usually restricted the number of architectures a company uses. Problems such as control, management, training, and the maintenance of multiple concurrent binary programs have challenged information systems managers. Maintaining multiple versions of a program is difficult, even if it is done automatically through electronic libraries.

Open systems architectures provide a framework for defining new systems, but the installations will still have unique program problems that can be simplified through the adoption of internal standards. The special standards within the company should define software frameworks for operating systems, communications, database, and user interfaces. Other internal definitions affecting software will be such items as security, reliability, recovery, and installation procedures.

Figure 5.1 shows the major considerations in determining open systems software. These include communications, control software, the DBMS, and the applications. The operating system provides connections between hardware and applications. It is the location of the control point for the autonomous processor. The operating system also balances resources among contending elements of software and hardware. Distributed systems require well-designed communications connections, which support the interaction between clients and the rest of the open network. Communications will conform to a corporate direction reflecting older protocols and desired new directions. At the lowest layers, it connects to hardware, and at the highest layer, it provides transparent interfaces to applications shared across a network.

The third element in open systems software is data code, which can affect multiple layers of the system. Sequential files are the simplest data form used in open systems, but most users support complex data structures supported

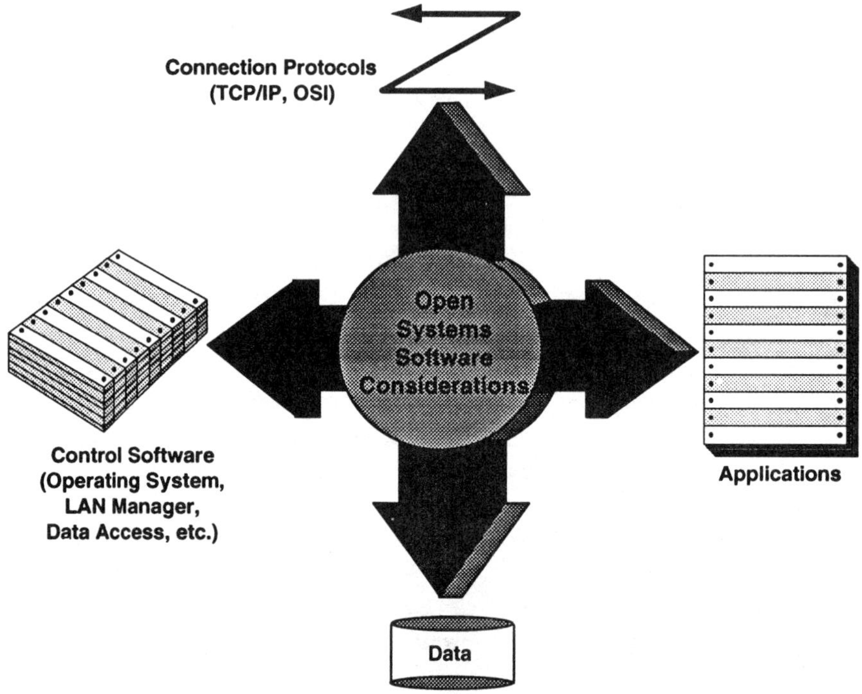

Figure 5.1 Open systems software considerations

by database companies. The data access language SQL (pronounced sequel) provides open access to different systems connected across the network. SQL support is found on most clients.

An important fourth element in the adoption of an open system is end-user interfaces. While graphical user interfaces (GUIs) are *conceptually* similar to one another (i.e., they all have menus, windows, dialog boxes, etc.), there are subtle distinctions in the look-and-feel attributes of any one versus the other major models. For example, the Apple Macintosh user interface has a small box in the upper left-hand corner of a window that, if present (and that box *doesn't* have to be used), closes the window when clicked. On Microsoft Windows, however, a different upper left-hand corner symbol is used (a horizontal bar within a box), and not only may a window be closed that way, but other functions—such as "minimizing" a window (transforming it to an icon on the screen)—can be selected from the same box. Along the same lines, the Macintosh interface has no concept of minimizing a window.

Therefore, it is important in an open systems environment—particularly one in which heterogeneous client software is used—to achieve as much commonality among user interfaces as possible. This is the motivation behind the Common Desktop Environment (CDE) mentioned in Chapter 4.

The value of the open system to a company is measured in ease of producing and managing applications, which is the fifth element in client software. The ability to develop applications that use the full power of the distributed system becomes an important criterion in accepting a network implementation. The entire concept of visual programming (using tools that facilitate screen building and application generation) is based around the philosophy of easing the applications development burden. Further, it's not just the development side for which "easy operation" is a goal; tools that enable the *management* of large networks of distributed workstations are becoming increasingly important for corporate acceptance of open systems.

Just as operating systems have been shifting, there has been an increasing movement to adopt languages that permit portability across multiple hardware platforms. An important ingredient in this effort is C language, which has facilitated ports across multiple hardware platforms. Hypertext tools are popular on systems such as the Macintosh. These tools are spreading to other platforms.

5.2 SELECTING OPEN SYSTEMS OPERATING ENVIRONMENTS

Although many operating systems and operating environments can be used on clients, it is well to carefully consider the alternatives before making the final choice. In Chapter 3, we examined the design of alternative operating systems that could be used for open systems platforms. Any or all of the alternatives can be used in the installation while conforming to the objectives of open support. Many companies choose to limit support to one or two options, thus reducing the support costs and also the potential transitions of software.

Most companies prefer to reduce the number of systems maintained within their installations. It is well to consider the qualities that make the different systems important as client systems. The available options, circa mid-1990s, might be divided into the following categories:

- MS-DOS or MS-DOS with Windows
- OS/2

- Macintosh Operating System
- UNIX
- Object-oriented Operating Environments.

MS-DOS is perhaps the most widely supported system in the history of computing. It is the base for the majority of IBM PCs and their clones and dates back to the early 1980s. The wealth of personal productivity tools available for MS-DOS has not been duplicated on any other system. Much of the code is targeted to individuals working alone and has been limited by inherent design constraints within the system itself.

For the most part, though (other than with "PC-based legacy applications," e.g., those applications which were developed in the mid-1980s or earlier and are still in use), "plain old DOS" isn't used much as a client operating system any more. Microsoft built on the acceptance of MS-DOS by introducing Windows, which removed many constraints found in the original operating system. Many applications have shifted to Windows support, but even this support has limitations, which will restrict the eventual long-term value of continuing MS-DOS support. Microsoft originally developed the Windows NTas an evolutionary path from the DOS/Windows world into UNIX-like functionality. Some studies suggest an explosion in Windows NT use by the late 1990s, though others claim that a divergence in Microsoft's operating system products (the touted "Chicago" upgrade to Microsoft Windows as contrasted with the Windows NT path) may cloud the operating system/operating environment picture from that front. Regardless, Windows-related environments (whether NT or some other variant) will be a major factor on the client desktop throughout the rest of the 1990s.

OS/2 was the original intended replacement for MS-DOS, but it has been slow in reaching a critical mass. Originally a joint effort between Microsoft and IBM, the environment has fallen into the IBM camp as Microsoft placed its fortunes in Microsoft Windows. Although not as "popular" (in terms of an installed base) as the DOS/Windows tandem, OS/2 nonetheless is a viable option for many organizations on the client desktop.

Apple's Macintosh operating system is another operating system alternative for the desktop, although it has never gained the prominence in open client/server environments to the degree that it has in stand-alone PC systems. While some might argue that it is less open than other desktop operating environments (in terms of running only on Apple hardware), there has been discussion in recent years about Apple's licensing the operating system to other vendors—in effect creating a portable operating system.

UNIX is the primary operating system used in many open systems solutions found on client hardware, primarily those that feature workstation clients (as opposed to PCs). Since the system is available across multiple hardware systems, it is popular with application vendors. Programs written for UNIX can be ported to different hardware systems with minimal impact on the code. The primary problem for clients is the complexity of the user interfaces. These interfaces have been masked through a number of software solutions, which effectively build a layer of usability code on the UNIX base. As noted earlier, though, there is no such thing as "standard UNIX" or even standardization among the various consortium-led standardization efforts (although every year seems to bring yet another consolidation). For the most part, there will likely always be divergences in the UNIX world.

Although UNIX is infamous for its relative difficulty of use (as compared with other operating systems), the increased use of graphics has introduced elements similar to Macintosh OS for end users who are familiar with this system. As UNIX was extended to the desktop, additional effort was placed on defining simpler user interfaces. Windowing and graphical user interfaces help make the system more usable and competitive with PC operating systems.

At the heart of desktop usability is the X Windows system, which was developed at MIT during Project Athena. Support from major vendors, such as DEC and IBM, contributed to its early acceptance. The common interfaces provided by X Windows represent a basis for creating windows across multiple desktop computers in a transparent fashion. X input events are driven from the keyboard, pointer, or from windows. Output capabilities include images, 2-D graphs, windows, color, and multifont text. PEX was introduced as 3-D graphics for X-based systems on the Programmers Hierarchical Interactive Graphics System (PHIGS) standard. The support has been extended to desktops, including PCs, workstations, and X terminals.

Additional support has helped to make X advantageous to use. Programming interfaces to X, called Xlib, were introduced, which provide a C interface to the protocol. Toolkits have been introduced to facilitate the use of X in different environments. These toolkits provide a higher-level abstraction than Xlib and provide standard GUI and programming interface. Three types of toolkits are available: X based, Xlib based, and intrinsics based X-based toolkits include CLUE from Texas Instruments and Garnet from CMU. Xlib-based toolkits include Andrew from Carnegie Mellon and XView/OpenLook from Sun Microsystems. X intrinsics toolkits are Athena from MIT, Xcu from Cornell, OLIT/OpenLook from Sun Microsystems, and Motif from the Open Software Foundation.

Focus on user interfaces was carried another step farther with the acceptance of Motif as the user interface for X Windows. Using the power of modern graphics devices, the software supports 3-D images that appear similar to what is seen on the Macintosh. Users of modern interfaces get accustomed to pushbuttons, pop-up windows, and pull-down menus. A number of significant features permit users to use advanced interfaces.

A growing number of packages are becoming available to create and modify user interfaces. These packages permit the developer to build a system more easily while connecting into the database available on the local system. For example, there is a User Toolkit for Motif. This provides a tool to build the GUIs that connect with the database. Pop-up aids are in the toolkit to facilitate screen creation. These toolkits make it possible for application developers to define their own windows.

Although porting between systems has been touted as the primary reason for the acceptance of UNIX, IS executives have questioned the value of ports versus complete object compatibility found in PCs. It is clear that complete binary compatibility is simpler than porting. Porting, however, does not appear to be as complex as opponents fear, nor is it as simple as the zealots would have us believe. Few hard statistics exist that document the time required to make a port from one vendor's UNIX to another. The perception is that the process is very easy, although complications can exist in, for example, porting from 32-bit to 64-bit platforms.

Finally, it is arguable that object-oriented client operating environments will play an ever-increasing role throughout the rest of the 1990s. The apparent leaders (circa 1994, at the time of writing) include:

- NeXTStep, from NeXT Computer, Inc. NeXT, originally conceived as a company dedicated to university and higher-education computing, has shifted its focus since its early days to a software company focusing on object-oriented, multiplatform operating environments.
- Microsoft's "Cairo," an object-oriented toolset for Windows-related environments
- The Taligent operating system and object development toolkit. Taligent, a joint effort between IBM, Hewlett-Packard, and Apple Computer, is expected to have marketable technology by the 1995–1996 time frame.

As operating systems are considered, it is well to balance the value of the control point code with the need to interact with many other processors. Control point distribution becomes a critical point in determining which operating system will be used.

5.3 USER INTERFACE SOFTWARE

As mentioned above, the client is the location of the user interface to network software and therefore is the focal point for software packages that support usability. Early user access to the computer depended on toggle switches and wiring boards, which required a good deal of training and skill. When the accounting card became a software tool, it was adopted to batch commands into a system. Elementary processes depended on simplistic cards, but as software grew in complexity, the command structure also adopted new complex parameters. Early command languages relied on 80-column format to enter the control information.

Many command structures supported in modern computers were created in the era of the punched card and still retain vestiges of the design. For instance, IBM's Job Control Language (JCL) is still part of the structure of MVS, which is used in open systems. The initial input device for this language was the card reader, and the language was built accordingly. The languages were also built in an era in which the control program was limited, and the user needed to specify more information about the computer I/O devices. Even such popular desktop operating systems as UNIX descended from this period of card input and truncated commands. As a result, there is a complexity in the command structure that often challenges even programmers.

Significant studies have examined user interaction with computers and proposed software approaches to facilitate human interaction (Abelson, 1987). Some of the best systems have had human factors experts as part of the design team from the beginning. User interfaces were designed first, and the system was built around the assumption that the user could rely on simple approaches. Other systems have learned from work that originated at Xerox.

The work performed on smallTalk at Xerox Corporation's Palo Alto Research Center provided a base for desktop computer interfaces through the 1980s. The use of menus and icons replaced the cumbersome command structures from the earlier stages of computing. Unfortunately, there is a wide body of applications still tied to older command structures that are difficult to use. An icon is a picture representation of some computer task. Apple adopted the interfaces first in LISA and then in the very popular Macintosh, which provided the impetus for Microsoft Windows and other GUI environments.

5.4 PERSONAL PRODUCTIVITY ALTERNATIVES

An important goal of any desktop computer is to retain the personal productivity gains made during the past decade. Applications that enhance this capability have been introduced throughout the decade, each increasing the amount of processing the individual could gain from the computer.

A number of tools moved from machine rooms and laboratories to desktop computers. These new tools enhanced individual capability to respond to requests and often avoided the need to turn to skilled programmers for special packages. Many stories exist about productivity tools introduced to unskilled people that, through simple modifications, they have been able to improve significantly. The environment changed radically, and individuals could control their output. Packaged software was not only less costly to develop but was easier to use and change.

Although knowledge of the operating system continued to grow, there was less preoccupation with control code and more with ease of use. There is a constant shift in both hardware and software usability features. The mouse, icons, and menus changed the connection to different processors and made the system far simpler to use.

Advances are continuing in personal productivity products that will affect the acceptance of desktop computers. These individual productivity tools have important roles in distributed processing. Each individual will wish to retain the productivity tools that have helped him or her, but management will want to incorporate these same tools into a larger picture. Personal productivity must be extended to group productivity and the tools discussed above can help that process.

5.5 MOVING TO GROUP PRODUCTIVITY

The introduction of applications that enhance group productivity on the desktop assumes the existence of interfaces that complement the existing code on the desktop computer. Mission-critical applications have been built on desktop computers that can augment existing off-the-shelf products. These applications provide user code that supports the mission of a specific application with the company. Mission-critical applications are often competitive leverage points and therefore need to be protected from tampering.

Many examples of mission-critical applications exist. The engineer will use individual design tools that augment the company's specific product goals. The manufacturing manager will have written specific applications that perform a chemical or mechanical process better than the competition. Stock traders will find an edge in calculating time of trade for large blocks of stock and make significant gains from the results.

In addition to mission-critical applications, there are also a number of applications specifically designed to support a professional discipline. The most obvious sets of applications are those created for design and manufacturing engineers. Based on the heavy compute and graphics work inherent in engineering, the computer was a natural tool to replace the unwieldy drawing boards and calculation techniques. With the introduction of electronic data interchange, it became possible to create products that could be shared in different locations or by different groups of designers. The accepted discipline has helped to make engineering faster and more reliable in the 1990s.

The engineering discipline was able to use client/server models at an early stage, because there is a good deal of individual work that must eventually be shared with other engineers. Design performed on individual workstations must be combined with the work of other engineers in a completed product. Even CAD/CAM products supported on mainframes and minicomputers provided an environment for individual productivity. Integration of complex products became a control point for the development of shared applications.

Financial companies are building a repertoire of packages that can help the trader or the manager. Changes in modeling have permitted the individual trader to benefit from the use of UNIX-based applications that provide simulations of alternative purchase directions. Coupling workstations with high-speed parallel compute servers can be an edge that helps win unique business for a firm.

Major operations, such as the Toronto Stock Exchange, have implemented UNIX solutions to augment existing trading operations. The stock exchange introduced UNIX on the trading floor in 1988 and by 1991 had shifted major applications to open systems (Fowler, 1992).

Personal productivity tools that aid the professional will continue to flourish in the coming computer generations. Additional support of group interaction will permit widespread interaction between global members of professional teams.

5.6 PERSONAL DATA SOFTWARE

The wide acceptance of desktop computers has caused a major shift in the data placement within a network. It was discovered that PCs could support large and mixed databases, and the introduction of workstations extended the capability. Large-capacity data files can now be purchased for relatively low cost, and higher-capacity units are promised for the near future. The era of locally large files of information has begun.

Selection of data handling routines is something most end users are not accustomed to performing. Typically, the management information group within a company would select the file systems and the software needed to support them. When individuals bought their own desktop computers, they were faced with unique questions of managing and using data locally. Important selection criteria for the end user may be different from the corporation making the selection. End users will look for simple ways to store and retrieve data, while corporate managers will look for questions of longevity and durability.

Initial database applications were simple, but with the introduction of powerful workstations, additional capability has shifted to workstations. Initially, a limited number of database companies focused on the PC as a desktop alternative, and many of these products are still available on desktop computers.

Equally important, major database companies, which produce server products, are offering counterparts on desktop computers. These products are designed to interface with servers. Companies such as ORACLE and Sybase have products that interact with their code on servers.

ORACLE was a pacesetter for department computing in the 1980s and has shifted emphasis to desktops and high-performance servers. Their portable relational database, which operates on many different computers, has made them very successful across a broad range of computers. ORACLE was a late entry on the PC but used its support levels to create a single database image across multiple computers.

The variety of PC databases presents a challenge and opportunity for workstation users. Database vendors have learned a good deal from the PC experiences, and we can expect to find many of these packages migrate directly to workstations.

Although there is great promise for distributed data systems with portions of databases residing on different processors spread through the network, the reality is that databases on clients are primarily focused on individual data handling. Capacity is measured by the ability to support individual productivity at desktop computers and augment information stored in servers and large data farms.

Individual data handling involves an awareness of the specific applications and the need to shift data from one to another. This data movement is accomplished very well in Macintosh applications and promises to work well in applications built around object processing.

Individual desktop databases begin with specific databases, which include the day-to-day working systems. Sequential data dominate client operations, since it is found on output from printers, tapes, disks, or diskettes. Paper data represent the largest sequential data source and are the most difficult to manage. Until recently, paper was the only medium used for many operations.

A good example is federal income taxes, which by 1989 represented over 200 million tax returns with an average of five pages per return. Although some returns were submitted electronically, the majority were handled in paper form. Even with extensive new support for electronic filing, the growth of paper handling is expected to continue through the century.

Open systems designs have created new opportunities for relational databases. New design paradigms assume mixtures of data that include images, mixed media, and animation. These data requirements challenge older data handling routines and provide opportunity for new designs. New compound data raise questions of storage techniques, which reduce image and graphic information to compressed digital formats that can be used for storage and transmission across networks.

Databases are driven by languages that enable end users to access their facility. *SQL* is a popular alternative provided on most computers today. A data manipulation language (DML) is a language that facilitates query and update on databases. Queries are formulated against portions of the data.

In open systems databases, access determines the overall completeness of the system. Open approaches have adopted the relational model as the standard. They have extended the support to use the SQL language to access the data. Requirements for security raise additional design considerations on databases, and the issue of security will grow in importance during the next decade.

5.7 CONSIDERATIONS

The operating system was once the major interface to the end user. With the introduction of modern user interfaces, the user has layers that isolate applications from the specifics of a single operating system design. Improved graphics are making the interfaces to the operating system simpler for unskilled users, who may not even know there is an operating system in their computer. Further advances of user interfaces result in the production of artificial reality solutions, which can enable users to experience the full power of open systems.

Also hidden under these transparent interfaces are connection protocols, which resolve the access to different protocols within the system. Although in the PC and workstations the access to the protocols is not clean, it is getting better. Application Programmer Interfaces can be common to all LANs.

The desktop computer is the location for user interfaces in an open system. PC designs created innovations in designs that make desktop computers appealing for the nonprofessional. Increasing use of windows, icons, and menus has created a protection layer that shields the average computer user from the complexity of the network design.

The increasing power of desktop computers forces additional applications to individual clients. This increased power also raises unique challenges for managers who must determine the correct code and ensure its steady execution in an operating environment.

Personal productivity packages helped to spur the rapid deployment of PCs. This individual productivity introduced in the era of the PC is being augmented by newer packages that improve group productivity. The introduction of these new paradigms presents the manager with challenges and opportunities to improve the productivity of the entire group.

Database design is continuing to advance the interconnection between desktop computers and the larger servers. The local user has access to very large amounts of storage and tools, which help to manage this storage.

Clients will utilize central services found in more powerful shared programs located in servers. The servers augment the capabilities of desktop processors and provide an environment that presents the open systems user with unique capability.

5.8 REFERENCES

Abelson, Robert P. "Psychological Status of the Script Concept." In *System Design for Human Interaction*, edited by Andrew P. Sage. New York: IEEE Press, 1987.

Fowler, Wayne A. "The Toronto Stock Exchange Case Study." *Proceeding of the Third Annual Executive Symposium on UNIX and Open Systems*, Toronto, March 4, 1992.

6

Servers

The increasing acceptance of PCs and workstations precipitated a need for shared services that could reduce costs. Servers are dedicated computers optimized for processing tasks that serve multiple intelligent workstations (Wheeler, 1991). Interconnected users can rely on a single server to perform common functions to avoid replication of code and hardware. Initially, larger PCs were used as servers, but many departments selected familiar minicomputers to provide faster processing or increased function. The initial shift to servers was limited to shared data or high-cost I/O devices. Eventually, servers were extended to different communications protocols through bridges, routers, and gateways.

Servers emerged as a solution that appealed to departments with many PCs. Sharing resources, while retaining personal autonomy, met the needs of both individuals and departments. By 1984, an increasing number of servers were being used to share data and expensive I/O functions. As the increasing power on chips enabled designers to create powerful redundant environments, additional functions shifted from desktop units to shared data environments. Acceptance of connection standards permitted the use of more powerful processors as servers. Acceptance of open systems standards has further pushed the threshold of power for the many different machine configurations used as servers.

After the initial introduction of servers, it became clear that additional hardware could improve the performance of servers. Dedicated designs for servers improved their performance. New dedicated servers provide high-speed access to special functions with higher redundancy for shared devices. Servers have shifted from being a simple extension of a workstation to a dedicated hardware design.

Many ask what the difference is between the client/server model and the mainframe and minicomputers. In the past, computing philosophy depended on shared logic or programming facilities, which assumed little or no compute intelligence on the terminal interface. The modern server communicates to the workstation as a peer, which requires that a portion of the work be performed on the centralized processor. Modern servers use lower-cost hardware to replace minis and mainframes.

A number of hardware considerations help determine the configuration best suited for a specific application. Figure 6.1 shows four elements that

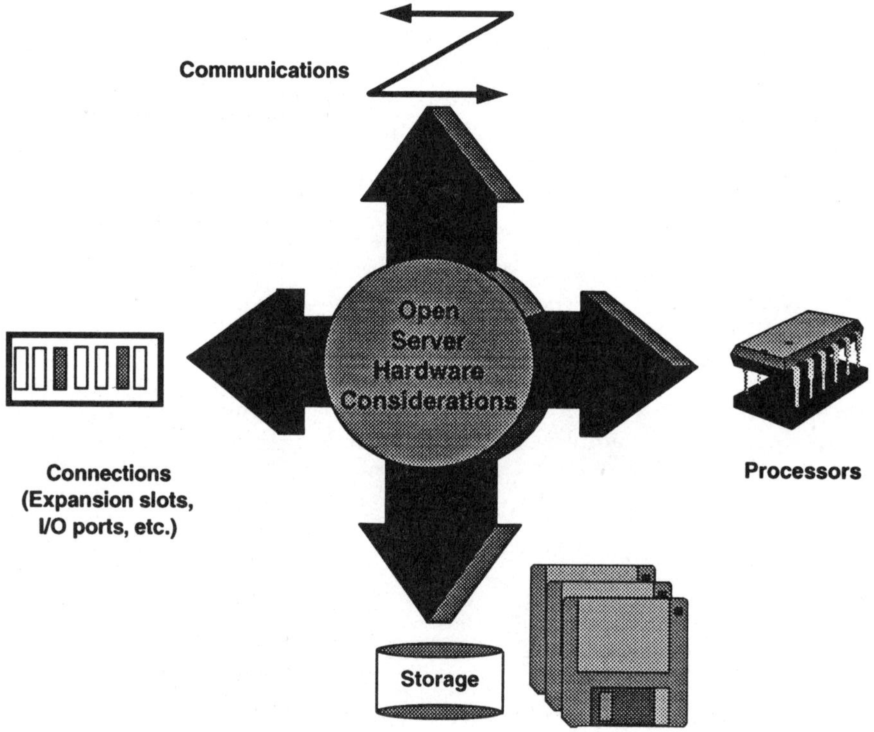

Figure 6.1 Elements to consider in server selection

must be considered in any server selection. The first element is the processors, which determine the response to requests. The second is the internal server connections, including the various types of I/O connections and support hardware that enhance performance. The third is communications, which defines the support characteristics for the network. The fourth—especially important for data servers—is the storage characteristics of the server.

The selection of servers often begins with a determination of functional and performance characteristics needed to complete the job for multiple users. Often, this involves identification of required functions and connection protocols, which map to the client architecture adopted by the company. Although different server functions require unique software and hardware to ensure successful implementation, the protocol connections can be common to varying performance levels of hardware. We will next examine various hardware platforms that can be used by servers.

6.1 HARDWARE BASIS FOR SERVERS

Users of computer networks will find various types of servers with different processing power, storage capacities, and I/O capability. Each server that supports open systems connection standards can be accessed easily through the network. Multiple hardware and software architectures provide solutions to user-specific requirements for increased performance or capacity.

Figure 6.2 shows examples of different open server technologies with a wide range of performance options. From the simplest servers, which use single chip micro hardware, the user can design a system that steps through higher performance levels and degrees of redundancy without modifying the connections from the clients. Low-end servers use single microprocessors. Parallelism is introduced by placing multiple processor chips in the server. At the highest end are parallel processors, which provide high performance using the same chips found in workstations.

For a number of years, minicomputers served as departmental alternatives to mainframes. Although they used shared logic support similar to mainframes, they provided local autonomy similar to servers. Many functions supported by today's servers were found on these computers. Minicomputers shared complexity with mainframes but provided autonomy for departments to support their priorities. Business minicomputers were generally optimized to support shared functions, such as accounting, personnel, and billing applications. Minicomputers provided functional and price availability, which made their use advantages for many companies.

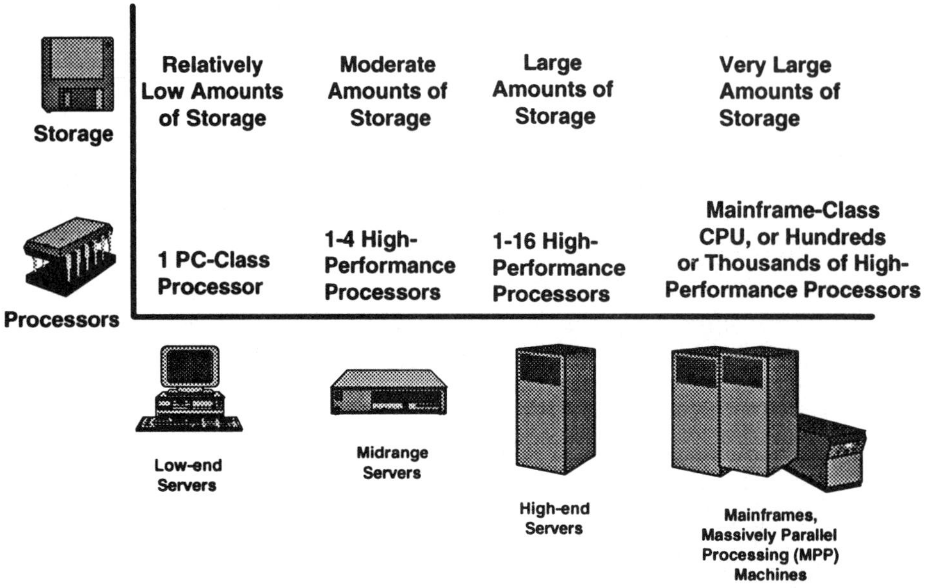

Figure 6.2 Examples of open server technologies

Initial minicomputer architectures provided an open systems base that relied on programmers providing support packages to augment initial system functions. Hardware optimization provided for advanced programming through design paradigms, such as stacks, registers, and rich instruction sets. Initial products were complex and difficult to use, but by the third generation they were powerful and had many easy-to-use features. High availability or fault tolerance became popular in minicomputer architectures. Redundancy became an important purchase consideration within the scientific community and those applications that could not afford significant downtime. Redundant computers ensure the completion of a function when a single portion of the system has problems. Redundancy achieved widespread acceptance in a number of critical industries, such as banking and chemical processing.

The data and communications handling was as varied as the processor capability found in the systems. The wide variety ranged from simple wire attachments to sophisticated architectures. Servers were used to concentrate database or specialized hardware handling.

Servers began as simple devices shared across LANs, but they have continually expanded to handle common functions for many users connected together. Prices for dedicated servers have continued to decline, making them competitive with minicomputer and mainframe alternatives.

6.2 DIFFERENT TYPES OF SERVERS

Figure 6.3 illustrates some of the different types of servers available to the open systems user. Database servers represent the largest single server category in use today. These servers provide users data from many sources. Database servers provide support for reading, writing, or updating databases and also facilitate the connection between open systems data files and existing databases. Device servers access costly devices shared by many end users. Although these are typically printers, they can also be expensive multimedia devices or plotters. Communications servers are gateways to different protocols, which facilitate access by masking the different communications protocols.

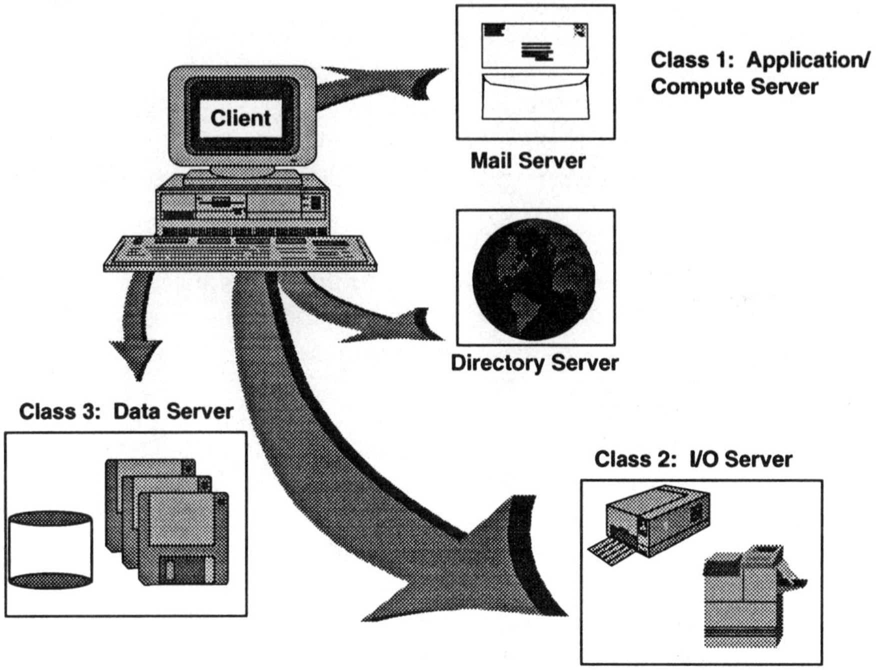

Figure 6.3 Servers available to the open systems user

Other servers provide specific functions, such as simulation, that can be used by multiple workstations. Office servers provide word processors and spreadsheets, which are typically used in office computing. Executive support system servers are repositories for executive information accessed by different levels of management. A language server could be used to support fonts for different letters in Japanese or Chinese alphabets. Name servers support directories of file names, which facilitate data searches across the network. Yellow-page functions are built using name servers.

6.2.1 Data Servers

The sharing of data among many workers has been a significant challenge to application developers since the introduction of computers. This challenge continues as open systems provide services across multiple processors. Data have been spread throughout the network using different software products to provide access to information.

Early engineering servers addressed the demand for extensive storage capacities. Designs use extensive graphics and numerical information, which consume data space. As the designs migrated from workstations to servers to large data farms, the server began to require additional storage. Storage farms of servers were needed to contain complex designs, such as nuclear reactors or complex jet engines, which have over 35,000 parts per engine. These large storage servers support both engineering and business applications.

As usual, commercial requirements followed the lead of the engineering groups. Massive financial and inventory data could be temporarily stored on local data servers. The processing performance and capacity matches that found on engineering processors. Transaction processing requirements can be easily met with modern data servers.

Initial storage capacity has been met with low-cost magnetic (disk) media. Magnetic capacity has continued to grow, as technology advances and price reduction are making high-capacity magnetic storage servers reasonable alternatives.

Expanded requirements for massive storage systems were answered by the introduction of optical servers. These devices can store terabytes (trillions) of characters, in relatively compressed space. In a server configuration, workstations send massive data information to the optical storage. Since optical storage has high reliability and is relatively unaffected by traditional magnetic problems, these large servers are important to certain industries.

Early servers on PCs used sequential data files. With the introduction of database support, many of the servers use relational databases supported by SQL access. Since additional redundancy has been added to parallel servers, high availability has been added to a limited number of servers. Reliability and availability are assured for critical databases using these design paradigms.

6.2.2 Compute Servers

Specialized compute functions often require servers optimized for high computing. Initially, these were thought of as high-speed processors designed for engineering and scientific applications. Engineering often requires large-scale numerical calculations that exceed the processing power of local processors, even when they are coupled together to reach large aggregate compute levels. Problems such as predictive simulations, eigenvalue operations, and finite element analysis require large amounts of processing, typically unavailable on desktop processors.

Commercial applications that provide large-scale simulations of market forces, population shifts, or large amounts of financial modeling consume processing power comparable to those required by engineering departments. The introduction of expert systems, which require calculations on many parameters to reach a solution, is another area in which high-powered computing may be used in the commercial environment.

Yet it continues to be the engineering and scientific applications that require process-rich computers to complete their tasks. Computer-aided engineering (CAE) has used more powerful servers to augment the capability found at individual desktop computers for several years. The modeling and testing of engineering problems can be facilitated through the creation of a model on a larger computer. Often, engineering problems cannot be resolved without using more powerful processors.

As an example, fluid mechanics represents a challenging branch of CAE. Often, fluid problems will have effects that depend on nonlinear relationships with a high degree of time dependence. There are many examples of complex problems that challenge even the fastest computers available.

One such example was a cavitation problem discovered by General Electric engineers on a hydro-turbine runner in James Bay, Canada. The turbine is a large multistory device, which provides hydro power to a large geographic area. Once the problem was discovered, it was clear the turbine could not be disassembled and investigated in detail. Using a Cray supercomputer as a compute server, the engineers were able to find the source of the problem and design a solution without unhooking the turbine.

Powerful compute servers are required by engineers in many fields of new design. The calculations of fluid dynamics for the Orient Express, a modern high-speed airplane, will require the services of supercompute servers. The flow of air through and around the engines as well as the flow around the airfoil can be calculated by these compute servers.

Parallel compute servers are also useful in the financial markets. Calculations of stock changes will affect many trades. A simple calculation on a high-powered server can affect trading time and eventual profit derived from a trade. In commercial applications, it is necessary to move data from large storage devices found on mainframe computers to the parallel processor. Parallel processor companies have adopted the use of the high-performance connection HIPPI to achieve these connections.

Users in many fields benefit from the use of parallel processors as superservers. Since many parallel processors follow design paradigms used for open systems, they can be connected to the workstations with little effort once standards have been adopted. The server performs the compute operation and returns the results to the engineer's workstation. Frequently, these computers will provide specialized types of computing, but the standard connections to open networks make them a critical part of the entire process.

There is a body of even more complex problems, which often require extensive calculations that can exceed today's most powerful computers. The term *grand challenge* application has been applied to those scientific and engineering applications that can take the fastest computer and use it dedicated for a year at a time. An example of a grand challenge application is the model for global warming. Most massive parallel computers are being designed with the capability to connect to the network.

There will be increasing demand for high-powered computers to perform mathematically loaded tasks. The types of applications will change, as commercial businesses become more aware of the potential to improve business through high-powered compute servers. Later, we will examine the technology that will permit high-powered compute servers to be connected to the network and function well.

6.2.3 Communication Servers

An open systems user must communicate to a company's legacy network, which was defined before industry standards. Each computer vendor defined protocols that matched their architecture and were significantly different from other vendors' protocols. Attachment requires overt translation to communicate with different network protocols. The translation problem has been made more difficult by differences in data structure between different vendors and even within a single vendor.

Popular protocols such as TCP/IP, IPX/SPX, and SNA are different from each other, but other vendors with smaller market shares also have unique communications standards. Each of these different systems required a translation either in the sending or receiving computer or in a neutral processor such as a communications server. Communications servers combine hardware and software to package messages in a way that permits transmission between different processing elements. Separate adapter boards are included for the physical hardware interfaces from the sending processors. These signals are converted into a common form and transferred to software programs that adjust the protocols. Software converts incoming protocol by encapsulating it with new information, which transmits the data to the new system.

An early design concept was similar to inserting different protocols in envelopes of the new protocol. At each level in the process, the necessary information is either added or removed. In this case, each subsequent layer becomes a receiver layer, with the final intermediate node responsible for final protocol form.

As with other servers, the communications server began as a PC that connected into a network, such as the IBM SNA network or Digital's DECnet. The specialized PC mapped the protocols from standard interfaces to the vendor interfaces. In addition to the backbone network, the system also permits a client to communicate with different LANs. This type of problem is not unique to open systems. Major corporations have had dedicated computers to connect to different systems for some time.

6.2.4 Input/Output Servers

A number of expensive devices have been attached to servers to permit sharing by many users. A good example is the high-speed print server, which provides access to higher-quality printers. The print server has proven valuable in connecting open systems desktop computers to facilities that individual workstations could not afford. In an era in which the workplace has become more portable, the need to access print servers on telephone lines will also increase.

The printer was identified early in PC networks as an essential item for sharing and cost savings. Simply queuing access to printers through the use of the PC could have large payback in relatively short time frames. Logic could be shared across multiple processes and reduce the need for costly printers. As the cost of printers has continued to change, it is now possible to get high quality at the desktop, but there is still a requirement for high performance and high-function printers.

The print server performs many functions commonly allocated to the local computer. The simplest function is to serve as a font server for the attached printer. This provides centralized font manipulation and storage. Extended protocols carry information about the fonts, page alignment, and control features. As a result, sophisticated protocols have been defined to communicate to high-speed printers with additional functions. Modern protocols have been extended to compound document information. The intelligence in print servers enables the company to reduce the protocols from individual workstations and focus the process in the server. Functions such as expanded font management can be handled locally.

In countries with complex languages, the print server assumes an expanded role of providing additional language support. Printers from major vendors in ideographic language environments will find additional functions embedded in the print server to handle these differences.

Another shared output device is the plotter, which provides precise line drawings of completed designs. Although plotter costs have also fallen due to advances in technology, precision high-quality devices are still too expensive to attach to individual workstations. Two separate designs are the pen-based and the electrostatic. Additionally, devices are usually mounted on flatbed or drum configurations. The flatbed plotter draws on paper on a table surface. These plotters are available in sizes up to many feet. Drum plotters use rolls of paper to perform the drawing. The paper is mounted using prepunched holes, which contribute to its accuracy.

Pen plotters can provide many color drawings, while electrostatic plotters are usually limited to black and white.

6.3 DESIGN CONSIDERATIONS

Design considerations are important in defining a well-balanced server system. One important design consideration is synchronization of clocks between the workstations and servers. Fault avoidance, tolerance, diagnosis, and correction are characteristics shared across the open system. The server has special needs for each of these qualities, since it is a shared resource that can affect the work of multiple users.

Fault avoidance is the first step in producing a reliable design. This step begins with the design of the computer chips and continues through the development of the applications on the server. In designing the chips, automated design tools facilitate prompt recognition of potential problem areas. Monitor chips located in the server and workstation can project potential errors. These devices can detect a number of conditions that can cause adverse results in a computing environment. A good example is a thermal detection chip, which can determine when a device has reached a heat level of potential failure. Another such device is the chip placed in portable workstations, which determines when the battery level has reached a point in which data could become lost.

Complex techniques have been designed for fault tolerance. Some of these include mirrored disks, which will copy information and ensure that the system will keep performing. Redundancy in processors, if properly applied, can guarantee the system will continue to function when one portion of the system fails.

In modern systems, advanced chips aid in the detection of faults in both the hardware and software. Additional coding is usually necessary to ensure that this is an ongoing process. Fault isolation code has been used in modern computers for years, but modern renditions of the code have the computer ordering the necessary parts on the network to make the corrections. Once a fault is detected, the next problem is to correct it in the shortest possible time frame. Again, this occurs using a combination of hardware, network, and software resources.

The principal design consideration is to ensure that the servers fully support open protocols. This is important to achieve portability of applications across multiple servers.

6.4 PARALLEL PROCESSORS AS SERVERS

Multiprocessing technology was originally introduced for mainframe computers in the 1970s. Originally, dual processors provided higher performance and redundancy, which could be applied to critical mathematical and design processes. The computers used for the NASA manned missions depended on redundancy through parallel processing in hardware and software. In this case, each processor had a complete copy of the operating system and application code. Redundancy was also a motivation behind the processors introduced for Wall Street applications. Early applications depended on identical copies in twin hardware.

As technology has advanced, multiprocessing technology can now be applied directly to workstations. Chips connected in parallel on single boards permit the balancing of work across multiple processors, providing a performance advantage and a potential reliability advantage. Workstations with many chips could be converted into multiprocessing servers, which distribute the work across many processors. Simple multiprocessors will have only a few chips that can give them higher performance and redundancy.

The use of multiple processing chips has been introduced in specialized servers for open systems. These functional servers provide support for fast access to data and high degrees of reliability. Parallel or multiprocessing architectures have achieved server fault tolerance. In other words, when a processor ceases to function, another processor with data will automatically switch into the network.

Larger degrees of parallelism have been reached by placing massive numbers of simple chips together in a parallel arrangement. Massive parallel processors can have thousands of processors and memory locations, which provide unique compute services that can often exceed the power of supercomputers.

Many of the massive parallel processors use standard workstation chips to achieve very high performance. Attached to the networks like any other open systems computer, these compute processors can solve complex engineering applications, such as structural and fluid flow analysis, electronic circuit design, thermal analysis, and simulations (Karin and Smith, 1987). Applications in financial markets involve complex modeling to determine the value of stock or other securities. Such simulations can result in a high payback in a relatively short time.

Parallel processor development is moving rapidly enough to ensure high performance. Parallel processors will have a growing role in open systems configurations. Since these devices are based on inexpensive building blocks, they will be highly price competitive.

6.5 MAINFRAME SERVERS

The desire to introduce open systems while retaining critical data on existing mainframe computers has created a challenge in defining effective connection protocols. A shift in the role of the mainframe computer from the primary network control point and center of all applications to the central repository of business state data has occurred. Application locations are shifting from central processing to local sites, as many are downsized to servers or workstations. At the same time, many mainframe vendors have adopted open systems solutions for their mainframes. The role of the mainframe is shifting from a central shared resource handling all processing to a server providing functions, which makes it especially strong.

The mainframe provides access to legacy applications, which are the backbone of business. Legacy software reflects 40 years of continuous development by thousands of programmers. The large amounts of completed programs represent a significant investment in problem solving, which cannot be eliminated with the introduction of new technology. As the backbone of processing within the company, this code is valuable for continuing business operations.

The challenge of open systems is to identify simple connection mechanisms from the large installed mainframe base to open networks. The initial attachment selection is to use traditional terminal attachments between the open systems component and the mainframe. These attachments carry an unnecessary overhead, which degrades performance across the connected link. In addition, since mainframes require proprietary interfaces, there is not a capability of transparently connecting them into the network.

Mainframe manufacturers have agreed to conform to standard POSIX interfaces, which will greatly enhance the attachment of different processors. Additional emphasis will then be placed on the attachment of data connections that can support the performance of other attached processors. Initial mainframe networks have used a channel-to-channel connection, which limits the performance of high-speed compute servers. Mainframes are also connecting into client/server networks. Channel extension architectures, such as HIPPI, provide faster connections between mainframe data and other components of the network.

Conformity to standard interfaces will usually be accomplished through the introduction of a standards layer on existing operating systems. This layer will convert UNIX interfaces to proprietary calls. Users selecting this option must become comfortable with additional path lengths needed to access system code.

The second challenge is to make the repository of state data—which has also been developed for years—available to the open systems users. Much of the history and culture of the corporation is buried in this data. More importantly, customer information is embedded in this valuable source of information. Innumerable data files exist that can only be accessed through these larger computers containing operational files necessary to the running of the company.

Since many mainframe applications run as batched programs, it is possible to activate these programs from a client. This treats the mainframe as though it were a large compute server. Data must be translated through routines that can convert the information directly into a form needed for the mainframe. Output from the mainframe must also be converted to transmit across the network.

Access to time-sharing functions is more convoluted. Initially, the client becomes a time-sharing terminal with more of the function being moved up front to use the intelligence on the desktop. Since programs are allocated logical time slices, it is possible for the client to perform other tasks while waiting for the interaction with the mainframe. Interaction between the processor and data is the same as discussed above.

The mainframe will continue to participate in open systems as servers having peer relationships with other servers. Access to mainframe code is provided through applications that connect to the correct repository of information. Overall costs for mainframes remain higher than server alternatives, so these solutions will be temporary.

6.6 CONSIDERATIONS

Servers are network resources that provide function to multiple users. The server can use different hardware designs if connection protocols are adopted to support transparency. Simple extension of existing microprocessors is the first step to installing a server. If the selection of the architecture is carefully made, the granularity of servers can increase to meet the specific needs of the applications. A single interface can connect the network into anything from a microprocessor-based server to a multiple parallel computer.

Shifting capability to department processing through the use of servers has a technical and organizational implication. There will need to be a consistent policy that reflects the power of the new attachments and also provides for open capability. The wide use of server-based data will increase the need for directory and global naming conventions.

In an open system, the server is a shared resource, which implies that it has the ability to stop the work of many people if there is a failure. Connections of very high performance servers to very high performance networks will press the support levels of the system. Additional emphasis must be placed on design for disaster recovery. A number of items must be considered to ensure server reliability in a network environment.

Traditionally, many installations will rely on weekly recovery tapes to provide the backup. With the introduction of servers, many companies have shifted to an arrangement where they back up more frequently.

Three traditional functions are located in servers. The most prevalent use of server technology is to support data access. Data servers range from simple file servers to more complex information servers. The second use of server technology is to support unique and different I/O devices. The third area of interest is compute servers, which perform special tasks within the open network. Available storage on servers has continued to rise, as the price and configurations of disks have improved. Redundancy in the processing of information has resulted in an increased interest in the use of high-performance and redundant disk units.

Multimedia is another application that is growing on servers. Coupled with artificial intelligence programs, the repertoire of server applications is expanding greatly.

With the introduction of parallel computing, new levels of computational performance can be found on servers connected to networks. They are used increasingly for simulation in engineering and scientific applications. As the performance improves in the systems, there can be further transparent improvement in performance found on servers. Eventually, multiple parallel processors will be used for this task.

Although the hardware has been steadily improving, effective use of hardware will depend on well-balanced software packages that use the hardware efficiently. The next chapter explores the software characteristics of servers.

6.7 REFERENCES

Karin, Sidney, and Norris Parker Smith. *The Supercomputer Era.* San Diego, CA: Harcourt, Brace Jovanovich, 1987.

Wheeler, Thomas F. *Professional Workstations.* New York: McGraw-Hill, 1991.

7

Server Software

Server software provides shared functions required by multiple network clients. This software provides functions that cannot easily be duplicated on smaller processors or be more effectively used when shared across multiple clients. Although many software building blocks are identical to systems found on workstations or mainframes, there is a growing uniqueness in the code provided on servers. Attachment protocols, which reflect the movement to standard interfaces, are unique from customary mainframe and minicomputer connections.

Standard system protocols (Figure 7.1) support a versatility in the level of hardware that can be used for the same server software. Many packages begin with offerings for inexpensive microprocessor configurations, which can service a limited number of users and provide restricted function. The same programs can be offered on multiple parallel processors without modifying system interfaces used on the lower-priced servers. Many different types of server software can be migrated across this wide range of granularity. Compute-intensive programs, which service engineers or mathematicians, can migrate from department servers to large supercomputers. Database server code has also seen the same migration direction, as offerings available on PCs have migrated to dedicated parallel processors.

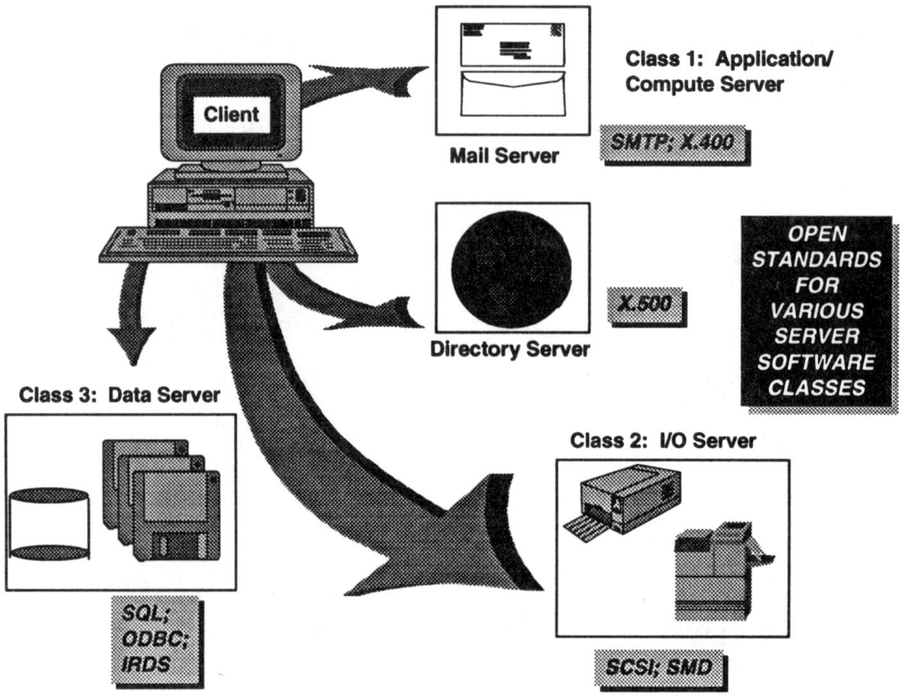

Figure 7.1 Standard system protocols for server software

The server is the source of executive code for the large numbers of X terminals. UNIX applications provide the major functions and facilitate sharing across multiple users.

Operating system and support control code are similar to comparable base support used in minicomputers and mainframes. This software includes the utilities that maintain the operation of the system and track developments within the network. Processor connections within a client/server environment require robust communications code, which is located in server software. Often, the upper limit for connection is determined by the amount of table and code space required for individual nodes to be connected. An upper limit is frequently established by the algorithms used to provide the connections. Since servers demand reliable connections, the server will also have detection and correction code as fundamental parts of the support.

There is a balancing between the functions contained in clients and those shifted to servers, as seen in Figure 7.2. Servers may support general applica-

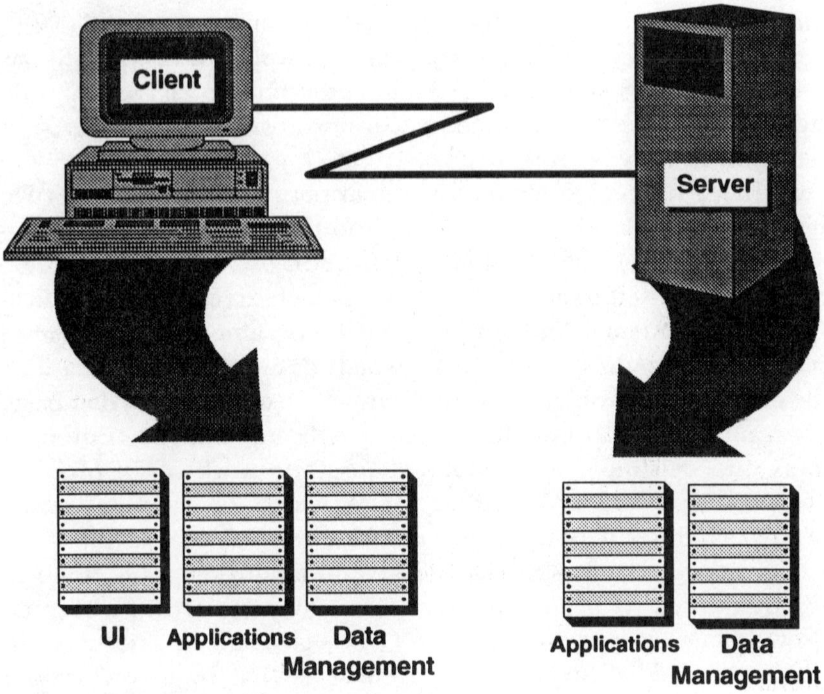

Figure 7.2 Balancing between client/server functions

tions with a special reference that performs special support tasks for the particular dedicated mission. The specific mission determines the type and extent of code. For instance, data servers that provide extensive relational support will have additional code that supports access to the information. Print servers will have special code that supplies font handling capability. Most servers will support additional code that supports an application-to-application protocol. Name servers have been introduced to locate data within the complex network. Central name servers have been designed to support the data structure across the entire system.

The largest single use for department servers has been database support. A database is an information collection accessed by either end users or application programs serving as agents of users. The information collection usually is under the control of a database management system (DBMS), which creates a method for a well-structured management of data. Advances in computer capability have created a demand for databases that include nontextual and textual information. The nontextual information includes graphics, image, audio, and even video information. This chapter will distinguish between elementary database servers and complex information servers, which include DBMS with expert system code. Simpler servers handle data as extensions to sequential data files. More extensive data and decision support mechanisms have been incorporated into knowledge servers.

Object databases have received increased impetus from the respective work of the *Object Management Group* (OMG) and the Object Database Management Group (ODMG). OMG issued a definition of *Object Request Broker* (ORB), which can be used to access data from object servers. The specification used by programmers to implement ORB is contained in the *Common Object Request Broker Architecture* (CORBA), which defines the specifications for both the client and the object server. In any active open system database, mapping becomes an important first step in defining the integration of open systems into existing operational systems. The work of ODMG has defined the ODMG-93 standard (Cattell, 1993), which, in a general sense, might be viewed as "the SQL of the object database world." That is, just as the early days of relational databases featured several languages (SQL, QUEL, RDML, etc.) that were used among the various products before SQL became "the" relational language, so, too, do today's object database products use several statements and constructs. The premise is that by incorporating ODMG-93 support into object database products, a more open flavor to object database servers will, over time, be achieved.

Print servers provide software that enhances the performance of the printers as well as providing basic hardware control. Many print functions, such as headers, which are used commonly within the department, can be placed on the server. Headings and trailers for specific pages can be stored and manipulated on the server. Using modern font management located on the server, different sizes or colors can be created through the use of the server code. The use of color printing has again emphasized the importance of shared print servers. Print servers support compound document protocols that shift the page arrangement of information to the server.

Compute servers provide a mix of functions often involved with high-performance problem solving. In this role, simulation or analysis programs reside on the server and complement connection code found in the desktop units. Increasingly, elements of expert systems have enhanced the role of the server by combining roles with the general support systems. Server software is growing in sophistication, as support expands with additional elements.

Since servers are shared by many workers, it is useful to provide fault tolerance in the processors. Fault tolerance provides a capability that ensures the system will continue to function after a major problem has occurred in the hardware or software system. Complex data have become so important to business that it is important to retain shared data servers even when the system fails. Equally important is to retain access capability when a portion of the system fails. Many readers who have been unable to access critical information when a computer failed can relate to the needs for this level of redundancy.

The server has become a logical control point within the LAN. Much of the structure of the application code relies on the definition of the control point within the server and its ability to manage the requests of many different users.

7.1 CONTROL CODE

Like other processing elements in an open system, the server operating system provides the functional base for support code residing on the system. The selection of a server operating system is not as critical to end users as the client operating system, since users will seldom experience the interfaces to the system directly. The client will access server capability through masked calls, which conform to standard user interfaces.

The performance and function of the server is dependent on the size and granularity of the operating system. Most accepted operating systems have been used in building modern servers. If a server configuration uses an IBM mainframe, standard support will be one of the major operating systems—OS/MVS or VM. Both systems will support POSIX standards and therefore connect into open systems network protocols. Since OS/MVS supports a high percentage of corporate data, POSIX support enables users of client/server computing to attach directly to legacy databases on existing mainframes, but it introduces a complexity of interface to the system.

Many engineers and production shops have used Digital Equipment hardware to preserve their design and manufacturing information. Support of their operating system VMS for POSIX has expanded access by engineering and manufacturing teams using open systems protocols. The existing DEC hardware can simply be treated as an active design server on the network.

Since servers evolved from PCs, the first server operating system was MS-DOS. This single-person system was not designed to support multiple users, but within the constraints of its capability it performed the tasks well. The wide and continued acceptance of MS-DOS helped to make it a critical support component for building open networks. Early server support code has been transferred to Windows packages, which is a more realistic level of support for multiple users.

With its initial introduction, OS/2 was believed to be a natural successor to MS-DOS as an ideal server operating system. The limited capability of the operating system and its slow acceptance helped to solidify acceptance of other operating system alternatives.

UNIX is growing in popularity as the operating system of choice for server vendors, including some mainframe manufacturers. Since UNIX spans a wide range of processor levels, it appeals to companies looking for continued growth in their server performance. It is possible for a vendor to introduce a low-powered server with full capability UNIX and plan a growth pattern that will continue to enhance the system through higher performance ranges without changing the operating system.

In the PC-LAN realm, Novell has produced subsystem code that resides on the operating system: NetWare. Novell provides many adjunct functions required for smooth network functions.

Operating systems provide an important base to build the primary server code. Advantages can be gained for the vendor and eventually the customer in defining commonalty to reduce the operating systems support. It is more important that the server achieve high degrees of granularity to improve the potential for growth. Each will affect the capacity of the resident subsystems to perform in the server environment.

Since the server is a part of the network, subsystem code provides communications connections between the different parts of the network. This code is part of the basic code of the server. Separate network operating systems have also been provided to support the complex communications needs of open systems. As the server begins to assume more of the role of the mainframe, additional software is necessary to complete the task.

Management of the local network includes administrative features that can be shared across different workstations. The simple task of determining the balancing of resources within the LAN is one of the many functions that need to be provided on this level of software. Backup and recovery of local UNIX systems are important applications provided on servers. Applications such as Sun's On-Line: Backup Copilot provide automatic and on-line network control. The software mirroring or duplicating information across different disks also provides a significant reliability level.

Beyond the simple services are the extensive application services provided for specific server configurations. Database and information capability are the most important and will be discussed next.

7.2 DATABASE SERVICES

Much of the history of computers is concerned with effectively using and producing data to meet business needs. Initially, most computer data were in card form and resulted in paper output reflecting manipulation of the card information. Even with the strong shift to magnetic processing, over 90 percent of business data is still found in paper form. A great deal of historical engineering data are found in libraries full of paper drawings. Access to this paper repository depends on filing systems that must be carefully tracked. Simple approaches to information retrieval began with the use of tape devices. Processing benefited from the speed of the tape devices, but the final output was still paper.

Early pioneers developing information retrieval, such as the National Library of Medicine and Chemical Abstract Service, used batched requests to large tape libraries. Even the initial information retrieval services found on PCs relied on cassette tape drives, which were often unreliable. The introduction of disk devices in the 1970s provided a base for more advanced browsing and accessing features and eventually led to the development of database systems.

Early database design relied on random and indexed data access techniques. Commercial offerings provided extended management to keep track of variations in data as updates were made. Engineering databases were built to ensure the close interaction between design screens and the graphics information in the database. Engineering used graphics and textual information, while commercial applications primarily used textual data. Modern databases for both engineering and commercial applications use compound data forms, which support textual as well as more complex digital information (Beeby, 1983). Modern database systems reflect the storage needs of applications that use audio, video, graphics, and image as well as text information. Documents that have included voice annotation are being passed from workstations to supporting servers. Output is being shipped to multimedia devices. Database servers are changing to reflect the balancing between shared capabilities and those found on local workstations.

The increasing use of network services has resulted in powerful network information servers that access information at different locations, as seen in Figure 7.3. When combined with increased processing power and disk capacity in servers, we find large amounts of storage accessed across the network. Large central databases in excess of multiple terabytes can now be found in many companies. In addition to the large central database, there is a great amount of data stored at servers and individual desktop computers,

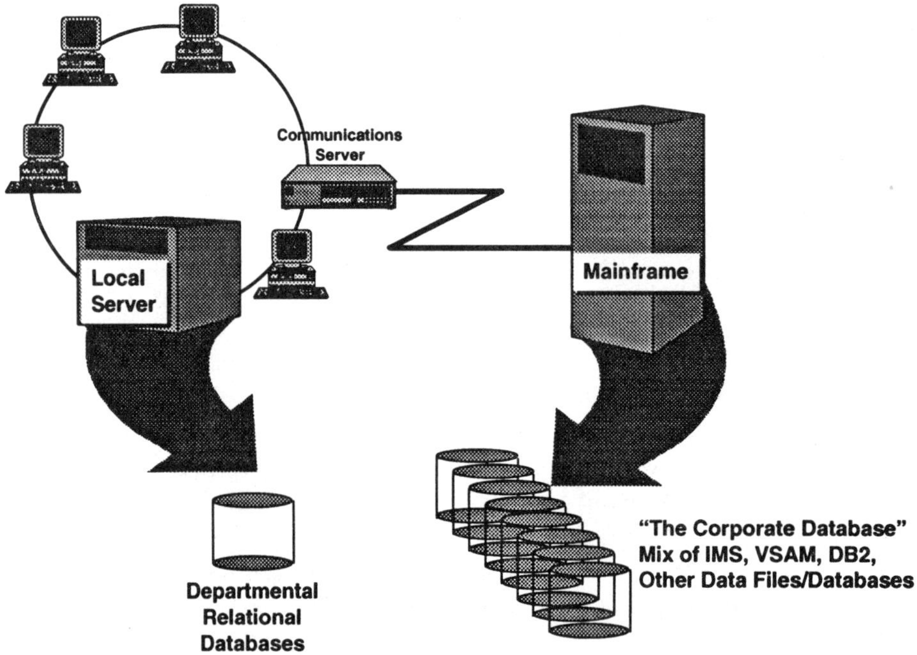

Figure 7.3 Network information servers access information at different locations

which can now contain data files measured in the billions of characters. Designers must consider this ever-growing capacity as they balance multiple locations in an enlarging network. Pointers will determine the location and type of database storage found on each server.

Traditional auditing functions must be expanded to track the status of information across the network. Balancing between different data locations is the goal of truly distributed systems, and the balance must be determined with sufficient information to make informed decisions. Locating data in a heterogeneous network strains the resources of simple file searches.

A number of factors have determined the acceptability of different data handling routines. Data currency and accuracy are required by many companies that control finances or life-support systems. In many systems, data are modified daily to reflect continual interactive transactions. A good example is the banking system, which supports daily deposits and withdrawals. Older data in these systems decline in value rapidly, but even these systems have a strong requirement for historical or archival information. Laws require the retention of financial data for seven-year periods, and the data systems must support this information.

Figure 7.4 shows the relative values of data and the required retention periods. High-value data often require a high retention period. High-value data may include patent information, historical financial data, corporate strategies, and critical personnel information. Some data, such as financial information, have mandated retention periods. Other data require either a short retention period or none at all. In assessing data routines, it is a good idea to determine the necessary retention period for the specific data.

Other systems do not change as rapidly as financial systems but require access for longer periods of time and across more functions. Engineering data change constantly until the final design is completed. It is then incorporated into state data or final product information, which must be retained for the life of the product. Eventually, the design will migrate to archive files that need to be accessed only for specific design problems. Engineering data may have an exceptionally long life, reflecting the specific design. For instance, some of Thomas Edison's designs are still being used 70 years after the original documents were created. The design data on nuclear devices must reflect the projected life of the device, which can be very long in some cases.

The introduction of PCs resulted in a shift of data across multiple processors. Sequential data were stored on PCs and workstations but often inter-

High Value Long Retention Required	Design/Manufacturing Data Product Archives Company History
High Immediate Value Mandated Retention	Financial Data; Criminal Records Maintenance History
High Immediate Value No Retention Required	Cash Transactions under a Certain Threshold Intermediate Designs
Low Value Low Retention	Interactive Sales Records

Figure 7.4 Values and retention periods of selected data

acted with more complex data structures found in relational databases on servers or mainframes. People consider data in a sequential fashion even though powerful parallel computers can use new techniques to access many items of information at the same time. Eventually, data return to a sequential form for many reports that use typical printed forms of output.

Open computers will be required to perform multiple functions in a complex system. Short-term data must be accessed through the systems. Archive data must be accessed when it is required. Data will be constantly changing to reflect the increasing value, and the access mechanisms must reflect these ever-growing needs of the open systems user. A wealth of information resides in computer systems, but often the challenge of retrieving it has resulted in only small benefits. Figure 7.5 maps the trend from simple files to more complex information gathering. Currently, open systems provide support for files and databases. As the level of data continues to grow, additional expert system logic is combined with database access to produce knowledge bases. It is expected that decision support algorithms will combine with data to produce insight systems. The trend affects the way data servers are evolving.

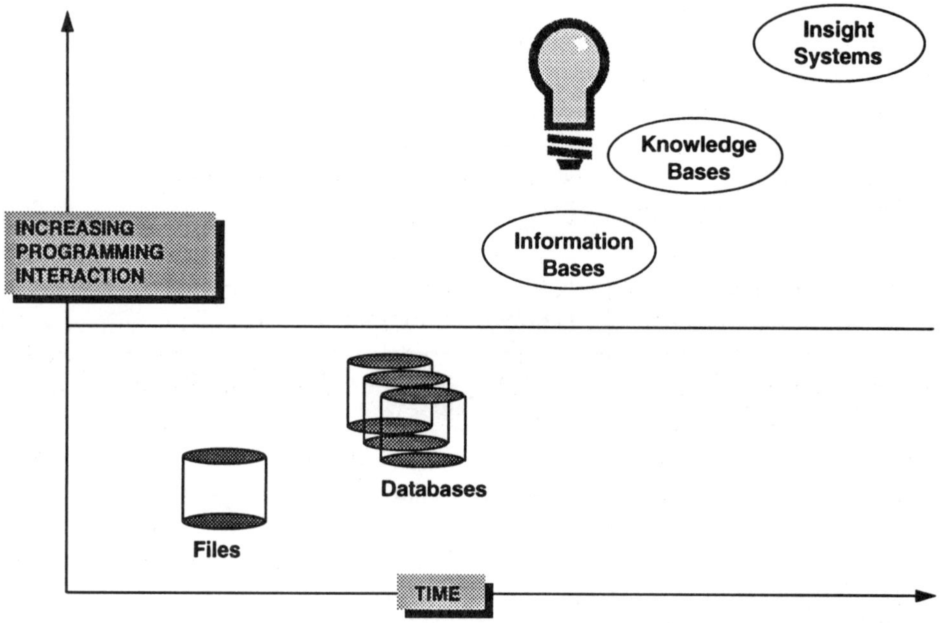

Figure 7.5 From simple files to complex information gathering

Database models have been shifting in response to the increased capabilities. Three separate models have been widely used in database support. The original network model was included in the CODASYL Data Base Task Group report of April 1971 (DBTG, 1971). As indicated by the name, network nodes use a network model to manage data. Each data record can have multiple access paths from multiple superiors or subordinates. Schemas are used to define the records, sets, and the connecting access paths. Sets are two-level hierarchies. Although network models provide high performance, they are cumbersome to use, since the user must provide a large part of the definition. Programmers could access network levels through high-level languages such as COBOL or FORTRAN (Martin, 1983), but even these languages did not fully mask the complexity.

To reduce the complexity, the hierarchical model was introduced as a special case of the network model. The close mapping to sequential processes used in hardware made it popular with database designers. Data organization relies on a parent/child relationship similar to the structure often found on organizational charts. The model has also been compared to a tree structure with roots, branches, and nodes. Access to specific records has worked well, but the update process has been a typical bottleneck in this model. Many vendors introduced their own languages to access hierarchical models, although they could be accessed using standard languages. Although popular in early computing, there have been no new database systems introduced using this model since the early 1980s.

Some older systems, such as IBM's *Information Management System* (IMS), remain important in open systems environments (Pugh et al., 1991). Many commercial customers have adopted the system and use it for their state data and therefore assume access in an open systems environment. IMS represented an easy use of terminals and databases and connected remote users to sources of information. Its database managers are a complex combination of elements, which include major pieces for terminal handling and for providing rapid access to the databases. Efforts have continued to improve the performance of this subsystem and keep it competitive with other, faster systems on mainframe computers. Based on OS/MVS, IMS remains important in many major corporations, particularly as they attempt to extend the life of their legacy systems and augment those environments with open systems technology. Connection to IMS is required for these companies to achieve acceptance of open systems solutions.

Many other critical databases exist on proprietary mainframes and minicomputers, which contain state data important to the operations of the businesses. Since there is usually a large investment in these databases and their supporting code, there is no plan to change them in the near future. Many of these databases use hierarchical or network models. Connection to legacy databases is considered a critical factor in the acceptance of open solutions.

The most popular server database model is relational, which combines features of previous models and permits real-time information sharing across different data structures. The relational database was developed through the work of Edward F. Codd of IBM's Research Laboratory in San Jose, California (Codd, 1982). The company introduced its relational Database 2 (DB2) based on this original work in 1985. The product has received increasing support on mainframe computers and is slated to eventually replace IMS. This product can be used as a relational server in an open environment.

Relational data are placed in tables that provide single-point location for access to multiple streams of data. Similar to a spreadsheet, the rows in the table are alike in size and content. A primary key is defined for each table, along with a domain and a foreign key. Logical relationships are established between data contained within the tables using a mathematical theory of relations, known as First Order Predicate Logic. Simple statements define the connections between the rows containing data to be retrieved. Predicates refine the selection criteria to improve access times.

Standard definitions for relational databases have been created to enhance the flow of information. Relational databases adopted SQL (pronounced sequel) for access in the early 1980s. The national standards group defined a standard for SQL, based on the original IBM definitions. The SQL Access Group (SAG) was created to validate the claims of individual SQL implementors and has been instrumental in defining changes to the standard in order to facilitate interoperability between vendors.

SQL is a database sublanguage, which can be used to access relational databases. The high-level user expression provides an easy access to the relational databases, which enables users to access data at a high level without the use of application code. The language was designed to facilitate learning but uses relational mathematics to connect with the different databases. This language is widely supported by different vendor databases and is the most popular alternative found on systems today. Some have contended that the language can be further simplified, and a number of fourth-generation languages have been introduced to simplify the access process.

A number of companies have extended the relational definition work to distributed systems. IBM, for instance, extended its basic research on relational from 1979 to 1987, when they investigated relational support across distributed systems. The research effort was known as R* (R Star) and assessed options across open networks. Additional work has been conducted by different database companies, such as Digital Equipment, ORACLE, and Sybase.

Many work assignments involve the manipulation and use of objects. For example, design drawings are objects that often define the drawing with attributes used for the consistent assembling of the designed part. Comparable examples exist in businesses where the customer contains specific attribute information about the individual account information. The use of object-oriented databases accelerates access and improves programs needed to access information. As a result, there is increasing use of object-oriented databases for modern applications. Since these databases meld with advances in workstation interfaces, they are becoming very important for systems design. Originally introduced by engineering as convenient ways to reference design information, their use has spread to financial and commercial applications as well. Objects identify both the data and attributes used to process the data.

Objects contain information about the use of data and its processing. Objects of finished parts will often contain information about processing the finished product or materials to be used. An important element in understanding objects is to understand class. Classes define the templates for common objects and are also known as object types that can provide modularity. Within the object type, individual objects are instances of the class with storage allocated to it. Each part of a finished product can be an object, and the total product can be considered an object. The attribute data contained in the object permits the designer to bind the data to the program at the latest possible moment. As a result, objects are important for the support of open systems where late binding to the system is a necessity.

A simple example of an object would be a bicycle that has different perspectives or attributes to different people. To the designer, it is a mechanical device with wheels. To the child, the attributes are those of a toy, while the parent views it as a potential hazard for the child. A racer will view the object bicycle from the perspective of a well-engineered piece of equipment. The data do not change; only the attributes used by the viewers to process the data change.

Object support is beginning to proliferate through open systems, as techniques are defined to support compound data types using objects. Binary large objects (BLOBs) are used to store multimegabyte files with compound information, such as images and graphics. The introduction of object-oriented languages has helped define programs that use object databases. The most widely used languages are variations of C.

Countering the existing state databases are families of server databases, which use the latest technology in development to create leading-edge support. These server databases have learned from their counterparts residing on minis and mainframes and have produced modern code that can become the base for an entire new family of applications. The databases are usually relational and provide significant support over many existing packages. Many of these databases execute on different vendors' hardware and are really examples of open systems working. ORACLE, for instance, provides its database products across a large number of different processors. Although much of the code was originally written for minicomputers, the code performs quite well on micro-based processors and has performed very well on the multiple parallel processor from nCube.

There are an increasing number of database companies that service open systems connections. Many companies began with solutions for minicomputers or mainframes and simply extended the support to open systems. Other companies have begun with open systems solutions and have provided significant solutions using either relational or object systems for servers.

A good example of an open systems database company is the ORACLE Corporation, which has been a pioneer in open systems database support. The company provides its primary database support on different types of hardware—from microprocessor servers to the nCube parallel processor. The majority of its support is focused on providing offerings across multiple machine levels. The company supports a wide range of hardware vendors within a relatively brief support window. ORACLE originally entered the relational database market with products on minicomputers and mainframes. Versions were later prepared for microcomputers and were used across an entire tier of processing power. The company products are used extensively in open systems solutions.

Another database company that has been in the forefront of open systems solutions for servers is Sybase. Their relational database (RDBMS) runs on open servers ranging from the PC to parallel processors, and newer products, such as the Sybase Replication Server and various database gateway middleware systems, have extended their base technology further into the open systems realm. The products support database storage while enforcing integrity, security, and recovery requirements across the network. Sybase products support stored procedures, which permit transparent access to other databases. SQL transactions and precompiled procedures aid in producing an effective tool for database access. A number of features make the products especially useful for accessing data across the open systems configuration. Stored procedures enable the database to replace workstation code in checking various options available to end users. Sybase software is structured on open systems architecture, so it can be ported to different hardware architectures.

There are an increasing number of companies that have made the shift from paper to the use of distributed processing on open systems networks. Although these shifts seem slower than projected by professionals, important advances have been made in these applications within the past year. Changes in income tax filings have also resulted in new business applications that rely on electronics. The federal tax problem is enormous, with over 200 million annual returns handled through paper processing. The IRS is attempting to resolve many of its technical problems through a massive Tax Modernization System (TMS) effort, which will continue into the next decade (past the year 2000).

Northwest Orient shifted their ticket handling from a paper operation to an open systems solution using Sun workstations attached to automated ticket scanners. Through the use of the powered workstations, the company was able to increase its return from the tickets and avoid lost revenue, which justified the change and presented a significant payback. A paper database was converted to electronic media, resulting in a significant payback in business.

A shift to object-oriented databases is expected to result in significant gains in productivity for many types of applications suitable for open systems environments. An object is equal to the data and the software or other instructions intended to handle the data. Objects have been effective in managing text, data, graphics, voice, and image information. Management data are encapsulated with the actual information stored on the data files. Since much of the work we do with complex images and graphics operations is really working with logical objects, there is widespread support for this type of processing.

Distributed databases have presented a unique set of challenges to all database vendors. Distribution eliminates single points of failure, since data are manipulated locally. Distributing data to servers increases the level of parallel access to information and removes traditional bottlenecks. Significant design challenges remain in the distribution of data with an open systems environment.

Referential integrity, which is the assurance the correct data will be obtained, is a challenge in a multidatabase environment. Each database must provide local referential integrity, which must be balanced through the system. An example is a disconnected workstation, which contains significant data for the enterprise.

Update synchronization has been a challenge to early implementors of open systems. Locking mechanisms have helped balance the different requirements of the network. When locked, the different records are no longer accessible to other programs. Modern database systems permit multiple levels of locking algorithms, which can support either file- or record-level locking.

Performance challenges design and implementation of open systems data server solutions. Developers must understand the different types of systems that benefit from the use of servers. Typical questions may include analysis of approaches that optimize the use of servers in open systems. There is also concern about duplicate copies of data spread through the network and the implications on performance.

The need to find answers to the questions of large-capacity data servers has caused the University of California to launch a research project to investigate the design and potential use of such large servers in a large network. Sequoia 2000 investigates the application of these large networks and servers shared across many university campuses.

The continued advances in data servers have enabled designers to define advanced data servers or information servers.

7.3 INFORMATION SERVERS

Modern databases can provide more complex information handling when connected to networks. Combinations of programs and relational databases coupled across open systems have led to the definition of information bases. Additional programming introduced directly on servers can provide for intelligent interaction between data and sets of rules. Expert systems have been introduced to search and connect different tidbits of data with specialized rules to produce information bases. These information databases search information from many sources and combine it in a form that can be used for management support systems. They also do other information search algorithms.

As data services have advanced, additional intelligence is added, which provides access to multiple databases. Data navigation describes the process that performs complex searches for data through a heterogeneous network. Simple navigation is performed today by operators using specific file identifiers, but electronic navigation will use electronic naming systems to ferret out information from multiple unrelated databases. A cascading information search will move through different levels of electronic information and also point to relevant paper references. Since large amounts of data are retained in paper form, searches—especially for engineering parts—are designed to include paper libraries.

The navigator provides automatic searches that can locate information anywhere in the system with little description from the end user. Navigators use correct retrieval mechanisms to search data in any system and add the information to appropriate group-generated reports. Expert system capability will be embedded in the navigator as it searches multiple courses across the network. Data navigation is in the early stages and will take time to develop, but we can expect to find products with this level of support in open systems.

Simple navigation programs, which remove the requirement for individuals to understand different target databases and their interfaces, have been introduced to specialized users. The power of the client is directed to perform the transparent connection to the different server databases.

Another important application is routines that permit the assembling of documents with parts from many different creators. Called dynamic documents, these documents use the efficiency of automated search facilities to find the location of document parts and then put them together.

As the use of artificial intelligence (AI) has evolved, additional information has been uncovered about the same data. Another transition is being made as we move to knowledge bases. Although knowledge base servers can use existing databases, they receive additional benefit from the use of object data. Object data contain information about the environment of the data as well as the simple information. Attributes provide a form of additional information, which enables the data to be transported across multiple nodes in a network for execution.

The next step is to combine additional processing power into the server to create a data insight server. Using the power of artificial intelligence combined with decision support tables, the next step seems to be insight systems that can aid in the production of decisions and provide management with additional information on how to run the business.

Automatic switches, which enable the end user to access data in whatever form and whatever system it resides, are being provided by server vendors. There is an increasing use of special software to provide easy access to multiple system points.

7.4 COMMUNICATIONS SUPPORT

Communications servers provide translation between different protocols used in open systems networks. Communications translation augments the data server to connect to computers that rely on different communications protocols. Vendor-specific protocols will be mapped into open protocols. The most prevalent vendor protocols, such as SNA from IBM and Novell's IPX/SPX, can be mapped to TCP/IP standards or eventually to OSI layers. As different systems are introduced, the server is employed to map the bridge between the different systems.

The increased use of different systems will extend the need for communications servers. Whether these servers are called routers or gateways, their function is simply to connect to different communications systems.

Software included in these systems will translate the different pockets of information between the systems. This code enables the system to handle applications as though they were local. Remote access is achieved through transparent interfaces.

7.5 COMPUTE SERVERS

An important and growing server function is high-powered computing. Using open systems interfaces, it is possible to introduce servers that provide high-performance compute operations. Compute programs will migrate from low-end servers to multiple parallel processors containing thousands of processors. Balancing the work across multiple processors has become an important challenge to software designers.

Traditionally, compute servers using parallel processors will use conventional languages such as FORTRAN, but there is a growing use of advanced languages that augment C. Languages such as C++ have been used to program lower-performance servers. Languages are being explored as vehicles to provide seamless program migration from low-end workstations to multiple parallel processors.

Once compute-intensive programs are coded in common languages, the software can be migrated to the system with sufficient power to perform the intense compute functions. Thus, applications that operate on small servers can be migrated to the larger parallel processors. As long as the interfaces conform to the protocol conventions of accepted standards, the compute operation can migrate to the location of the most intense performance.

Many engineering and scientific applications fit into the area that can use high-performance compute servers. Applications requiring intense calculations can migrate to the highest power point in the network. Fluid flow analysis can be performed on modern workstations, but analysis programs requiring large amounts of power can be migrated to supercomputer centers.

In the financial world, there are applications that can also benefit from the ability to shift from low-powered servers to ever-increasing capability. Financial market simulation is a good example of an application type that could benefit from migration to an intense power computer.

Computer software provides a unique dimension to the network. In powerful processors, it provides the means to execute applications that provide calculations in the complex environment of engineering or financial operations. From the simple calculations of engineering models to the more complex applications that require the fastest computing power, a broad range of software will reside on calculation or compute servers.

Distribution balancing is a distribution technique that shifts information to the nodes of the network with sufficient computer power and storage to perform the necessary functions. Some systems have already defined mechanisms to balance between different processors with sufficient power to perform tasks. This is especially important when coupled with compute servers.

7.6 CONSIDERATIONS

The growth of client/server computing has been much slower than anticipated—mostly because of delayed software packages that can support the full capability of the network (McCarthy and Bluestein, 1991).

Servers are used to meet the shared needs of many clients. These different tasks reflect the types of software required for servers. Specialized code reflects the need for high performance and quality, but underlying the special code are general operating systems that provide system functions.

The primary use of servers within a network is to support databases. The complexity of the server software is directly proportional to the data support requirements. Initial data servers were simple processors that handled large numbers of data files for many PCs. Eventually, relational database servers, which combined sophisticated processing with higher data capacity, were introduced.

There has been a shift from relational databases to object support, as knowledge processing replaces simple data handling. Objects encapsulate additional attribute information about the data and permit a shift in the processing location. Additional control information moves with the data and enhances the probability of correct processing.

Additional shifts in function will occur as insight systems are introduced. Additional use of implementation products for AI will be the result of this paradigm change. Also, executive support software will be included in the software supporting insight code.

Increasing use of different data sources has led to the development of data navigation tools for the network. The data navigator will find data wherever it may occur on the system. It reflects a concept of anywhere search for correct information.

The selection process for servers will probe questions of sufficient function to meet the needs of the projected number of users. The server software should provide sufficient scalability so that, as users increase, the data and processing requirements can also be expanded without disrupting the operations. Equally important, the server must accept standard industry protocols to permit movement to large processors if the application demands it.

7.7 REFERENCES

Beeby, William D. "The Heart of Integration: A Sound Database." *IEEE Spectrum,* May 1983, pp. 44–48.

Cattell, R. G. G. (editor). *The Object Database Standard: ODMG-93.* San Francisco: Morgan Kaufmann, 1993.

Codd, Edward F. "Relational Database: A Practical Foundation for Productivity." *Communications of the ACM,* February 1982, pp. 109–117.

DBTG. "Data Base Task Group of CODASYL Programming Language Committee Report." April 1971 (available from the Association of Computing Machinery).

Martin, James. *Managing the Data-Base Environment.* Englewood Cliffs, NJ: Prentice Hall, 1983.

McCarthy, John C., and William Bluestein. "Resizing Client/Server." In *The Computing Strategy Report.* Cambridge, MA: Forrester Research, December 1991.

Pugh, Emerson W., Lyle R. Johnson, and John H. Palmer. *IBM's 360 and Early 370 Systems.* Cambridge, MA: MIT Press, 1991, pp. 591–593.

8

Network Characteristics

Open systems assume a powerful network or communications capability between the components. We are approaching a networked society that will be able to access any computer from anyplace at anytime. Data transmission has benefited from advances in communications technology over the past 100 years. During the recent history of computing, we have shifted from simple voice transmissions to complex communications involving data and images. Many users have already benefited from open access to electronic data. Although the transition from paper to pure electronic transmission has not yet arrived, progress is occurring very rapidly. Advances in communications have contributed to the success of open systems.

ARPAnet is considered the practical predecessor of modern computer networks and the forerunner of the Internet. ARPAnet, sponsored by the Department of Defense, was developed to connect research organizations with relatively high performance and data accuracy (Booth, 1981). Commercial networks have been introduced that support business needs in global networks. Examples multiply, as airlines have adopted global communications for airline reservation systems, and manufacturing companies have defined worldwide design systems. Many were introduced to communications networks through remote access to mainline computers. Certainly, advances in communications products have enhanced interconnection between local and remote sites.

Early networking protocols used less reliable communications systems. Protocols were mutually defined handshaking agreements between implementors. Information often was lost in the network, and it became necessary to define redundant routing techniques for transmitting information. Modern devices have reduced reliability problems and the need for redundant systems. System complexity has introduced additional problems. Modern dependency on network reliability was demonstrated in September 1991, when a generator failure caused the communications network to cease operating. This resulted in the cessation of landings at New York airports. Reliability of the network became an important and costly problem for travelers and the airlines.

Communications involves transmission of information from a sender to a receiver. Often, this communication can be directly between computers, but even in this case, the network must be dependable and predictable. Open systems communication assumes any device meeting the open protocols will be able to connect to the network. Open access to data in the network is achieved through conformity to standards that can be duplicated across the world.

Information networks are in active use around the clock. International banking shifts large amounts of financial data across satellite links around the clock. The daily shift of financial information often exceeds the gross national product of many countries. Engineers have adopted global networks to perform international design and manufacturing. Product information must be reliably transmitted to remote plants for manufacturing processes. Each of these efforts depends on international standards to transmit data across multinational telephone systems.

As we examine open systems, our concern will be with different aspects of communications use. Data building begins on LANs supporting departments in a building. Many of these networks began with wiring hubs that connect different systems together. Few workstations were originally connected to the LANs, but eventually the numbers have expanded. Many LANs are interconnected as departments share data locally. Our first focus will be the local connections within an establishment. LANs are used in conjunction with backbone connections to connect individuals within a location. Since their introduction in the 1980s, LANs have become the basic building block for corporate networks.

Connections between networks have challenged integrators, who have attempted to bring many different connections together. Figure 8.1 illustrates the large number of potential connections that can be found in system

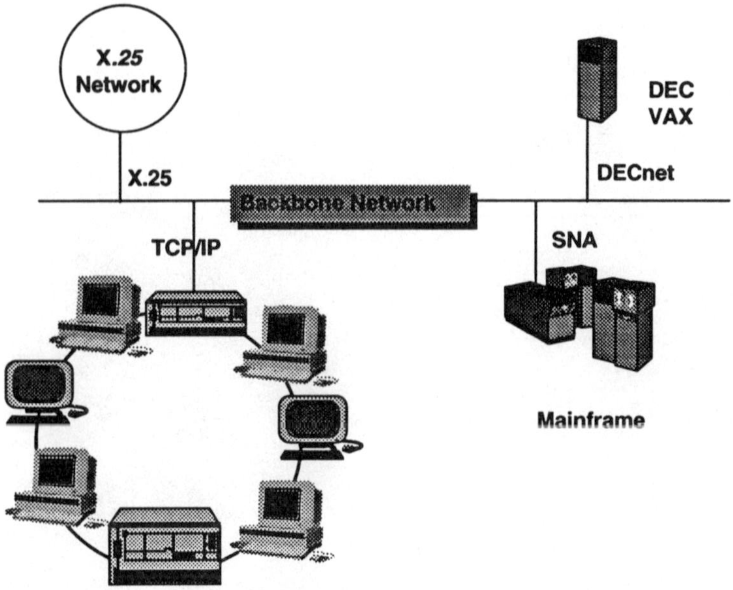

Figure 8.1 Potential connections in system configuration

configuration. As communications are established between different pairs of computers on the network, a conversion is required that will map specific protocol features from the sending node to the receiving node. At one time, the prevalent philosophy with respect to open systems communications was that connectivity and interoperability would occur under the Open System Interconnect (OSI) model, but the continued rise of TCP/IP as the de facto open communications standard has put the earlier philosophy in doubt. Primarily, the need for internetwork conversion is no longer viewed as a stopgap measure but rather as a long-term reality for many organizations.

Conversion between networks is usually supplied by three different levels of combined hardware and software projects. As seen in Figure 8.2, the lowest-level conversion is accomplished through the use of a bridge, which provides connection at the physical level. The bridge assumes that identical protocols are used in the connecting networks. Since most protocols are different at higher levels in the network, bridge conversion is augmented by routers, which convert the protocols at the data link and network levels. The highest-level conversion occurs at the logical level, which represents the level between layers of software. These network conversion products enable open systems implementors to connect between different systems.

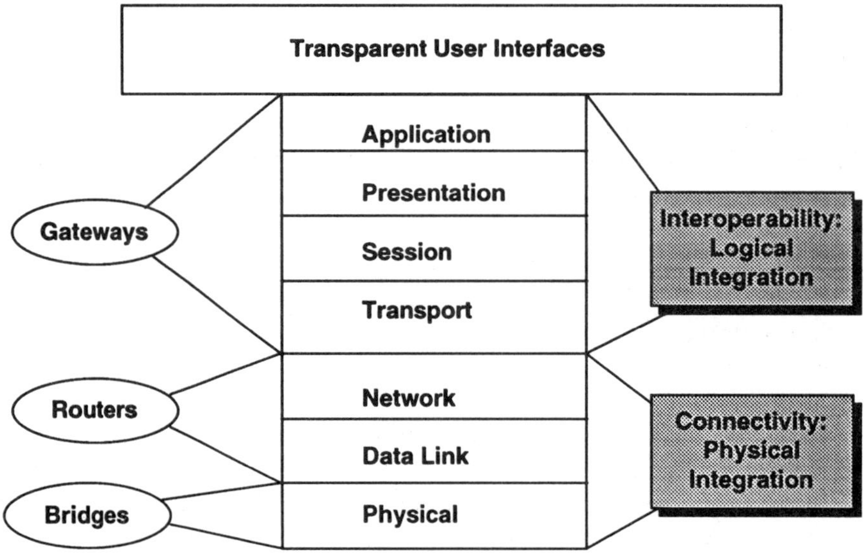

Figure 8.2 Three levels of hardware and software projects

Metropolitan area networks (MANs) augment local connections and provide reliable connections within a city. Many companies extend their networks beyond the local campus and create an enterprise network spanning the nation (or world, in the case of global companies). These networks, called *wide area networks* (WANs), use high-speed connection techniques to reach performances in the billions of characters per second (Bartee, 1985). The increasing transmission of compound data, which includes images and video, will place additional requirements on these WANs.

The entry price for communications is being reduced to the point where emerging nations can participate in data networks. Advanced nations have extensive plans for high-speed communications networks that will provide a backbone for business. The Nippon Telegraph and Telephone Company has some of the most advanced plans in the world for connecting homes and businesses through optical fiber linkages. The U.S. government is supporting research to build a high-performance network across the country.

The adoption of communications protocols has enabled users to avoid specialized handshaking agreements between different users. De facto standards have ruled many networks, but these are being replaced by industry standards that can access many different vendors' hardware. Yet, there are large networks that support multiple protocols without any adverse effects on the day-to-day operations.

Electronic mail has received wide use, as organizations adopted approaches to send messages to key people. Message handling applications have been in use since the 1960s but required single-vendor solutions. Modern mail networks use open systems to connect between different vendors. In addition, while historical electronic mail systems have focused on textual information, research systems have embraced architectures that include multimedia support. A voice annotation can be routed through the network with the same performance as textual information. Standardization has helped define a more advanced environment, which can have many processors sending messages.

Electronic bulletin boards, which are popular techniques used to broadcast information, represent variations on electronic mail. Information is exchanged on bulletin boards about many popular subjects. For example, bulletin boards about car mechanics will collect comments on developments in the area. UNIX users access bulletin board information to acquire current coding information or even to critique specific releases of the system. Rapid dissemination of information was popular by the middle 1970s across mainframe-based networks. These networks enabled early application of central information files for PC users.

International businesses have invested large amounts of development dollars searching for effective communications support. Both local and remote communications are connected to the high cost of producing a network that will interconnect different computers. With the use of modern electronic technology, the hardware costs of communications networks have declined faster than computer technology. Equipment represents less than 20 percent of the total network budget.

Network efficiency is critical when large amounts of complex information are transmitted. Efficiency has improved during the past decade, but the volumes of information and the complexity have also increased. As compute power of information continues to increase, it is believed we will face rivers of data moving across the networks during the 1990s. The network components are being improved, as technology permits changes to the network.

Many characteristics that we expect from open systems will depend on the reliability of the network. The ability to interconnect across a world of data structures depends on reliable systems below the network. In addition, the complexity of the network demands advanced tools to be able to manage changes in the network.

Networks, in the management sense, contain technology, but more important is the interaction of different departments within an organization. Computer networks are a combination of hardware and software that work together to ensure a successful operation. People are considered the third element in a successful network, since they must interact with the technology to produce the desired results. Failure in any component can result in a significant problem for the complete network. As network growth compounds and the power at each desktop grows, the requirement for capable management will increase to ensure easy and accurate connection by the systems.

8.1 GENERAL COMMUNICATIONS HARDWARE

The open systems delivery system begins with elementary pieces of communications hardware that serve as building blocks for the networks. Hardware networks can be found in many different configurations. Although each system node, whether client or server, is a participant in the communications network, there is specialized hardware that drives the communications system. The hardware may reside on the customer premises and be part of the private network, or it may reside in the public network and be a part of shared equipment utilized by anyone using the communications systems.

If we begin from the end-user perspective, we find a communication adapter embedded in many workstations and PCs. The adapter provides the link between the desktop and the local networks. Adapters provide hardware connections for an entire range of potential network protocols. For instance, adapters available for connections to protocols include Token Ring, Ethernet, SDLC, FDDI, V.35, T1/T3, Wireless, and X.21.

Many workstations and PCs have built-in modems to connect to analog networks. Since computer data are in a digital form, and many transmission facilities use analog, the MOdulator and DEModulator (Modem) (Pickholtz, 1985) was introduced. Modems provide a digital-to-analog translation connection between analog networks and digital devices either synchronously or asynchronously, based on the presence of a clock. Since synchronous modems can operate at any line speed, they have a larger portion of the network than asynchronous modems, which usually work below 1,200 bits per second (bps). A good modem performance for open systems is 2,400 or 9,600 bps. Another important classification is whether the modem can transmit in both directions simultaneously, which is full-duplex modem. Half-duplex modems operate in two directions, but only one at a time.

Modems have benefited from the cost reductions for electronic technology. Once offered only as separate processors with discrete power and diagnostics, they have been embedded in workstations of all sizes. Even palmtop computers have embedded modems, which enable the device to communicate with open networks. Many functions have been designed on single chips, permitting the modem to use the power of its host. Pocket modems, which connect to portable devices for transmission on the network, are also available.

The user will connect the working unit into a wall telephone plug, which simplifies the connection to the wiring that connects several local nodes together. Common outlets can be used for workstations, printers, or database servers. At one point, many corporations used shielded coaxial cables, which were included in the design of new buildings. In older buildings, the cable is pulled through the walls, which is often expensive. The shield protects against penetration of unwanted signals. Many companies use unshielded twisted pairs, which are used for local telephone networks, to connect local terminals.

Wires on a building floor or portion of the floor will be concentrated in wiring closets, which serve as hubs for multiple users. To the uninitiated, the wiring closet appears as a labyrinth of wires. The wiring closets will be connected to other floors in the same building through a backbone cable, which can carry multiple transmissions. Modern switching rooms have replaced the earlier mazes of wires.

It is possible to connect distributed workstations to multiple networks using wiring hubs. Wiring hubs enable companies to focus their communications in a single accessible location. Concentration in the closet enables easy repair and replacement of the different connections. When a new station is added, the technician can make the change in a single point. Even loop connections benefit from the local wiring hub. All connections or changes can be focused in the wiring closet, avoiding the need for the repair person to call on each site to make changes.

Optical wiring has become important in long-distance and local area networks. Transoceanic optical cables have replaced earlier copper installations. Optics have increased the bandwidth and the numbers of users that can attach to a network.

Large installations introduced fiber-optic backbones to connect LANs using either coaxial or wire connections. Fiber optics improved performance and quality of connections between networks. Optical reception is clearer and more reliable, since it is not affected by electromagnetic interference. As fiber optics have continued to develop, companies are shifting to local fiber optical connections. Vendors that initially offered copper wiring products now provide optical cable systems, which provide higher reliability and performance up to 100 Mbits per second. The closet becomes a connection point for optical networks. In the transition stage, combinations of both optical and copper connections will be used within the department.

Fiber Distributed Data Interface (FDDI) products offer high-performance connections that were introduced as backbone networks connecting different LANs. Continued developments in fiber optics have led to the acceptance of fiber optics not only as backbone but also as primary LAN connections. Hub vendors such as SynOptics Communications Inc. and Cabletron offer concentrators and modules that support FDDI.

Alternative forms of communications are being adopted to reduce wiring and permit more flexibility in hardware placement. Infrared has been used in communicating between local nodes in the network. Another form of communication with desktop units is cellular or radio communication with the network. If the workstations become mobile, as in the case of sales or delivery services, a direct advantage can be achieved using cellular connections. IBM and Motorola have pioneered this connection for their service representatives.

One form of hardware that has aided this process is the communications switch. These switches connect LANs to the overall network. Terminal controllers have been used to connect multiple terminals to a mainframe and perform the logical function of a switch. Most systems also use combinations of gateways, routers, and bridges, which enable different protocols to connect and transmit information between their systems.

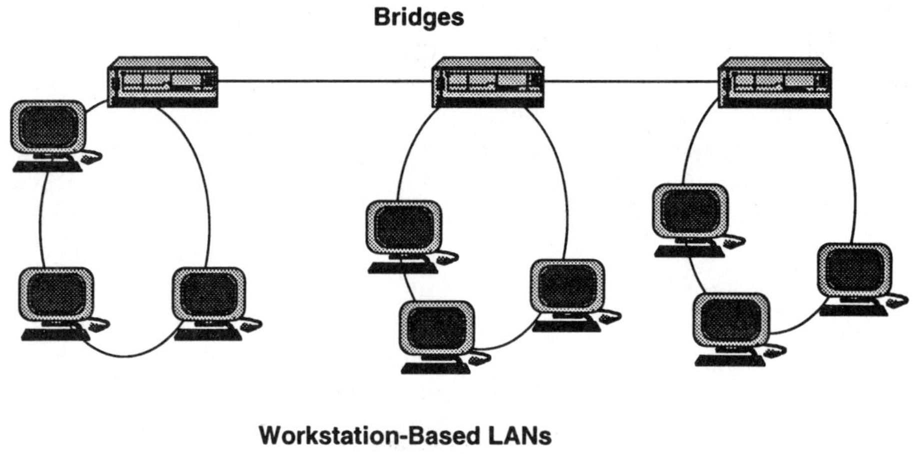

Figure 8.3 Bridges provide connections between identical LANs

As can be seen in Figure 8.3, bridges provide simple connections between identical LANs. Routers, as seen in Figure 8.4, connect dissimilar networks. In our example, they are connecting Token Ring and TCP/IP networks. Routers have become popular and have achieved a rapid growth rate. Companies such as Cisco, AT&T, IBM, and Kentrox have all produced router products. SynOptics has coupled routers with smart wiring hubs to bring together multiple LAN connections.

Smart hubs are wiring hubs that have been augmented with additional network management capability. These intelligent hubs represent a significant advantage over dumb wiring closets. Buyers are ready to pay premium prices to manage the network with smart boxes. Concentrators were introduced with terminal communications to provide common processing for the terminals and to pack their signals together for transmission across the network. High-speed lines can be shared across the network, thus reducing the costs of network connections. Many concentrators were used as store-and-forward facilities. The front-end processor (FEP) is a special-purpose concentrator for collecting communications messages. Originally, it was believed a high percentage of communications connections to computers could be handled by these concentrators. The IBM 3705, 3725, and 3745 are

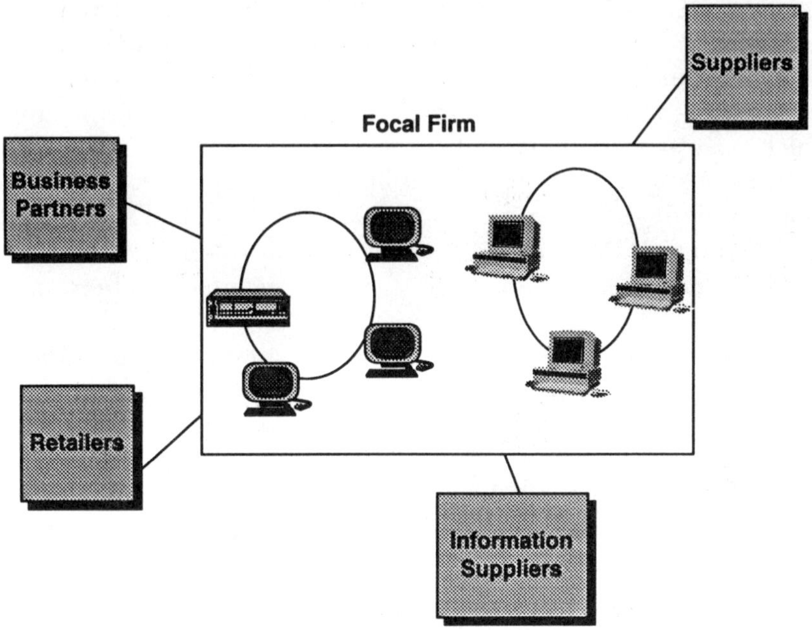

Figure 8.4 Routers connect dissimilar networks

widely used front-end processors that provide connections to mainframe processors. These processors will be found in open systems configurations that connect to mainframes.

An early device used for communications is the *Private Branch Exchange* (PBX). PBXs were based on using idle time to reduce line costs leaving the premises, since only one-sixth of the telephones are active at any time during business hours. Significant savings resulted from using these devices to reduce external trunk usage. Initially, PBXs used plug connections, but newer technology enabled the designers to reduce the configurations significantly. Eventually, the Rolm company introduced the *Computer Branch Exchange* (CBX). Programming replaced wiring, and PBXs shifted into the electronic era. These breakthroughs have helped make private networks realistic.

Although transmission costs continue to fall, they still comprise a high percentage of the money spent in connecting open systems within an enterprise. The introduction of digital communications (ISDN) has reduced these costs and made worldwide networks a growing reality. Digital communications has grown since the introduction of ISDN networks in the United States and Europe.

Multiplexers have adopted two forms for data communications. Frequency-division multiplexing (FDM) has been the most widely used technique for voice transmission. FDM breaks bandwidth into smaller units of frequencies, which are stacked in and shipped across the transmission medium. A 9,600 bps line could be broken into 32 300 bps lines, with each subchannel ending at a different location. Time-division multiplexing (TDM), which uses pulse code modulation, is widely used for data. TDM divides transmissions into time units, combining pieces from slower transmission units into high-speed communications connections. Statistical time-division multiplexing (STDM) allocates a time slot only when there is traffic for the slot. *Wave-division multiplexing* (WDM) has supplanted FDM for optical networks

Once communications leaves the local premises, it moves into global transmission networks noted for their high performance. This has not always been the case, since people have tried different techniques for long-distance communications. Couriers, beacon fires, or drum beats were all limited in mileage and duration by the capability of the medium. Intercontinental communications were equally frustrating until the first communications cable was completed in 1878.

Today, textual data and voice data can be commingled with complex video, graphics, and image information in transmission using modern high-speed networks. Advanced transmission facilities have accelerated traffic.

High-speed digital transmission continues to get better with the use of technology. T1 multiplexing with its high performance (1.544 Mbps) and large capacity became available in 1974. The lower prices, combined with the high transmission rate, made the connections sufficiently appealing for companies to use them for corporate networks supporting voice, data, and images. Enhancements over the original AT&T electronic switching system 4 (ESS4) have resulted in further improvements in performance and capacity. T3 provides higher performance (44 Mbps) with an option of reaching the equivalent of 28 T1 lines. It is also compatible with existing fiber-optic standards.

Satellite linkages have provided voice and data transmission for some time and are used by engineering and manufacturing organizations to transfer design information across continents. Satellites achieved almost instantaneous connections in a few short years without the problems encountered with underwater cables. Transmissions can be accomplished in seconds and redundancy achieved through the use of second satellites.

Whether the network uses microwave, satellite, or optical fiber, modern transmission gives the appearance of being local. Interactive teleconferencing has promised new dimensions of capability by moving the video interaction from a conference room to individual desks.

Across the external network, we find a wide range of diversity in tariffs and devices. The organization of the public system varies with the specific countries and the capability for communications. Specialized wide area systems have benefited from the introduction of electronic technology. Continued improvement will improve hardware capability both locally and remotely. Optics will continue their acceptance within the different network nodes and produce significant cost advantages for system designers.

8.2 LOCAL AREA NETWORKS

Pivotal in the definition of open systems are local area networks. Initially, these networks were formed through informal connections using wires strung between offices to connect small groups of PCs. Since the connections were mutually defined, it was relatively simple to add additional members to the network. The increasing population of PCs connected to LANs has created challenges of support and management that have been answered by standardization.

The LAN was introduced to facilitate communications and sharing within workgroups. It transported information between computers on locally connected nodes. With increasing capability on the network, traffic can be mixed and require significantly higher bandwidth than originally designed within the systems. LANs were originally confined to single departments but have been expanded in scope to include entire buildings and even entire campuses (Stallings, 1987). As the hardware has improved, it has become possible to increase the number of people connected to the network.

Advances in LAN technology have created products that are faster and simpler to use than their predecessors. Capacity across the network has expanded services through faster attachment mechanisms. Simplicity has been achieved with the introduction of easier and more descriptive support software. Support across the network has resulted in clear definitions of problem areas. Fixes can be transported across the network using the LAN. Originally, LANs required special wiring, but newer LANs are using twisted-pair telephone wiring within the building. Requirements for advanced performance will result in the wider use of optical LANs.

Another consideration in attaching LANs is the individual unit costs. Early adapters connected directly into PC slots using the bus performance of the device. Recent connections have used accelerators to reach high performances in the actual connections and also to reduce the costs.

LAN communications uses two distinct electrical protocols to provide required local services. Baseband transmits encoded signals as one continuous stream, with each node sequentially placing messages on the transmission medium. Repeaters are used in the transmission system to boost the overall power and ensure correct delivery. Reduction in the repeaters can reduce the cost of the network but may cause errors in receiving messages. Baseband networks can achieve very high performance.

The second electrical protocol used to transmit messages is broadband, which is a high-speed transport for multiple analog signals using various transmission media. High-speed data connection to broadband is achieved through the High Speed Serial Interface (HSSI), which is used in internetworking. Broadband supports different types of traffic, including data, image, video, voice, and multimedia. Multiple broadband channels can achieve parallelism, which provides redundancy to the network.

Broadband has been applied to a wide range of applications affecting open systems. These include LAN interconnect, used by both engineering and commercial computing, and video signals to workstations. Broadband has been used to connect to mainframes and database servers. More advanced potential applications include the use of protocols to support multimedia, video, computer networking, and high-speed image transfer.

A number of protocols have been used to transmit messages across the LANs. The most popular for open systems has been the *Transmission Control Protocol/Internet Protocol* (TCP/IP), which was designed originally for ARPAnet (Advanced Research Projects Agency Network) by the Department of Defense in 1972. The network uses a set of protocols that was designed for internetworking and are simpler to implement than most other protocols used on LANs. Extensions for shared file access, file transfer, and electronic mail have helped extend the life of the support.

Ethernet is associated with TCP/IP, since it was introduced as a vehicle using the protocol in 1973. From the introduction of the first operational board, continued developments have improved the design to the point where it can support 10 Mbps transmission using twisted pairs. Ethernet provides many basic network functions and furnishes a target for subsequent designs. Its support of variable-size packets and the immediate and random access by users are both important features, which help make it appealing. The IEEE recognized the value of the support and began standard work for the system in 1979.

The acceptance of TCP/IP and the growing demand for standards have resulted in additional definitions of the values of different technical approaches to the interconnection problem. Standards work by the IEEE has resulted in the definition of three LAN standards, which provide a basis for open systems design (Dixon, 1987) and represent three different philosophies for open systems interconnections. Any of the three standards could be adopted for specific implementations.

1. The *Carrier Sense Multiple Access/Collision Detection* (CSMA/CD) uses carrier sensing to determine active traffic on the network. Since a node determines the availability of the network, it is possible to determine when circuits are idle and transmit a message across the idle node. Collision detection enables the detection of simultaneous transmission, which terminates transmissions. CSMA/CD is the most popular design used in open systems, since this mechanism is used in TCP/IP protocols. It is simple and cost-effective to implement and appears adequate to meet the reliability of most installations.
2. The second important architecture is *token bus.* Tokens represented a natural way to design communications connections, since they have been used in other forms of human communications. Like a marker, the token represents permission to initiate sending of data. Two separate implementations have been used in token architectures, repre-

senting either bus or ring preferences. The bus represents a dedicated bidirectional transmission facility with high degrees of reliability. It was originally introduced in the factory environment and is important to the manufacturing automation protocol (MAP) standard.

3. The third architecture is *token ring*, which connects nodes in a unidirectional closed path. Each node regenerates signals as it reaches its station. Using the ring network, tokens are initiated from the sender to the receiver and regenerated throughout the network until the token reaches the destination station. The destination station makes a copy of the information in its own storage and continues passing the data around the ring. When the token combined with information reaches the sender, it is removed and the token freed. Any station that detects a freed token may begin transmission but is limited to a maximum period of token retention. The asynchronous priority level makes token ring appealing for many applications.

The wide acceptance of LANs with their required administrative structure has provided a new challenge for designers. In many companies, each LAN has a separate administrator, which represents costly overhead to the installation of open systems. It has been estimated that the middle of this decade will find millions of LANs installed. The overhead for LAN administrators can become very high. The challenge is to develop techniques to administer LANs that do not require one administrator per LAN. Some companies are already introducing programs to solve this problem.

LANs may be located on separate floors or in multiple buildings. The connection between LANs is called *LAN Interconnect* (LIN), which is achieved using either routers or bridges. When multiple LANs exist in a company, LINs are required for open systems support. Bridges connect LANs at the lowest protocol levels and are most appropriate between two similar networks. Routers recognize the existence of higher protocols and are most appropriate for heterogeneous LANs. LANs are connected in enterprise networks using protocols that extend beyond a single building or campus. We will discuss next alternative connections beyond the local domain.

8.3 BROADER NETWORK CAPABILITY

Considerations for broader network attachment will assess networks outside the location. These networks may use either private or public facilities to achieve broader connection. Private networks use architectures originating from either a computer vendor or the using company. The private network will use leased or owned facilities with private channels.

Public networks use existing communications equipment with local, national, and international connectivity. In public networks, the interfaces to the network are based on standards that use shared bandwidths. Public networks are more economical but have the same characteristics of any other shared facility.

An examination of the available data services will find that they are broken into three categories.

1. Packet switched provides long-distance packets with current connections using X.25 protocols. Packet-switching performance improvements will result from the introduction of advanced packet networks during the decade, but X.25 will continue to be important in many countries.

2. Circuit-switched alternatives include current circuit switches and the 64 Kbps. Connection from office equipment to circuit switching is through modems.

3. Dedicated lines use the analog or digital systems that are prewired into many buildings. In performance levels above 64 Kbps, these lines can use T1 at 1.544 Mbps and T3 at 45 Mbps.

Networking exists beyond interconnected LANs in a given site. Metropolitan area networks (MANs) provide networking support to citywide or suburban locations. Local offices can be interconnected on an open systems network with compound data using this public network. Although copper has been used in many sites, fiber-optic cable is replacing traditional linkages in many cities. Since MANs are local public networks, they can be used to connect to suppliers and other business partners not on the private network.

Large companies have long supported wide area networks divisions within the company. These networks use many different media to communicate across the enterprise. Technologies as diverse as copper wiring and satellite transmission have been used. Ground-based fiber networks and optical connections have also been used. These networks have traditionally used specific vendor implementations but are being shifted to standard interfaces. Enterprise networking extends across the entire business and supports distant offices. Using the WAN, enterprises can continue their communication across different regions of the world.

A number of companies have used enterprise computing to run their businesses. Boeing has used the network to provide designs for their aircraft. IBM has a worldwide network connecting not only their development operations but also their marketing groups.

The adoption of network protocols that work across global systems has made an open approach appealing to companies that must use the best hardware available in different countries. Logical workgroups can span many locations and yet be able to use open communications devices.

8.4 NETWORK ARCHITECTURES

Local computer networks started with a hodgepodge of protocols and wiring to connect different processors together. Informal wiring within PC installations included the wire thrown over the wall to connect the PCs together. The protocols between these initial systems were simply handshaking code agreed to by connecting processors. Since the early days of networking, sophisticated protocols and wiring schemes have modernized the entire approach to support.

As networks continued to grow, there was an apparent need for the organization of the hodgepodge into organized systems to meet the needs of heterogeneous connections. Although standards have made good progress, multiprotocol, multiwire connections remain prevalent in many companies and are expected to continue in use through the rest of the century.

If we examine the network from a purely functional perspective, three separate levels can contribute to the required organized approach. Communications processing modules handle the creation, transmission, error detection, and monitoring of messages through the system. These modules will use protocols, which are interfaces that define the connection rules between communicating nodes. Combinations of the processing modules and protocols represent the operational networks that exist across local and remote connections. Each of these logical functions provides unique capability to the open system and must be investigated to understand the power of the network.

The same advances in technology that have sparked a revolution in data processing have also affected the communications environment. Early terminals required close proximity between terminals and supporting computers. Breakthroughs permitted remote but—by today's standards—primitive connections for end users. Advances in satellite and optical communications have created remote environments with the apparent ability to match local communications capability. Networks were once dedicated to voice or data transmission but can now sustain mixed communications. Data transmissions were once low-speed and of dubious quality, but today's high-speed bandwidths can transmit exceptionally high quality processing information.

With the use of advanced conversion products, remote communications has achieved an effective transparency between different network protocols. Modern switching techniques enable the connection between local networks and large data farms with repositories of valuable data. Many companies, such as automotive manufacturers, are involved in external networks, as shown in Figure 8.5. These networks include the focal firm that is the hub of the connection and the suppliers, retailers, and business partners. Advances in remote connections have helped to make these intercompany networks a reality.

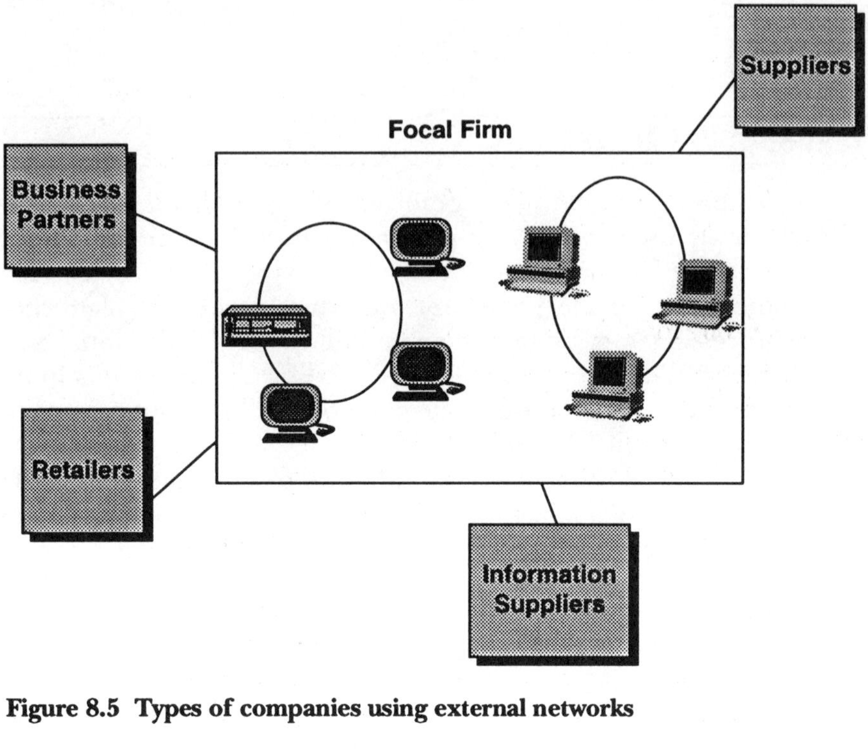

Figure 8.5 Types of companies using external networks

Compound data records can be very large with text annotated with voice or graphics and image information being transmitted. The use of expanded graphics for business application has provided a challenge across the network. Early in the design of communications, network reliability was a challenge, but later architectures and advances in electronic chips have improved reliability.

Transmission of engineering parts was an early reason for the creation of robust designs. A single imprecise bit can affect the design of critical components. Since millions of characters are transmitted, it is important that the system be designed to transmit accurate data. Every evening, billions of dollars of electronic information are transmitted by the world financial network. This area also demands high precision.

Each of these data files contains information that must be protected across the communications network. Remote intrusions on telephone systems are possible, and more sophisticated equipment can obtain a large amount of industrial intelligence from the airwaves. Eavesdropping by an experienced professional can penetrate systems, making them vulnerable to attack.

8.5 DISTRIBUTED PROCESSING

Distributed processing represents a significant opportunity for many businesses to effectively use the growing performance of desktop computers. With a well-developed distributing system plan, it is possible to leverage existing resources and at the same time introduce lower-cost platforms. Distributed processing represents a flexible alternative to individual and group productivity. Widespread use of distributed processing results in increased network traffic. The cost of management and installation is much higher than central system solutions.

A number of technical challenges exist in the implementation of distributed processing systems. For some years, designers have been attempting to create distributed systems that worked well in many environments. It soon became apparent that transparent communications support was integral in any distributed system solution. A naming system that understands the distributed nature of the information is also a prerequisite for support.

The Open Software Foundation (OSF) introduced the *Distributed Computing Environment* (DCE) to define a framework for distributed computing.

One of the first steps in their definition is to create an environment to handle many PCs, with future definitions for other distributed problems. Also included are distributed file services, which retain management and security considerations. Time and directory services are fundamental to the definition of this work.

An important early protocol in the DCE definition is the *Remote Procedure Call* (RPC). Originally introduced by Sun Microsystems, the RPC accesses services in distributed open systems using commands and defined application programmer interfaces (API). A library of distributed routines, which can provide access between clients and servers, is available through the command. Using RPC, the end users perceive all functions as local to their specific computers.

Major vendors have adopted the DCE standardsto define new distributed processing problems and are providing software to support the standard. Although DCE has been around for some time, widespread implementation isn't expected until the 1996 time frame; most current work by user organizations has been in the area of experimental pilot programs rather than full-scale deployment.

Universities have also launched research into the advanced aspects of distributed open systems. Project Athena helped define characteristics of large local networks of workstations. As a follow-up to this work, the University of California has joined in launching a study of multiple campus-large networks of open systems. Called Sequoia 2000, this effort connects open systems across multiple campuses and supercomputer computer centers.

8.6 DEVELOPMENT TRENDS

Increasing network traffic has created intensified attention to techniques to handle compound information at very high data rates. Many of these efforts will result in future offerings that will further enhance open systems computing. High-speed networks will permit the introduction of technology that facilitates anywhere computing. In addition to traditional communications developments, there is increasing interest in cellular communications, which will facilitate portable computing connections.

There is increasing emphasis on the need for gigabit networks both at the local and long-distance support areas. Projected performance improvements make the network critical to social and scientific computing. Five separate gigabit networking experiments have been established by the Corporation for National Research Initiatives. These include the Aurora project, which is focused on high-speed packet switching; Nectar, which is concentrated on large-scale distributed computing; and CASA, which is working on distributed supercomputing.

The continuing work on FDDI and ISDN-B channel support will provide a communications base for powerful enterprise networks. In addition, dedicated line switching improvements are resulting from work in Synchronous Optical Network (SONET) at 51.84 Mbps, which provides fiber transmission services compatible with existing digital hierarchy. All regional companies have either trial or deployment systems available in the United States, and major countries in Europe expect a phased deployment over the next few years.

Packet switching will benefit from the introduction of frame relay, which improves the performance of private and public networking applications. Frame relay arose from work that Telecom Finland initiated with DataNet, which was the first public LAN interconnection service in 1989. Applications using low- or medium-performance LANs attached to the system, using IP protocols. IBM protocols were bridged to the network, using TCP. Although the network was a success, customers required additional capability. Benefits from this system included cost reductions for solutions using X.25-type protocols.

It became clear that the next level of DataNet would provide a data link layer based on backbone technology with congestion control. Frame relay has the advantage of providing virtual networks that can improve the selection of OSI layer 3 protocols, permitting a wide range of networks to be attached to the system. Frame relay is based on international standards and has been tested for its effectiveness.

Switched Multi-megabit Data Service (SMDS) is a public datagram packet-switched MAN service developed by Bellcore for U.S. regional telephone companies. Comparable work is underway in Europe and Australia. Performance of the network provides throughput ranging from 1 Mbps to 45 Mbps. Eventually, it will go up to 155 Mbps using SONET access. SMDS provides high-speed networking to existing distributed processing software and applications. The high performance rates make it a natural to access high-performance servers such as supercomputers. Initial SMDS pilots were introduced in the United States and major countries in 1991, and the datagram is projected to be in full production by the mid-1990s.

8.7 CONSIDERATIONS

Network hardware has benefited from the advances in electronics. Hardware that was once complex and located in central processors has been shifted into chips incorporated directly into individual workstations. For example, modems are included in portable processors. Wide area networks can augment copper connections with the use of fiber, satellite, or radio transmissions.

Wiring systems represent a complex labyrinth, unless the wires are collected in a single organized closet. Hopefully, the cable system will already be in place before the implementation of open systems begins. Combining intelligent network management with an organized wiring closet has definite advantages for network management teams. Eventually, wireless communications will eliminate the need for extensive building wiring.

The effects of bandwidth have captured the imagination of system and communications designers. Advanced applications that support multimedia transmission can strain existing network bandwidth. These applications transmit a very high number of bits and require sufficient bandwidth to ensure the accuracy of the information.

Significant alternatives are being developed by communications companies to expand services across the various networks. The continuing work on FDDI and ISDN-B channel support will provide powerful enterprise networks. In addition, there is increasing attention to the introduction of SONET and SMDS. Many believe there is a pent-up capability in the network that will benefit open systems developers.

Routing across multiple paths will permit alternative paths to be selected by the network manager. Route switching will enable users to move data across multiple routes in a transparent fashion.

Industry standards do not often move to acceptance with the same speed as de facto standards. As noted earlier, it has been anticipated that OSI will become the predominant standard; even if this eventually occurs (and this is in doubt), TCP/IP will remain the most important transmission protocol for open systems for a long time.

Multiprotocol networks rely on combinations of hardware and software solutions to resolve conflicts between systems. A great deal of this support will be concentrated in the hardware, but more software tools can be used to provide much of the conversion. The next chapter will examine in detail the different alternatives available in network software.

8.8 REFERENCES

Bartee, Thomas C. (editor). *Data Communications and Network Systems.* Indianapolis: Howard W. Sams, 1985.

Booth, Grayce M. *The Distributed System Environment: Some Practical Approaches.* New York: McGraw-Hill, 1981.

Dixon, Roy C. "Lore of the Token Ring." *IEEE Network Magazine,* January 1987, pp. 11–18.

Pickholtz, R. L. "Modems, Multiplexers, and Concentrators." In *Data Communications and Network Systems,* edited by Thomas C Bartee. Indianapolis: Howard W. Sams, 1985, pp. 63–117.

Stallings, William. "A Manager's Guide to Protocols for Local Networking." *Telecommunications,* September 1987, pp. 38–39.

9

Network Software

The proliferation of open networks will continue, creating a challenge to define the connections and perform the interactions between users and the network. An environment must be formed to simplify the creation, maintenance, management, and modification of networks that are a part of the open systems environment. It was estimated in the early 1990s, that over 11 million networks will exist by the middle of the 1990s and each will require an LAN administrator (Grove, 1991). This trend appears to be holding (circa 1994). This expansion of network hardware has emphasized the challenge of finding automated techniques to provide the monitoring, care, and feeding of these essential links in the open systems chain. These expanded requirements have resulted in software packages that aid in network management.

Exploration of network software begins by examining the different programs used to control and run the network. Network platforms contain software that provides conversion for different protocols, basic operating system support, network control, and network management. Typical network software must connect to a variety of protocols to monitor and debug problems on the system. The goal is to eliminate the need for the application developers to understand the complexities of the management process. Most important, the computer network should work with the same transparency and reliability that the local telephone system provides.

We will examine four different types of network software (Figure 9.1) in this chapter. The first is the network operating systems, which are actually additional programs that reside on standard operating systems and provide connection and monitoring support across the network. These operating systems are the heart of connectivity and provide easy growth as additional users are added to the network. Next, we will examine the control code, which is so important to network flow. Malone and Rockart emphasize the essential nature of coordination of efforts across worldwide enterprises (Malone and Rockart, 1991). We will then examine the network management programs that support active network management. Network management supports the different subnets and provides the network administrator with tools to debug and correct problems on the network. Finally, we will explore applications that are embedded in the network and provide value-added enhancements to the communications process.

Network applications must be tailored to reflect their use on communications nodes. The application must address specific application tasks and then be extended to support full network communications. Since the controlling structure of the process is computers connected across the network, operating systems supporting the network are important parts for the success of network software. An important feature of all systems is the ability to balance different system functions from a single logical control point.

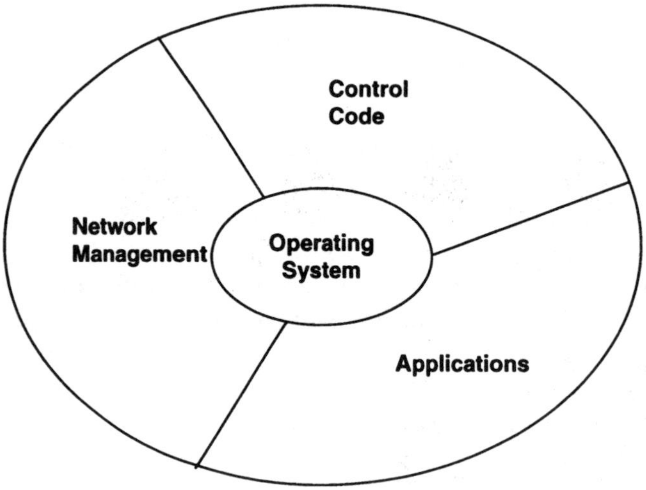

Figure 9.1 Four types of network software

Have you ever noticed that the aggregate compute power of workstations and servers attached to networks easily exceeds the compute power found on your supporting mainframes? It would be useful to capture and balance this power across multiple users. It is especially challenging to use inactive compute power of idle workstations and PCs. Programs are emerging that create a logical parallel processor comprised of idle workstations. A good example is Linda, developed by Scientific Computing Associates in New Haven, Connecticut. These programs become schedulers for larger numbers of heterogeneous computers attached to a network. The design is similar to programs that balance massive parallel computing (Figure 9.2). These control programs enable installations to balance distributed multiple processors connected on a TCP/IP network and treat them as a single programming resource with the potential performance of a parallel computer.

At the heart of operations on a local area network are network operating systems. These subsystems were introduced to augment functions found on PC operating systems. The subsystems use the operating system as the primary access point to the hardware but add many required functions that ensure the operations of the network. Originally, these programs were developed for MS-DOS, but they have been extended to other major systems used on network hardware.

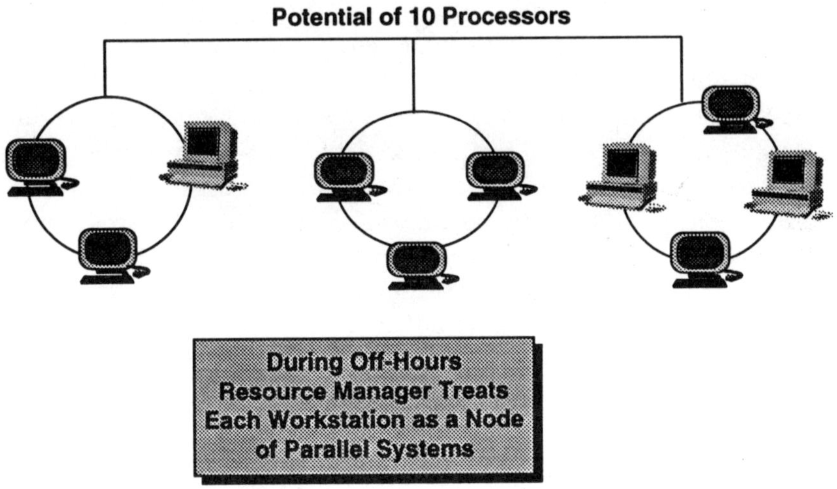

Figure 9.2 Balancing massive parallel computing

9.1 NETWORK PROTOCOLS

In discussing networks, it is worth considering different protocols used to communicate between workstations and servers. A *protocol* is simply an agreed communications technique for programs residing on electronic computers. Network architects consider that symmetrically balanced layers between discrete functions are the best approach to ensure long-lasting designs. As a result, most protocols follow a symmetrical arrangement that provides corresponding layers within network processors. In early implementations, each pair of computers or programs established an agreed protocol between them. As functions grew and the numbers of communicating computers increased, general agreements or standard approaches were adopted.

Initially, the champions of standards focused on specific vendor computers that could provide matching protocols for their own software. Larger computer vendors established their own protocols and enforced them by providing only software that conformed to the proprietary approach. Smaller computer companies followed the lead of the large vendors and provided the special architectures to get a portion of the market. Obviously, the large vendor had a lead on the design by at least two years and could maintain an exclusive market for a long time. The two most important proprietary protocol sets were developed by IBM and Digital Equipment Corporation. The similarity between the proprietary architectures and the standards can be seen in Figure 9.3, which shows the layered protocols of IBM's SNA, TCP/IP, and OSI.

In 1974, IBM introduced *System Network Architecture* (SNA) as the backbone of its communication strategy. This protocol provides consistency across IBM's systems and those companies that have adopted versions of the protocol (*IBM Systems Journal*, 1983; Sundstrom et al., 1987). The SNA designers recognized the value of symmetrical layering and created sufficiently clean interfaces between layers to permit reproduction on different sizes of hardware. The architecture facilitated asymmetric data flows through variations of the basic design (Cypser, 1978). The architecture was greatly supported within IBM's product line and has a wide acceptance among vendors desiring to connect to IBM processors. Many lessons learned from SNA have proven valuable in defining other open systems protocols. SNA continues to be the backbone of IBM's support strategy and will serve as their base for developing open systems solutions.

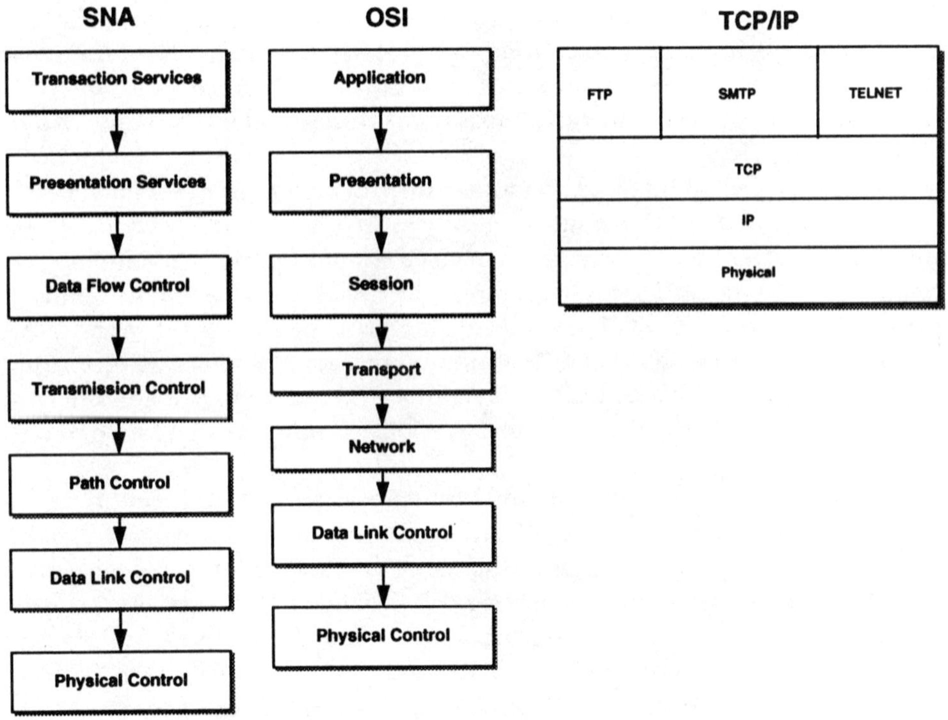

Figure 9.3 IBM's layered protocols: SNA, OSI, and TCP/IP

In 1982, IBM defined LU 6.2 as the major protocol to support peer relationships on a distributed network. LU 6.2 is the base for Advanced Program-to-Program Communications (APPC), which is a foundation for IBM's network designs.

An important IBM product that introduced its own set of protocols is the PC. The first LANs supported on the PC were supported through additions to the Basic I/O system (BIOS), known as NetBIOS. Many communications products built to connect to PC networks have used NetBios as a primary vehicle for the connections. Common NetBios interfaces were created to connect across different PC protocols using LANs.

Digital Equipment Corporation (DEC) also provides an important layered protocol architecture, known as *Digital Network Architecture* (DNA). The network system, known as DECnet, is the backbone of Digital's support across their main processors and is the basis for their client/server computing. By

1980, Digital had expanded the network capability to support adaptive packet routing for communications to non-Digital systems. Digital was an early supporter of Ethernet and used it to connect their workstations. The fifth generation of DECnet supports a networking model that conforms to OSI (Bradley, 1988).

DEC expanded its network protocols to provide *Network Application Software* (NAS), which provides information sharing across the network. Their definitions were used to create interfaces for compound documents on heterogeneous networks. This support is valuable for multimedia communications but also connects into the existing base of network systems. NAS applications support standard X Windows and such services as electronic mail on existing networks. NAS uses standard protocols to provide the connections between the different heterogeneous components on an open network.

It was quickly recognized that a more universal form of connection agreement needed to be reached. Standard protocols were first introduced by the Department of Defense, which required all research centers to communicate their information across secured networks. Early DoD support for open systems was built on the *Transmission Control Protocol/Internet Protocol* (TCP/IP). Introduced in 1972 for ARPAnet (Advanced Research Projects Agency Network—see Chapter 8), this low-cost connection mechanism was initially accepted by defense contractors and universities, but it eventually spread to commercial customers . . . and is now known as the Internet, the wildly successful first step of the much-hyped Information Superhighway. Since it is widely supported by workstation vendors, it represents a natural first step toward open systems. Although originally developed for internetworking, TCP/IP was extended to support shared file access, file transfer, and electronic mail support.

The transmission control protocol (TCP) is the most commonly used protocol in the TCP/IP stack. It provides reliable transmission across physical networks. The internet protocol (IP) is the lowest level of TCP/IP and provides packet delivery across an internet. IP does not provide error detection or correction. The internet control message protocol (ICMP) is used to report messages in IP transmissions. TCP/IP has been supported across Ethernet connections, where it first appeared in 1973. By 1989, Ethernet represented 60 percent of the installed LANs in the United States and was continuing to grow. Ethernet performance has improved with advances in wiring and connection technology. By 1990, the performance reached 10 million bps over standard twisted-pair lines.

A joint effort of ISO and CCITT created the *Open System Interconnect* (OSI) model to facilitate open communications. Work on OSI began in the 1970s with a target completion by the mid-1980s. Actual progress has been much slower than originally hoped. Further, many of the protocol efforts that comprise the layers of OSI (examples: X.400 for message handling/electronic mail and X.500 for directory services) have undergone several variations and subefforts to fix "deficiencies" (such as X.400's addressing mechanism, which is significantly more complex than that used on the Internet under TCP/IP).

OSI focused on open systems interchange across local and wide area networks. The designers used clean symmetrical layers between functions to facilitate implementations on different hardware architectures.

OSI has seven symmetrical layers between nodes in the network. Each layer is clearly structured as entities to permit clarity of services. High-level entities use services of the next lowest layer. As can be seen in Figure 9.4, the OSI layers are similar to those found in IBM's SNA.

1. The Physical Layer is the lowest level, providing basic physical connections on twisted pairs, coaxial cables, and fiber-optic connections. The Physical Layer is normally implemented in the hardware.
2. The Data Link Layer is an important layer for open systems since it provides data transparency and data flow control for the connections. Error-recovery mechanisms are found on this layer. Recent definitions from standards working groups have broken this layer into two segments—the Media Access Control (MAC) and Link Control levels. The Data Link Layer is sufficiently well defined that many hardware implementations exist.
3. The Network Layer is the routing layer, which determines the path information to send messages across the network.
4. The Transport Layer provides error-free data transfer between two nonadjacent nodes. In this capacity, it provides data sequencing.
5. The Session Layer synchronizes data interchange between logically adjacent senders and receivers.
6. The Presentation Layer reformats and presents data in the architecture of the intelligent node receiving the information.
7. The Application Layer connects different end-user application programs. This layer is the highest layer of the standards and represents the point in which applications will access open systems.

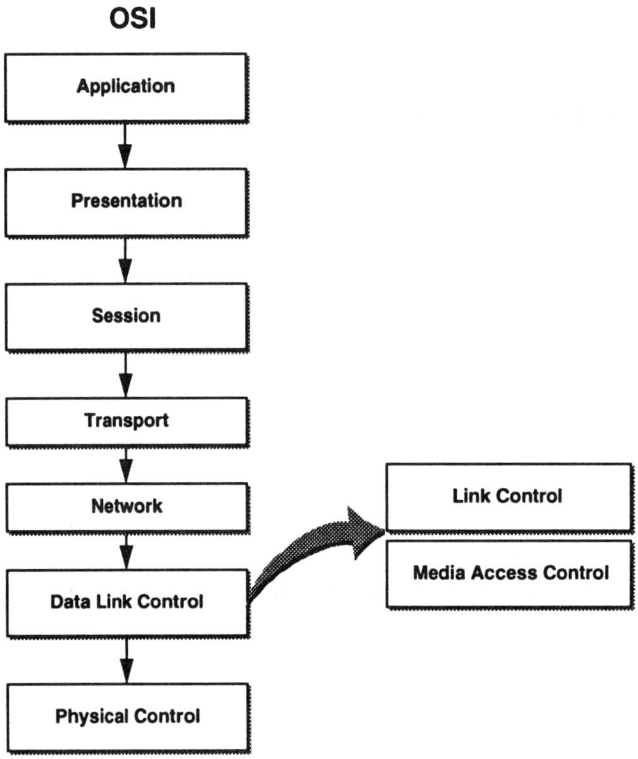

Figure 9.4 The OSI reference model

Other functions have been included in the open systems definitions. Some include the *Association Control Service Element* (ACSE), which provides a mechanism to establish connections or associations across open networks using application context names and entity titles. *File Transfer Access and Management* (FTAM) provides file transfer and file access in a single protocol for network users. Many of the upper layers of the standard have been ignored by implementors, suggesting there will be other iterations on the standard.

Joint work between ISO and CCITT has produced two important standards used in open systems connections across distributed networks. The wide acceptance of the message handling system or electronic mail protocol X.400 has provided a common message passing technique for the industry. Equally important in distributed networks is the X.500, or directory standard. Network systems require a directory containing the network locations and identifiers for users and data connected to the system. Directories provide pointers to information as well as routing information for primary and alternative transmission paths. X.500 version defines a global service providing connections to national name spaces and private networks, supporting a wide search capability. Definitions of directory services that could be accessed by directory user agents provided a naming convention that has been adopted by a growing number of network developers. A number of elements in the standard have been supported and implemented in different vendor systems. An authentication framework that supports attribute and naming models has been developed.

The manufacturing companies recognized the rich smörgåsbord of alternatives provided by OSI. Since many companies shared specific industry requirements, General Motors led an effort to define standards within the automotive industry. High demand for communications compatibility caused the high interest in this effort. *Manufacturing Automation Protocol* (MAP) was the first specialized subset of OSI defined to meet the needs of a specific industry. Multiple versions of MAP have caused a good deal of confusion with vendors, and even this subset of OSI has not met the original expectations.

We have examined performance improvements under consideration in network hardware, but many bottlenecks reside within the systems that support the hardware. Problems with transaction sizes, protocols, and use of buffers can adversely affect network performance. To offset these problems, additional emphasis is placed on designing software solutions that provide sufficient power at the node to overcome potential bottlenecks. Much of this power has been designed in the operating system and subsystems that support the system. The next consideration is the effects of operating system code on the network.

9.2 NETWORK SERVICES

Network operating systems provide access to the functions found within the LAN. In their simplest implementation, they are built on existing operating systems to provide disk spooling and communications connections for shared network resources. In this configuration, it is possible to take larger PCs and have them perform shared services between connected nodes in the system. These computers can still support typical job streams for single-user processing. Network services use the existing control program and augment it with the error-checking and connection protocols. Since it is not a dedicated medium, it can reduce the costs of installation.

As we move up the scale of complexity and dedicated resources, we find more elaborate software packages that provide extensive support for larger numbers of users with a single system image. The high-end network services provide additional function and redundancy but are more complex. Examples of high-end network operating systems include Novell's NetWare, which is excellent for print and file serving and is the most widely used. Microsoft's LAN Manager, Digital Equipment's Pathworks, IBM's PC LAN, and Banyan System's Vines are all rich in function and are used by many companies. These network operating systems run on PCs with LAN manager requiring OS/2 support. Increasingly, many packages are being ported to the UNIX operating system as the base for future development.

Services include everything from communications support to time synchronization on the network. Distributed database services augment software capability from server companies. Network security is included in these routines. The operating systems provide the base for other network services.

Investigation will reveal that these network service routines vary in their ability to be set up rapidly or to support large amounts of storage. The use of imaging and eventually interactive sound support on the network will push the requirement limits for this technology.

The selection of network operating systems is critical to determining the characteristics of the network. Lower-end LAN operating systems may be an excellent choice for beginning a system but may limit growth as the network continues to grow. Systems requiring a high level of disk activity will benefit from the higher-end systems that can address large amounts of storage space. Some systems do not support multiplatform connections very well, and some do not support Macintosh or UNIX platforms at all. In an open system that will eventually use WANs, it is a good idea to check whether the system will operate using your company's WAN architecture. It is also important to investigate the support for fault tolerance, name service for multiple files, the connection to mainframes, and the security features found on the systems.

A number of critical questions should be assessed in selection of an LAN operating system. What is the performance of the system, and how does the performance support my network goals? Does the system support multiplatform clients? Does the system support non-DOS environments? What are the install and growth characteristics of the system? What is the real cost of installing the LAN operating system?

Local area networks will require an LAN administrator, who is trained in the use of the network. This can be a costly ingredient in the support of the network. It is well to assess the cost of the network in training and administration. What is the cost for the users desiring to install a network? What is the expected load on the network and the projected cost for the LAN administrator?

9.3 NETWORK CONTROL SOFTWARE

In mainframe computers, control for the network resides in a designated control point located in a specific computer or computers. Since the control point manages steady-state processes, it is relatively easy to identify the needed feedback requirements from the network. With the introduction of the PC, each individual controlled desktop occurrences. With the introduction of LANs, a control point could be identified that governed what occurred within the LAN. As both mainframe and LAN use has grown, there is a need to identify the enterprise control point.

A good example is the connection between the IBM communications controller and the mainframe. A degree of distribution of control is achieved through control code, known as *Network Control Program* (NCP). The control code and the mainframe resident code interacted to produce a great team. When network functions expanded, the size and complexity of control program code also grew. Complementary generation of code was necessary between IBM's mainframe communications access method, *Virtual Telecommunication Access Method* (VTAM), and NCP.

The network control point is subjected to continual change. This is especially true with the introduction of anyplace clients. Clients can reside on desktops or actually be in a moving truck communicating with the system across radio waves. In any case, in modern networks, users are introduced on an irregular basis, and the network can expand and contract rapidly. As in the case of the gas network, we are looking for a point of network equilibrium that is either real or induced through the architecture.

9.4 NETWORK APPLICATIONS

Once information is acquired within the network, a number of applications can provide unique services with the data. Unique data points for network administrators and managers can help determine many characteristics of the network. Using aggregate statistics, it is possible to perform traffic analysis and determine a correct balancing or routing through the network across the system. On-line applications connected with visual monitors enable system administrators to detect any problems in timing or balancing across the active network.

Debugging systems permit the user to determine errors and correct them in a timely fashion. Conversations can be traced to detect error information within the system. Other network applications include tuning for the different nodes within the network. Applications can be applied to the network that track different attempts to penetrate the system code. Well-positioned information gathering permits the application of monitors that detect variations in access information.

Shared applications across LANs provide services to multiple users and reduce the overall cost to the company. This assumes that an advantage is possible through licensing agreements obtained from the supporting companies.

9.5 NETWORK MANAGEMENT

As the complexity of open systems increases, so does the requirement for effective management tools. Administration costs can be high for a few simple networks with minimal workstations attached. Networks that extend across an entire company or division require additional emphasis on timely detection techniques. Three separate areas must be addressed in a distributed management environment. The network manager must understand the level of resources on the network. What heterogeneous equipment, programs, and data comprise the total network? In active networks, it is necessary to understand which networks are being used by the different nodes connected to the system. Often, multiple networks can connect to individual desks. With smart wiring hubs, it is possible to have network monitoring information collected directly at the hub. This contributes significantly to the ability to detect and correct problems in the net.

In addition, the network manager must understand personal configurations, which are part of the distributed system. Normal and exceptional operational conditions are also factored into information supplied to the network manager. The tracking of system evolution is helpful in balancing system resources and allocating connections.

The need to detect and correct network problems was the genesis of much of the early work. There is an increasing need to perform administrative functions through systems management code. Enhanced capability at each node increases the data collection potential and raises the amount of decision that can result from full use of the software.

Since network complexity was growing, there was a need for solutions that could be applied from central processors. Initial network managers resided on mainframe processors and regulated enterprise networks. Initial statistics were skimpy but continued to grow with each new release. These network managers focused on proprietary networks, where each data element could be tightly controlled and supported across all the products. Interfaces to communications lines were well defined, and deduction could be used to determine whether the problem occurred in the network node or communications system. If the error did not occur at the nodes, it must have occurred in the communications system. Major computer and communications vendors learned to work together to reduce mutual costs, but problems continued to grow in complexity. Although mainframe systems appear complex, they actually establish a point of equilibrium that helps in defining a sufficient management algorithm. A comparable state of equilibrium is never reached in open distributed processing, and the network management problem becomes more complex.

With open systems, we have shifted into an area of heterogeneous systems, where control is more difficult. Conformity to detection and correction protocols depends more heavily on agreement or standards. Any intelligent processor attached to the system must collect error information and provide it to the network manager. Not all processors can be modified to collect the ideal statistics, and those that do not conform could have unknown errors. In addition, attached processors can incorrectly collect or transmit error information to the network manager.

Change requests will often come from the system administrator to reflect changes in operating procedures. Synchronization of fixes across multiple processors remains a requirement in many operational systems. Equally important are synchronized hardware and software updates, which must be reflected throughout the network. After the errors are detected, it is necessary to supply fixes to the different nodes in the system. Initially, this work occurred by sending someone to the location of the failing node. Since the network nodes were large computers and relatively expensive, the overhead of servicing the failing unit was relatively low.

With the introduction of PCs and LANs, the equation for network management changed. Since intelligence resided on individual desktops, a need grew to collect relevant information on each desktop processor that not only allowed error detection and recovery but also provided a census of the status of each network node. With the introduction of LANs, there was a need to have the specific control of distributed computers reside within the local network. LAN managers were introduced to support the network and provide information from the LAN to central network managers.

Network management conditions have been exacerbated by the proliferation of workstations. Data sizes on individual nodes have continued to increase. Essential business data can reside at different nodes, which make network failures catastrophic for some companies. Network redundancy reduces this exposure, but effective diagnostics have grown in importance. Each workstation has the compute capability and, therefore, the error potential of larger processors, but it has a cost that makes it prohibitive to send service representatives to each site of error. Since workstations have more computer power, self-correcting routines can enhance network reliability.

Enterprise network management remains a significant challenge that has been exacerbated by the introduction of additional power on individual workstations. Each workstation combines the power of previous mainframes that must now be managed. In large enterprises, it is important to know the worldwide status of all systems. Older network management systems remain on large processors and provide sufficiently robust tracking mechanisms to predict major outages. Detection of global problems can result in significant corrective action, which can be generated centrally.

To retain the connections between open systems and the enterprise networks, it is often necessary to connect to older network management routines. These include network management products based on proprietary designs or older OSI definitions. Figure 9.5 shows some of the major network management routines for WANs. IBM and AT&T have developed products that manage global networks. AT&T's *Unified Network Management Architecture* (UNMA) uses ISO's *Network Management Protocol* (NMP) to track information across heterogeneous networks. UNMA is a tool that works well with AT&T's specialty hardware, such as multiplexers, communications switches, and PBXs.

IBM's NetView, a widely used network management package, is based on their ONM architecture. NetView was initially a mainframe-only program but eventually branched out to include PCs. A cooperative relationship was developed between the host monitor programs and collection programs on

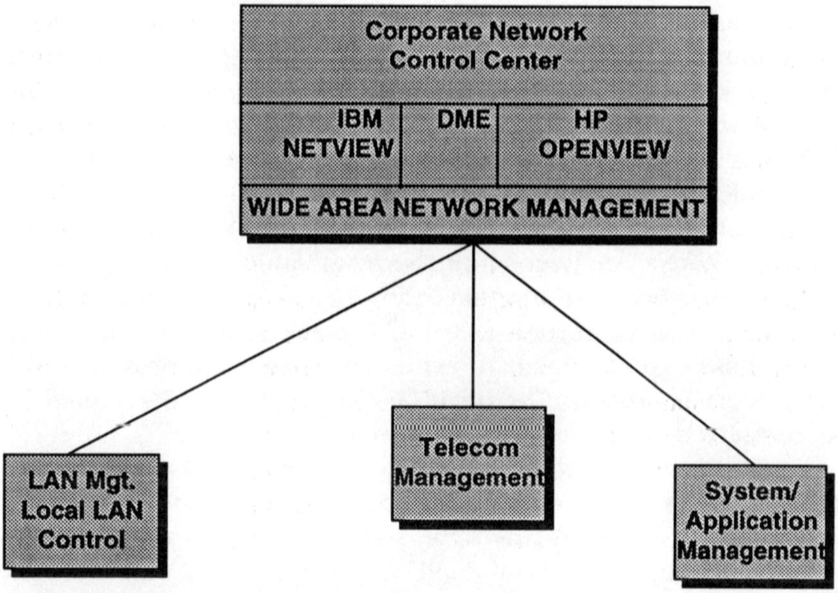

Figure 9.5 Major network management routines for WANs

PCs. Error statistics were architected in the early 1980s and eventually expanded to cover many other support features across the network.

Hewlett-Packard provides the popular network management package OpenView, which is based on OSI architecture and connects to other widely used management packages from IBM and AT&T.

The challenge of distributed management routines is to balance local network management with global tracking requirements. Autonomous routines provide significant capability, which is achieved by placing LAN management on a server. Local systems communicate with larger processors. Network management functions have continued to expand from simple beginnings. In addition to the diagnostic routines, network management now provides administration, performance tracking, and reports on daily network operations.

Using the power of open systems, it is possible to define modern systems that balance local autonomy and LAN network management with the needs of central network management. Design for these support packages recognizes that local units can take action or transmit information to the central processing units. Some worldwide networks have exceptional reliability specifications, which require redundancy. A loss of the network could mean significant lost business or potential loss of specific life-threatening information. Satellite launches required an international tracking mechanism sufficiently redundant to avoid outage. Comparable financial networks exist that will shift large sums of money across the network on a daily basis. Redundancy at all levels of the network is necessary to maintain these connections.

The communications picture has grown more complex as networks of LANs are interconnected with backbone nets. The entire system is eventually connected to WANs. Analyzer products are available for both LANs and WANs. Umbrella management programs track the status of distributed processing platforms but allow certain autonomy to the local network. These same programs use expert systems to achieve a balanced approach to the entire data gathering process. The details collected at the LAN should be able to be transferred to the upper levels of the network.

This complex network is best managed through distributed network management. Standards are helping to define enforcing criteria using network collection protocols. These are the same statistic collectors that feed the central network managers. OSF adopted a framework to define network management across the open system called *Distributed Management Environment* (DME). The framework is based on work performed by Tivoli Systems in Austin, Texas. The framework has also been adopted by UNIX System Laboratories in the *Distributed Open Management Environment* (DOME). Many vendors have accepted the framework and are beginning to create products on the definitions.

Two important network management protocols used in DME are the Common Management Information Protocol (CMIP) and the Simple Network Management Protocol (SNMP). Both provide APIs for software vendors to connect to their network management routines. A compatibility part allows multiple systems from previous systems to integrate to the newer system.

CMIP is a complex protocol defined by the OSI/Network Management forum and originally introduced in November 1990. CMIP is designed to provide comprehensive management of the network elements, with a basis for handling complex networks. It treats management resources as managed objects retained in a hierarchy.

SNMP was developed from the Simple Gateway Monitoring Protocol, which was directed at TCP/IP networks. SNMP provides an approach in which resources are modeled as variables and tables. In a sense, the development of the protocol was intended to slow the acceptance of the bureaucratic adoption of CMIP. SNMP used a subset of CMIP, providing rapid access for SNA, Vines, NetWare, and LAN Manager.

Standards organizations are moving rapidly to extend and expand the level of support available in network management. Certain characteristics are becoming relevant in all the solutions that help users avoid single-vendor support.

Large critical networks require sufficient statistics that can alert the network monitors of any potential failure. This is usually performed in central network monitoring centers, which can project failures and issue the necessary instructions to correct the problem. Normal execution information is compared with incoming statistics. Often, the central monitor will be able to predict an outage before the local site knows there is a problem and will be able to provide the necessary corrections or rerouting.

Gathering statistical information about the network also ensures that reasonable network accounting procedures can be determined. Simple procedures based on the number of network control blocks can be replaced by more accurate techniques when sufficient statistics have been collected. Basic statistical information collected on the network has focused on the hardware information, but extended programs also track the use of application programs in the network.

In massive networks, performance is a critical factor that can adversely affect the business. Fortunately, the nature of distributed open systems helps to reduce the toll on the network, but there are still nodes that can have serious problems if they slow down. Sufficient monitoring must be in place to ensure that the network maintains its performance in loaded conditions. As multimedia applications increase, there will be a growing need for this level of support.

Security remains a major concern in networks that contain a company's critical information. The first requirement is to protect the network against unwanted intrusions, but there is also a need to ensure that the network is not accidentally entered. A growing concern in the network is viruses, which are transmitted across multiple nodes. A number of viruses have been embedded in programs in networks and have even been packaged with network operating systems. Since there are so many different forms of viruses, it is usually difficult to protect against all of them.

The network management tools have as their primary objective the correct diagnosis of network faults. These faults must be identified and then corrected, using these advanced support tools. Networks with many thousands of nodes have a more complex problem in supporting the necessary intelligent diagnosis.

Typically, network management programs are expected to manage the physical networks, network adapters, bridges and routers, gateways, modems and multiplexers, terminal servers, and the applications that run across the network. The network manager also tracks information about PBXs and other electronic equipment that may be attached to the network.

Network management is considered a hierarchical system, which begins at the top level and continues to the lower levels of the network. Cross-enterprise information resides at the top of the network management picture and LAN information at the lowest level of the management picture.

9.6 CONSIDERATIONS

Networks have bridged workstations from personal productivity tools to business systems shared by groups of people. Pivotal to this role is the introduction of network software, which facilitates the interaction between heterogeneous platforms. This software provides connection and interaction between multiple clients and facilitates the full use of network services.

User interaction determines the usefulness of the network as a sharing tool. Although the interfaces properly reside on individual clients, the network software can facilitate the use of new applications. Effective applications that can be shared on the network help reduce the time spent waiting for services. Frequently used applications will continue to reside in individual desktop computers while shared applications will reside in the network. As workstations and LANs emerge, more of a group-think becomes possible. Systems provide significant gains for each individual, but, more importantly, they can provide productivity gains for the organization if they are used in the network.

The connection between installations has two major components. The first is simple interconnection between the different hardware elements, usually accomplished by routers and bridges and their support software. The higher level, known as interoperability, reflects the connection between applications and databases.

Network management in mainframe-based systems is established on a system in equilibrium. With the introduction of open systems, much system equilibrium is lost, and the network must determine characteristics that enable the effective use of the system. Network management must manage the resources of the system, which include all the different processors connected to the open system. It must also manage user accounts and configurations. The network manager must also track the operation of the total system and provide information on the evolution of the network.

The network problem is similar to the experience in neural computing and massive parallel processors. It is probable that the solutions for network management will result in solutions similar to those for massive parallel processing.

Groupware represents an important application portfolio for the future of network computing. The sharing of information by many people working together requires application knowledge coupled with a knowledge of network interactions. Good groupware will combine these two elements.

Companies that have installed open systems networks have rapidly come to the conclusion that network management is required for effective use. It is necessary to understand what is happening in the network while it is in active use. There remains a challenge to define sufficient tools that will support open distributed networks.

9.7 REFERENCES

Bradley, Bob. "Digital Network Architecture and the OSI Model." *Telecommunications,* February 1988, pp. 69–73.

Cypser, Rudy J. *Communications Architecture for Distributed Systems.* Reading, MA: Addison-Wesley, 1978, pp. 192–195.

Grove, Andrew S. Comments made during his keynote speech at 1991 COMDEX in Las Vegas, October 22, 1991.

IBM Systems Journal, vol. 22, no. 4, 1983. (This entire volume of the *IBM Systems Journal* is devoted to articles on IBM's System Network Architecture.)

Malone, Thomas W. and John F. Rockart. "Computers, Networks, and the Corporation." *Scientific American,* vol. 265, no. 3, September 1991, pp. 128–136.

Sundstrom, Robert J., James B. Staton III, Gary D. Schultz, Matthew L. Hess, George A. Deaton, Jr., Leo J. Cole, and Robert M. Amy, "SNA: Current Requirements and Direction." *IBM Systems Journal,* vol. 28, no. 1, 1987.

10

Applications

As we closely examine application development, we will discover an environment that has, on the one hand, been simplified by advances in technology but at the same time has been made more complex by the large number of options that still remain. The techniques adopted in building the winning application will also affect the selection and installation of open systems hardware platforms. Applications are the reason companies buy computers, and in this chapter we will explore some techniques for building applications in a network environment.

Large amounts of legacy code, which can affect the move to open systems, exist in most installations. This legacy code contains the operational template for the business and must be retained to ensure continued operations. New applications will be built around legacy code, and old applications will be downsized, with legacy code considered. Most legacy code has been produced in a disorganized fashion, using older computer languages, which were created before modern *computer-aided software engineering* (CASE) advances.

The first step in the development of open systems applications is the development and acceptance of standards that can be applied by your business across multiple vendor solutions. This reduces exclusive solutions while creating a software base that is portable to multiple processors. The standards should recognize hardware architectures as extensions of the principles of operations for software and should provide layers that enable systems to be built easily. The software should include the data, applications, system administration, and system management code. Software tools must be identified to facilitate development that can work on multiple system platforms.

Network technology is the assumed base for the new applications designed for open systems. Older applications will eventually change to use network frameworks and communicate to peer applications. Although there are still only a few network CASE tools, competent programmers can be shifted to use existing open systems development techniques in a relatively short time. Open systems can be designed and developed using modern design practices.

Eventually, success of any new technology is measured by the ability to effectively shift developments and create new code. Network applications can be either purchased or created. General applications will become available as the market reaches a profitability threshold. Specialized applications will, for the most part, be developed internally or through contracts.

A deterrent to a rapid movement to open systems is the number of programmers who can use modern development tools. Certainly, the tools serve as enticements for developers to produce large amounts of code simply. Software development groups within a company appear to be external developers when they provide code across the company.

Open systems applications were once confined to the periphery of mainline systems. These applications are increasingly becoming solutions for mission-critical problems, which are at the heart of business. Specialized programs require the use of design and application tools within the company to produce the unique applications for the company. These applications represent a significant advantage to the company and must be protected. Internal and external programming groups will look for modern tools to enhance the quality and productivity of programmers. Open systems solutions can adopt fourth-generation languages that enable end users to generate their own applications. These tools are expected to create a shift from the general stagnation in the software productivity of the past 30 years (Aron, 1974) by increasing homegrown solutions.

Finding the correct level of software execution has become more complex with the introduction of workstations. Rightsizing is the effort to place applications on the correct computer platform, which will optimize the solution for end users and the company. In rightsizing, some applications will remain on large servers or mainframes, other applications will be shifted to clients, and some applications will move to shared processors. More intense calculations may need to be shifted to high-powered servers.

The introduction of standard implementations has created an environment that supports portable applications. Portable applications are programs that can be easily shifted across dissimilar platforms. Popular PC code was made available on multiple vendors that conformed to the MS-DOS standard. Many vendors extended their application coverage to run on such operating systems as UNIX. Portability is a necessary characteristic of software used in open systems, since it can reduce programming and enhance the value of initial software investments. Ultimately, the value of open systems can be measured by the ability to create and use portable applications. Users and software vendors benefit directly from portability, while hardware vendors benefit from exclusivity. Portability reduces programming requirements while accelerating the move to different and advanced architectures. Selections can be made across a broader range of applications when there is a common interface.

Applications can be shifted to meet the best implementation. Some applications will continue to reside on servers and serve as hubs to multiple clients. Others can be shifted directly to workstations benefiting from the advantage of local access. Expert systems, for instance, can reside at the desktop of the individual. Immediate access to expert capability can enhance the value of the desktop for individuals. Portability has the advantage of ensuring durability and scalability. Long-lasting applications reduce the need to continually spend money on the same software problem.

With open systems, it is possible for many clients to share a single application residing on a server. This sharing has many advantages for the department utilizing it. A common server reduces the number of application upgrades that must be transmitted to service the clients. The license problem is complex in open systems. Application vendors have begun to change their licensing ground rules. License agreements can now be purchased that enable the installation to manage the number of users. It is necessary to install tools that poll the workstations and determine who has the license token for a specific application.

Other qualities expected in network applications include usability across heterogeneous processors, scalability to multiple platforms, and easy modifiability when included in the network. Scalability is the quality of an application package that permits its use on small processors or large processors. It is usually achieved by conforming to standards and has an open design that can take advantage of the local compute power.

A number of wild cards exist in developing applications in open environments. The most prevalent is the skunkworks, which is a small group of very skilled programmers who can create new applications in a very short time. Usually, the skunkworks have an abbreviated process and can create a prototype or even a full application in a fraction of the time required for standard development.

A second wild card is the demand for instant application support. Often, development schedules reflect a carefully developed project plan. User management will demand the application on a much faster schedule. Many steps in the process often will be deleted to meet the schedule but still retain a semblance of quality.

Applications are the driving force behind successful computer offerings. A well-written application in an open system will connect to servers and provide capability for end users on clients. Traditional approaches to application development have been time-consuming and have slowed down productivity gains from computer technology. Recent introductions of code generators promise breakthroughs in code production, since the generators have been able to take high-level definitions and produce reasonable operational applications.

10.1 RIGHTSIZING

Can applications residing in your department or company host computers be shifted to lower-cost platforms? What portion of the applications can be shifted to clients or servers while retaining the corporate control required by your company? Do you lose security by shifting more applications out to servers and away from central processors? All these questions and more are being pursued by managers considering the correct level at which to develop and manage new applications.

Many companies have adopted the concept of downsizing, or movement of the application to smaller computers. This means the movement of applications from mainframes or minicomputers to workstations and servers. Usually, this is driven by recognition of the advantages of lower costs. Individual productivity applications were early candidates for this shift. Benefits could be gained by providing individual workers the material they needed to complete their tasks. As larger applications were considered, it was recognized that not all mainframe applications and data should be shifted to individual processors.

The term rightsizing means finding the correct level of processing power for the application. This may mean moving applications to a smaller processor from a mainframe or minicomputer when this presents a clear advantage to the business in the form of individual productivity or lower computing costs. It may also mean shifting a shared application to a larger processor, such as a network server, or to a multiple parallel processor if there is a benefit from high performance. Finding the correct level processor entails assessing the needs of users and the application code and determining the correct processing level for the code. Can the processing level provide sufficient support to retain or improve the compute response the business requires? Does the application location retain or improve the levels of flexibility desired by the company?

An increasing number of companies are shifting from larger processors to clients or servers. Initially, it was found that applications that have a close relationship to end users benefited from relatively close proximity to users. Applications were shifted to PCs, which provided increased autonomy for individual workers and enabled them to perform more work without relying on mainframe software. Some control was lost in this shift, but it was considered sufficiently valuable to continue the movement.

As central processors are devoted to the role of data repositories, more functions found on these processors will shift to smaller computers. Initially, applications will be split between the different processors. The split or cleaved application challenges the design team to define clean interfaces to facilitate the shift. Additional performance on portable computers will find some split applications residing on mobile units.

Many applications are developed to meet the needs of specialized users. These applications should be developed with tools that facilitate their use in the complex network. We will discuss next different development tools.

10.2 APPLICATION DEVELOPMENT TOOLS

The quest for simple ways to create programs was initiated as soon as programmers encountered complex problems on mathematical computers. The need to simplify code creation and apply sufficient resources to problem resolution resulted in the introduction of language compilers and library tools. Originally, interfaces to hardware used direct binary coding called machine language, which proved cumbersome and time-consuming for all programmers and was a bottleneck to completing applications. Initial library mechanisms were card decks that were either retained in individual desks or department cabinets.

In the 1950s, assembly programs were introduced that matched machine instructions in a one-to-one relationship but used binary coded access to hardware. Macros were added to languages to improve their productivity, and, eventually, libraries of macro subroutines simplified programming. It seemed that early PC efforts duplicated the same cycle followed in mainframe computers.

With the introduction of macro assemblers, the search for simpler languages expanded, and a number of high-level languages were introduced. A first step in this direction was the definition of a language for commercial application developers. COBOL (COmmon Business Oriented Language) was introduced in the mid-1950s. The language was standardized early and has been constantly updated to reflect changes in hardware and software capability, such as the introduction of networks and object programming. Compilers were perfected to produce optimized code that could get relatively high performance from most processors. COBOL remains an important language to support the large amounts of legacy code.

FORTRAN (FORmula TRANslation) was first introduced on an IBM 704 computer in 1957 and was widely accepted by engineers and scientists (Pugh et al., 1991). A survey by the IBM users' group SHARE the following year indicated that a majority of respondents were using the language for many of their programs. After growing rapidly for years, FORTRAN's popularity waned in the late 1970s. A resurgence of interest in the past few years has found the language's acceptance growing again. In scientific applications, there does not appear to be an acceptable alternative. FORTRAN-90 is being used to provide support for modern applications in open systems and parallel processing.

Many languages have been introduced to replace COBOL and FORTRAN, such as Programming Language/I (PL/I) and Pascal, but none has demonstrated the wide acceptance of the early languages. UNIX provided early support for the C programming language (Kernighan and Ritchie, 1978). C was widely adopted across multiple operating systems that were available on workstations and mainframes. C provides both high-level and machine-level capability for system programmers. Many UNIX applications have been written using C, and extensions provided in proprietary systems have resulted in a wealth of applications across different processors. Many network programs also use C as the primary implementation language, so it is important for system designers and implementors to understand the language.

Objects have been introduced in programming and are proving increasingly important for open systems implementors. Variations of C have emerged that provide support for object programming on open systems hardware. C++ has proven popular for open systems implementations of applications. A number of languages use C as an intermediate step in the creation of operational code.

Computer compilers convert the simple language of the developer into something usable by the computer. Initially, this was a straightforward mapping into machine instructions, but it quickly was recognized that certain algorithms could be used to accelerate the run-time code on specific machines. Compilers became optimizers, which helped in the overall performance of the processors. The introduction of RISC architectures emphasized the role of language optimizers. These architectures reduced the richness of hardware instructions available for the programmer and shifted optimization to the programmer or compiler. Optimizing compilers permitted chip designers to reach near-peak performance from their processors.

Fourth-generation languages (4GLs) were introduced in the 1980s as simpler ways to access compute power. Fourth-generation languages couple information engineering with relational databases to minimize programming. Many of these languages are provided in conjunction with database support. 4GL raises the interface to the level where nonprogrammers can create code without recourse to traditional compiler technology.

"Nonlanguage languages" have emerged from PC implementations. It is possible to use simple functions within the PCs and create meaningful programs. Spreadsheets, such as Lotus 1-2-3 and Microsoft Excel, can represent programs to end users, and, given the rich set of functions, macros, and programmable facilities in packages such as these, spreadsheets represent another way by which application development can be done. The same is true for a package such as Lotus Notes, which can provide the foundation for groupware applications (see Section 10.4). These environments enable many end users to create their own task structures tailored to their specific needs, avoiding the complexities of typical software development.

Languages developed their own devotees arguing for the appropriateness of one language over another. Only a few languages received broad acceptance in any wave of computing. Efforts to define a universal language for both the scientific and business communities have generally failed. Some languages, such as C, can be adopted by combined communities.

10.3 CASE TOOLS

Engineers were the first to use the power of the computer to simplify the design, development, and testing of complex components with their *computer-aided design and engineering* (CAD/CAE) tools. These tools have provided engineering with significant leverage in product life cycles, which require careful design and testing. Automated tools provide functions that guide the engineer through the different steps in the life cycle and use the power of the computer to verify that each step is performed correctly. These tools have accelerated hardware design and perfected the quality of the end products.

CASE (Computer Aided Software Engineering) is a set of tools, which provides integrated approaches for building software. Combined with improved methodologies, these tools are replacing haphazard techniques for developing programs. CASE tools can be mapped to the open systems life cycle, as seen in Figure 10.1. The traditional cascading cycle can be divided into uppercase and lowercase segments. As can be seen from the diagram, the process of integration and operational support has typically fallen outside the traditional CASE definition.

Uppercase tools provide a high-level approach to business problems and can be used by planners or end users. Lowercase addresses the problem of making the application work with specific processors. Uppercase is based on object tools, which help the uninitiated learn more about obtaining results from the system. Lowercase requires a more in-depth approach to the system. Uppercase tools enable end users to become developers of complex code through requirement tools that cascade directly into final production code. These tools enable the user to define data and application structures that can be accessed on computers. Lowercase tools provide the accuracy required for high-performance and functional implementations. These tools permit accurate tuning in a system that is closely coupled to the that environment.

Figure 10.2 illustrates the major elements included in CASE as well as expansions of the basic tools. We begin at the top of the chart with the description of uppercase, or the front end, which is the design tools. Middlecase relates to languages used to create the output. Included in this category are 4GL and other products that can be used to create and build the software. Lowercase identifies coding and debugging tools as major components. An additional consideration included under the package of CASE is

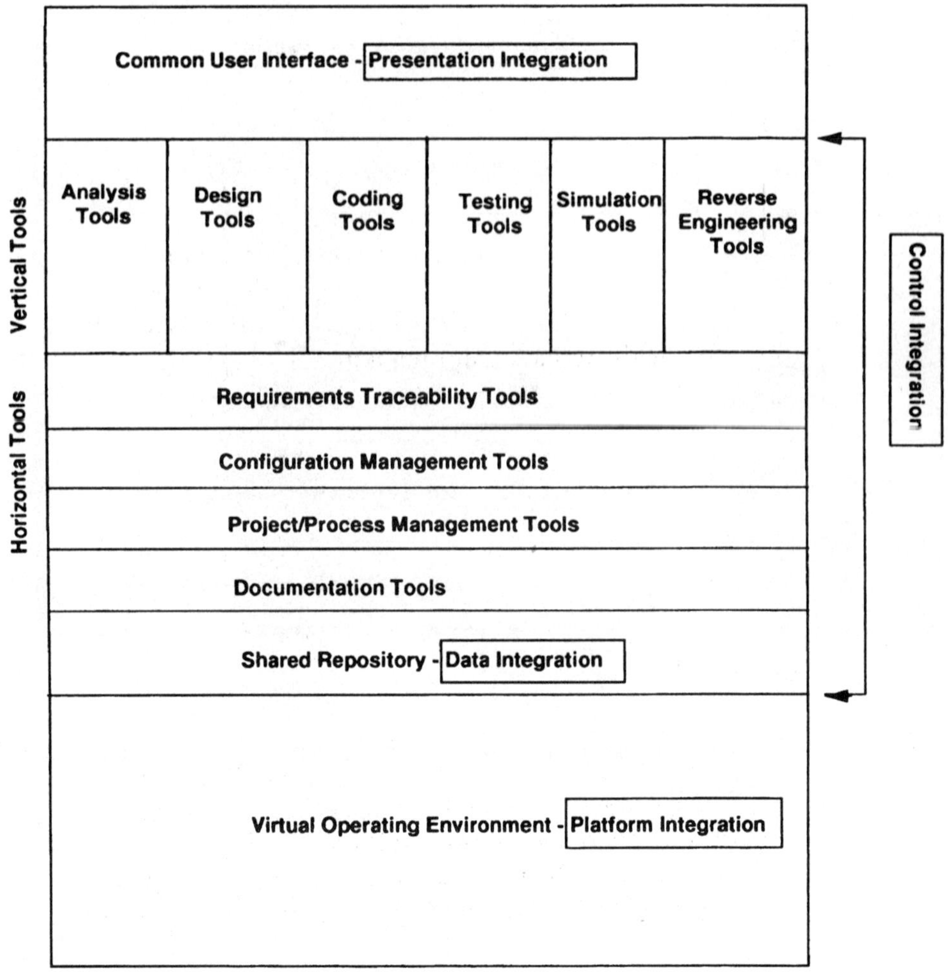

Figure 10.1 Mapping CASE tools to the open systems life cycle

reverse engineering, which permits the reconstruction of missing pieces. The CASE framework supplies the underpinnings of the set of CASE packages and also provides commonalty to the integrated package. Finally, CASE management enables the department to track the different portions of the completed code.

The increasing use of relational databases provides a vehicle to move design elements from one stage of the development process to the next.

Uppercase or Front End	**Analysis and Design Processes**
Middle	**4GL and Prototyping**
Lowercase or Back End	**Code Creation, Compilers, Debuggers**
Reverse Engineering	**Fixing and Modifying Legacy Code Preparing for Migration/Transition**
CASE Framework	**Integration Support Environments**
CASE Management	**Tools for Tracking Development Process**

Figure 10.2 Major elements of CASE

Unlike mechanical engineering, which requires synchronization between 2-D and 3-D renderings of the design, software design can be transmitted in 2-D form, which can be dynamically adjusted as the process continues. Each program will communicate with the open system through the relational database. Thus, a simple engineering application can be created on a relational database and can depend on a report writer to be defined with access to the same data.

A number of CASE tools provided by open systems vendors extend support to the open environments. A good example is Hewlett-Packard's SoftBench, an open CASE solution through which tools from multiple vendors can work with one another (Simon, 1993).

Programming often appears as the cobbler's child in relation to electrical engineering. The rich capability of automation possible for the engineer has not yet been reached in programming. Although existing CASE tools facilitate greater productivity, they miss the capability to provide connections between different operational processors. The addition of new features will continue to make these tools more useful to developing open systems solutions. Eventually, it is hoped that CASE tools will provide functions to match engineering with automated testing, which will result in better quality and higher productivity.

Many CASE tools have been built for central computers, but few have yet been produced that adequately reflect the needs of open distributed systems. The analogy to engineering is still good. Central processing design requires a different set of tools for the engineers than the production of large-scale integrated circuits. Open systems design requires design tools that factor connectivity and distributed function into the design. Test tools must simulate multiple processors resident in different nodes. A challenge exists to produce these tools during the next decade. The next few sections will consider some important applications that contribute to the acceptance of open systems in different companies.

10.4 CREATING GROUPWARE APPLICATIONS

Traditionally, central processing supported groups of workers though a hierarchy based in the mainframe computer. With increased desktop power and added function on servers, traditional reliance on an information hierarchy has changed. Work-flow automation and management products enhance the virtual workgroups. Individuals find themselves interacting with many groups and logically becoming parts of different groups. Figure 10.3 shows a number of workgroups in which individuals at the Sun workstation participate.

As we examine the figure, we discover the individual is connected to professional groups within the company and other groups outside the company. Individuals are members of many real and virtual groups. The personal network includes combinations of different protocols and operating systems. To function within the groups, there is a need to map across the different protocol connections. Groups now interact using software residing on individual desktop computers and shared across many sites.

Research has focused on an understanding of the interaction between workers participating in groups. Interesting corporate-sponsored research has been launched at The Institute for the Future (IFTF) in Menlo Park, California (Johansen, 1988). Examination of the Institute's work will help in understanding the interaction between scattered professionals working jointly on projects from different processors. Group working environments

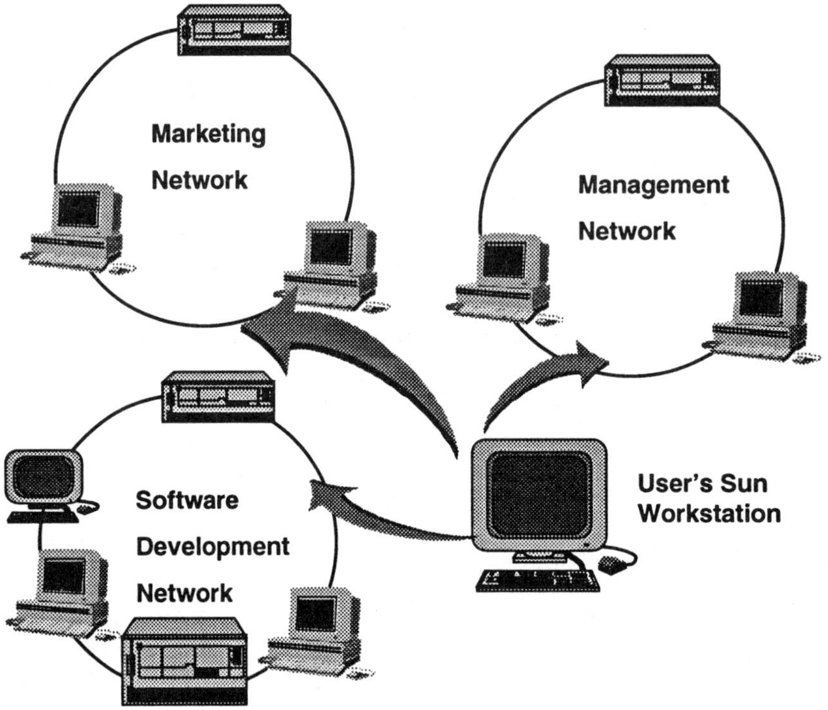

Figure 10.3 Sun workstation workgroups

differ by company, but group members often work in different locations and often different hours of the day.

Software is being developed to provide for anywhere computing in the network. More importantly, tools that provide a common base with identical user interfaces are now available. Group members will communicate using desktop and portable clients and have the work correlated in group servers.

High-technology meeting rooms built around client/server models are being tested by universities and private research groups. The University of Arizona, EDS, IBM, and ICL have experimented with technology rooms designed to facilitate meetings. Electronic blackboards replace the traditional whiteboards and provide ongoing minutes of meeting results. Different hardware was used by the groups, but all the hardware has emphasized capturing the dynamic interaction between groups involved in thought work as it occurs. When the participants leave the meeting room, they can leave with copies of the completed documents of the meeting. It is clear that network computing can facilitate teleconferencing from any location using the open systems designs.

Although only a few products are available, increasing attention to the subject has provided an incentive for further product activity. Five categories of groupware applications have emerged. The first is the electronics and communications programs, which provide the conferencing backbone for local or remote connections with other members of the group. The second is scheduling programs, which facilitate synchronization of key schedule points for members of working groups. Third is work-flow management, which facilitates data sharing between group members. Fourth is data sharing, which permits members to interact and use the real-time data on the network. The most popular is the data sharing that covers the creation of joint documents or joint designs using network connections as a tool to facilitate the application. The fifth category of groupware is electronic collaboration. Examples of collaborative work are numerous. Collaboration occurs locally or across a wider network span, which assumes a database access for all members of the group. Local brainstorming can be augmented by electronic brainstorming, which encourages the formation of new ideas across the network. Electronic brainstorming facilitates sharing of ideas across the network. A dynamic conjecture and refutation cycle can be created using electronic collaboration tools.

The creation of documents was facilitated by the introduction of the typewriter. Yet, modifying the textual output typewriter remained difficult until the word processing unit was introduced. Word processing provided end users with the ability to modify and change documents rapidly. Group word processing extends the capability by facilitating the building of a document by an entire group of developers.

10.5 VISUAL APPLICATION DEVELOPMENT

Pictures are worth more in understanding complex problems. Network computing has provided a natural platform to support visualization across a broad range of problems. *Visualization* is the ability to turn data information into pictures that aid in understanding complex numerical information. Initially introduced as scientific visualization to provide engineers and scientists a three-dimensional perspective of complex information, the work has extended beyond the initial concept and has been adopted for complex engineering equations. Scientific visualization was begun by the National Science Foundation in 1987 but has experienced rapid growth, as a richer set of programs was introduced to support the various implementations.

This work has expanded beyond the engineering and scientific arenas to financial visualization in commercial applications. Complex financial problems could be modeled in a visualization world just as easily as oil seismic information. Financial visualization benefits from examining different parameters in three dimensions and in color. Advanced visualization projects are using animation to emphasize specific functions.

Since visualization applications can require complex computing, they are often associated with powerful compute servers, such as supercomputers or multiple parallel processors. The supercomputer handles the compute-intensive applications while the powered workstations portray the 3-D images that result from the model. In larger commercial applications, data mining is employed to delineate useful data from terabytes of state data. Smaller computers with less power have been used for some visualization applications, but powerful and low-cost parallel computers are becoming important for many visualization applications.

A visualization center can be a natural adjunct to a supercomputer center. A good example is the visualization center established on the UCSD campus as an adjunct to the supercomputer center in San Diego, California. Access to the supercomputer is achieved using standard protocols, but large data pipes permit the rapid transmission of information between the supercomputer and the visualization center. A parallel processor is applied to ensure the easy movement of this information across the workstations.

The technical challenge for visualization is to convert data from non-graphical form to a form that can make it usable in graphical systems. Often, the first stage of a visualization application is to search through large amounts of data and determine the correct data to be used in the final product. Some companies have used neural algorithms to provide the basis for this search.

Once the correct data are defined, it is put in a form that can be shown on powerful 3-D workstations. Although more powerful PCs with graphics acceleration boards have performed visualization support, it is preferable to have workstations that have sufficient capability to support imaging. Large screens (1,024 × 1,024 pixels) are assumed with a capability of processing at least 30 repaints per second. Visualization stations will process large amounts of data, which requires fast access to large resident memory and storage devices. It is not unusual to find workstations with multiple megabytes of memory. They must be able to transmit pixels to screens at very high performance levels. Early CAD designers learned about the need to have sufficient floating-point power to exercise the correct figures on the screens. Graphics imaging is also another important element of a well-designed visualization workstation.

Large visualization centers, such as those found in conjunction with large supercomputer centers, only introduce the reader to the potentials of modern computing. A number of groups have placed visualization applications in direct use. A good example is the Harvard School of Medicine, which uses Stardent's *Advanced Visualization System* (AVS) to examine brain tumors. AVS enables the medical school to predict and control the radiation used in treating tumors, thus reducing some of the potential exposure.

10.6 MULTIMEDIA APPLICATIONS

Multimedia is an application area that benefits from the increasing power on open systems. It defines an application area of the human visual systems and enhanced media. Applications support multiple-presentation media representations, including audio, video, text, graphics, and animation. Each of the media is combined to improve the connections between humans and the computers. Ideas are expressed using the intertwined media, providing additional access to individuals. Although multimedia represents a tool for graphics artists, it also enhances the media capabilities of occasional users.

Multimedia begins with a capture program, which translates electronic media into forms that can be used by digital application programs. Input devices, which include scanners, TV cameras, and microphones, provide information to the digital computers. Once the data are entered in the computer, a digitizer program converts the information so that an authoring process can handle the data. A story program will define the boundaries of multimedia applications. Authoring provides for editing the complex media and permits the design of a well-structured presentation. Sounds and images can be refined using the authoring capability. Drawings are refined through the manipulation of the various forms in the complex system.

Advanced audio and video devices will often require specialists to provide support for quality devices. Audio translates typical analog input into a digital form so it can be used in computing. For instance, the electronic music industry has defined the *Musical Instrument Digital Interface* (MIDI), which facilitates the compression of musical data (Moore, 1990). The output devices translate digital information into audio form for reproduction on traditional audio devices.

The final stage of the multimedia application is the presentation. Presentation routines combine different output media into a total production. Video and complex graphics are mixed to support animation across the network. Audio annotation provides the ability to add special instructions to the completed product.

10.7 ELECTRONIC MAIL

Humanity's dream to instantaneously reach others at anytime from anyplace for the lowest cost seems closer to reality. Many tools remain too complex for most people, but simplicity is coming with processing power. Many have predicted the demise of paper documents for the past 10 years, but the transmission of paper has actually grown. However, the hope remains, and many have reached a capability with electronic mail to share information through paperless media.

Electronic message delivery systems were first introduced in the 1960s, using terminal systems based on mainframe computers. By the 1970s, DARPA had initiated a primitive electronic mail system to connect research laboratories. Simple messages were defined and each user had an electronic mailbox, which held information until the user was ready to receive it.

By 1978, UNIX systems were offering a heterogeneous e-mail system, which had its own protocols between the different systems. The *UNIX to UNIX CoPy* (UUCP) was introduced to facilitate connections and let the different systems define techniques for connecting through multiple processors. Simple networking addresses were developed that worked well across multiple processors.

Electronic mail originally handled brief messages but was expanded to handle larger documents. Using e-mail, scientists could circulate papers and obtain professional comments. More recent expansion has grown to support compound documents with audio, video, and image information included. Companies use e-mail to connect engineers with manufacturing plants but also have expanded its use to include marketing and sales users or any employee. A new generation of companies has begun to rely on e-mail as the primary communications medium between all levels of employees. Mail systems have become simpler as user interfaces have improved, and broader ranges of end users can access the mail system.

Early PC users achieved simple connections that were expanded by LANs. This is the first stage in worldwide communications links, which can connect desktop computers with others across the world. Some companies have the capability to interconnect their computers and achieve desired results through e-mail. Others are still struggling with simple peer-to-peer connections. Mail systems must be rapid and secure with an assurance that the message will arrive at the targeted destination. Network users live in a world impatient with the slow delivery systems found in traditional mail systems. Competitive variations provide almost instant response to the system needs. With e-mail, the user can attain response to simple requests within an hour, and complex design variations can be answered in slightly longer time periods.

The ideal e-mail is a single corporate system, but with many mail systems, it is useful to have a single client resident on the user's desktop that communicates with any required system. The user should be able to transmit information in any logical organization within an enterprise or communicate to external peers using the same workstation. E-mail should reflect the simplicity of the interfaces found on modern desktop clients (Huffman, 1987). In keeping with the Macintosh simplicity, AppleTalk provides a straightforward approach to mail. Yet, when Macintoshes are connected to other mail systems, they assume the complexity of the mail system.

Modern e-mail requires the capability to send compound data containing combinations of text, image, video, and voice information. Recent standards activity has defined compound document interfaces, which facilitate the sending, transmission, and reception of such data. E-mail moves in an instant to different addresses on global networks, driven in part by technology and in part by the acceptance of universal protocols of conversing. Chains of processors and communications links bring together users on diverse local area networks. Using protocols and logical envelopes, the chain of information moves across different processors that will pick off local information and translate it into forms readable on the local level. The power of the processors eliminates overt actions on the part of the user, who can access remote links or local electronic mailboxes to obtain the latest information.

At each level in the communications network, specific hardware provides either specialized functions, such as switching, or generalized program execution, such as that found in servers. Power processors are used to perform switching routines in the complex system known as the network. Once-simple mail systems, which supported only data, are now being expanded to handle compound data types in transmission. The introduction of requirements for consolidated efforts of groups has also provided an impetus for interaction between workers in remote sites. Many companies have developed partnerships with other companies that are suppliers or help sell specific products. These companies are also connected electronically. The network represents a significant power point, which is being exploited in open systems design.

Companies will find a wealth of alternatives for e-mail. Both private and public offerings are available, which provide sufficient interaction to make them interesting in an open systems environment. Private mail systems have been developed around office systems provided by computer vendors. Both DEC (All in One) and IBM (OfficeVision) have offerings that have been adopted by end users.

E-mail standards have emerged from the work of CCITT. Message handling across different networks has been defined in the X.400 standard approved in 1984 (Schuett et al., 1987). Much of the groundwork for using e-mail is defined in X.400, which defines protocols for many embedded envelopes to pass information across the network. The actual creation of the different pieces is handled by software that begins by defining a logical envelope around the transmitted message.

Most e-mail systems define simple protocols, which are similar to envelopes containing routing information between the sender and receiver. Message transfer agents (MTA) create the logical envelopes to simplify the tasks of shipping the mail through multiple protocols attached to the network. Mail is received in a mailbox that is an electronic equivalent to its physical counterpart. Transmission is through the network systems, which can carry the electronic letter to the receiver's desk in less time than it takes to walk to the office mailroom.

Gateways connect different mail systems and provide the necessary conversion routines to facilitate the connections. One of the more common e-mail networks is IBM's, based on PROFS and SNADS. This network is widely used in mainframe environments having a large nontechnical community. The basic naming protocol uses eight characters for the user's name and another eight for the node address. X.400 uses a complex, open-ended naming convention. Typically, four to six elements are found in the user's portion of the name, and there is no theoretical maximum. A number of algorithmic and directory-based mapping programs have been applied to the problem of SNA addresses mapped to X.400. Although UNIX e-mail has been implemented on X.400 systems, it does not require its use.

A number of the available mail systems are cumbersome to use. Mail depends on its ability to entice and keep users from adopting other techniques. Difficult-to-use mail systems should be replaced before they defeat their purpose. E-mail is an important application combining computers and communications. It is the first step in achieving close group interactions. Companies that have adopted the mail system will not surrender its use. Since mail uses many different hardware and software supports, it represents a microcosm of the total network. E-mail is a first step into network computing and has proven valuable in achieving close cooperation between companies.

10.8 CONSIDERATIONS

Applications will come from two sources. The first source is external packages, which can be purchased and installed throughout the organization. The second source is development within the company. Creating applications for open distributed systems will require different talents from those that are usually employed to create mainframe applications.

Companies wishing to downsize programs to run on workstations or servers have benefited from tools that permit the shift. Increasingly, there is a recognized merit level in achieving a level of rightsizing for different applications. Certainly, one of the advantages is the partitioning of the application functions to reach the highest level of response time.

Downsizing is often equated with reductions in staff. Although this possibility can arise from program downsizing, the usual result is freeing resources to develop additional applications. Faster turnaround in application code has permitted developers to reduce large backlog of programming. Debate will continue as to whether specific applications should be located on the client or the server. A good rule of thumb is to determine whether the application is used by many users or only by small sets of users.

Development tools have shifted from the simple need for programming languages to tools that aid the design process and assist in the placement of applications across the distributed network. Complexity in distributed systems has resulted in a need for more refined tools that can assist the complete management process.

10.9 REFERENCES

Aron, J. D. *The Program Development Process: The Individual Programmer* (Systems Programming Series). Reading, MA: Addison-Wesley, 1974, p. 11.

Huffman, A. J. "E-Mail—The Glue to Office Automation." *IEEE Network*, October 1987.

Johansen, Robert, with contributions by Jeff Charles, Robert Mittman, and Paul Saffo. *Groupware: Computer Support for Business Teams.* New York: The Free Press, 1988.

Kernighan, B. W., and D. M. Ritchie. *The C Programming Language.* Englewood Cliffs, NJ: Prentice Hall, 1978.

Moore, Daniel J. "Multimedia Presentation Development Using Audio Visual Connection." *IBM Systems Journal*, vol. 29, no. 4, 1990, pp. 494–508.

Pugh, Emerson W., Lyle R. Johnson, and John H. Palmer. *IBM's 360 and Early 370 Systems.* Cambridge, MA: MIT Press, 1991.

Schuett, Thomas E., James B. Stanton III, and William F. Racke. "Message-Handling Based on the CCITT X.400 Recommendations." *IBM Systems Journal*, vol. 28, no. 3, 1987.

Simon, Alan. *The Integrated CASE Tools Handbook.* New York: Van Nostrand Reinhold/Intertext, 1993.

11

Interoperability

System managers find themselves challenged in leading departments that have implemented localized automation solutions. These departments have usually exceeded expectations for departmental productivity, but often the solutions cannot easily be explained to other departments. Often called "islands of automation," the achievements of these departments represent a terrific local accomplishment as well as company challenge. The challenge is to connect these leading systems to the existing company structure and to other leading systems in the company. The first step is to connect different pieces so that information can flow between different departments.

Two separate terms are used to indicate the connection between different systems. Integration is the process that melds computer solutions from multiple architectures and creates an apparent single-system interface. Integration usually refers to the physical and programming connection between systems and usually represents a tight binding between the integrated system. It affects the implementation of applications within the business and the acceptance of new technology in a business. Integration is driven by organizational culture as well as technology. Each company tailors a process that combines the power of technology with the needs of the organization within the management structure of the company.

The term "seamless integration" describes the process of adding technically advanced solutions to existing business environments without disrupting the existing operations. This transparent integration means new processes can be added to an enterprise while continuing normal operations. This assumes the design of the new processes and defines the affinity between the old and the new clearly enough to permit replacement of older routines by advancing technology. Unfortunately, it is easier to write about seamless integration than it is to actually accomplish it.

Interoperability is an exchange of useful information made possible by interconnections between different systems. Usually, the information exchange is between open systems solutions and existing networks. Interoperability is usually a looser term than integration and can be accomplished with less detail merging than integration. Figure 11.1 illustrates major interoperable technologies, which are driven by functions more complex than simply connecting computers together. The interoperable network will contain many different elements of enterprise computing. Mainframes, clusters of minicomputers, and even supercomputers may be included within the network. Interoperable networks will usually contain a heterogeneous network of different workstations connected using different protocols.

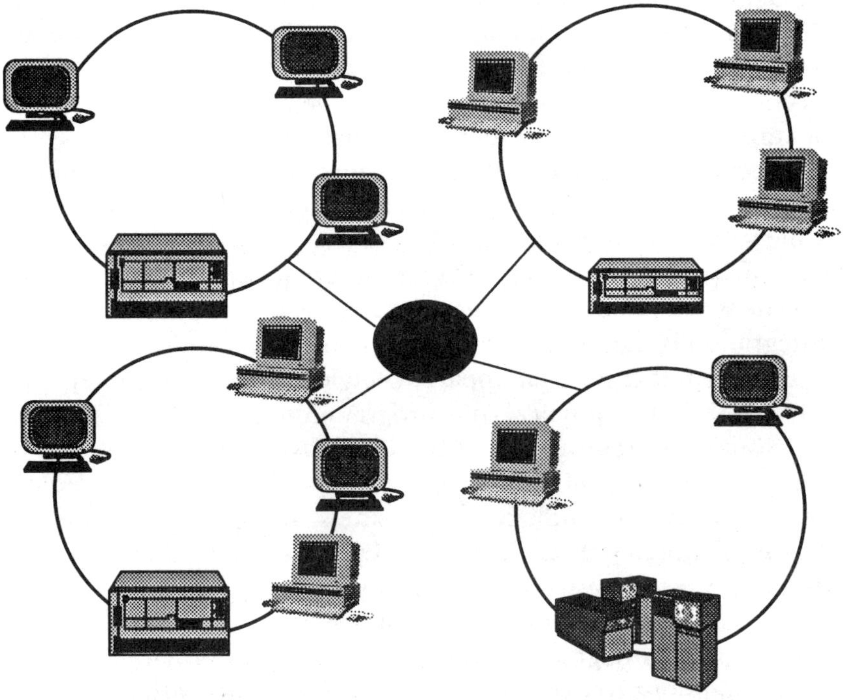

Figure 11.1 Major interoperable technologies

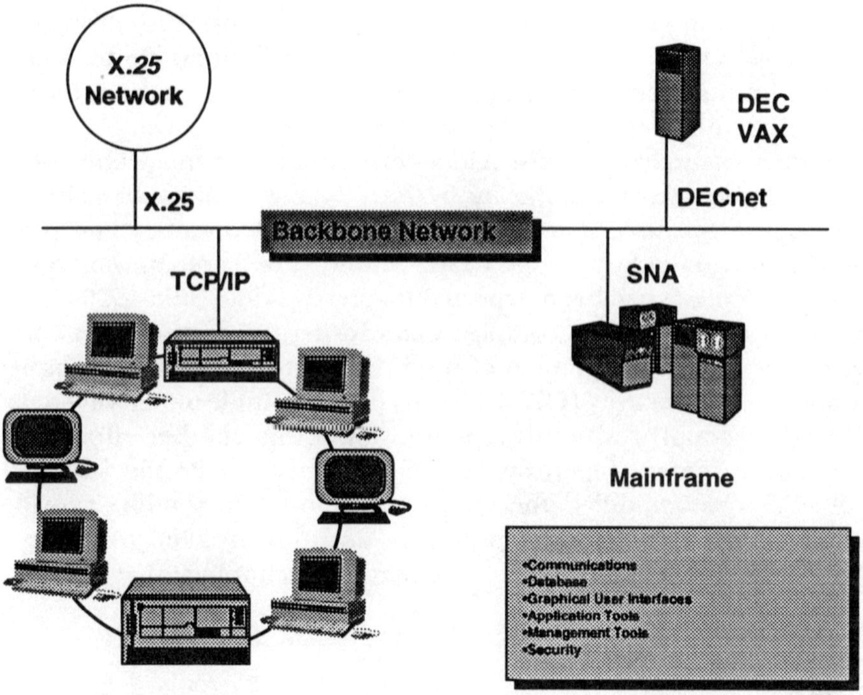

Figure 11.2 Technolgies to be resolved in the interoperable network

Figure 11.2 shows the major technologies that must be resolved in the interoperable network. Communications is assumed, but database and graphical user interface interconnections are also mandatory. The application development tools and management tools will be included in the complete interoperable network. Users can select a single vendor that would supply all the necessary technology at a reasonable cost, but competitive price and advanced functions have driven companies to many competitive and heterogeneous vendors. No single vendor can supply a complete range of alternatives or retain leadership in technology over time. Interoperability enables multiple vendors to be connected.

A good analogy is the telephone system, which provides a worldwide connection mechanism. Any person with a telephone can call another, and with cellular telephones it is no longer necessary to connect to a wiring system. Yet, once the link is made, there is another step, which is establishing an understanding with the person called. This is more complex, since it involves speaking the same language and then reaching an understanding of the ideas of the other person. Interoperability is similar to the telephone analogy. Connection can be made across computer systems recognizing the same protocols. Once connection is established, it is desirable to access information in the connected computer transparently. Once the information is acquired, the need is to interpret it correctly.

Open systems standards promise a long-term solution to the problem but have induced short-term complexity by introducing additional mapping alternatives. Interoperable systems must now map to proprietary interfaces among existing and newly developed applications, as well as to the emerging standards protocols. It had been expected that by this time (mid-1990s), this process would have been less complex than during the early days of open systems; however, the combination of newly emerging standards (example: Open Database Connectivity [ODBC] for access to multiple underlying database managers) coupled with missteps and slowdowns in other efforts (example: the Government Open Systems Interconnection Profile [GOSIP] protocol stack) has muddied the waters. Also, multiple vendors provide competing solutions to the same problems, and this installed technology must be modified to accommodate an emerging technology that provides

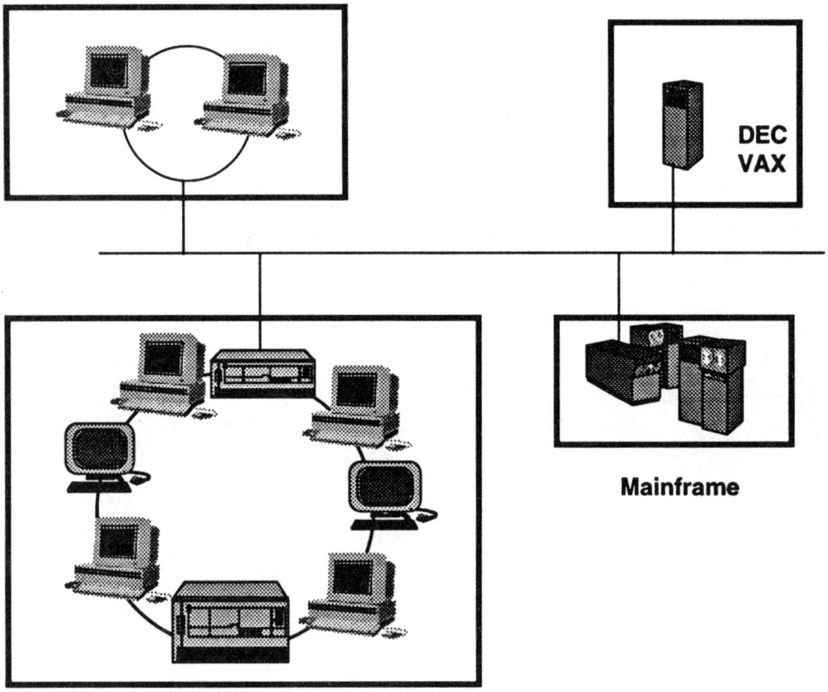

Figure 11.3 Data domains

competitive leverage. Bringing the pieces together involves definition of an architecture.

Complexity of data and the location and extent of data domains (Figure 11.3) will also affect the level of interaction between interoperable systems. Thus, it is easier to achieve interoperability with a text system than it is with compound data types. It is easier to interchange with a system that conforms to a limited number of protocols and has a limited domain as opposed to an open approach that accepts multiple protocols.

The definition of interoperability begins with the architecture that determines the framework for the system implementation. The architecture must be defined to permit early installation of pieces while permitting an ordered growth with the introduction of new technical solutions. The interoperable system must be successfully installed from the architecture. Finally, the system must reflect changes necessary for the changes found in daily operations. Let's examine interoperability from the architecture consideration first.

11.1 THE CHALLENGE

It is relatively easy to create software for distributed processors and call it an open system. It is far more difficult to create an interoperable system architecture that meets the needs of end users and provides a growth platform for the future. To create this type of system, a number of requirements must be met. It is useful to understand the immediate needs and vision of users. In speaking to end users, the author has compiled a list of requirements, which appear to reflect the needs of most using managers.

The first requirement expected is the *ease of installation.* Connections to existing systems should be done in a way that ensures their continual operation but also in a manner that makes it relatively easy for nonprofessionals to install the system. The concept of out of the box and operational within 15 minutes is a good guideline to request from vendors.

The second requirement calls for the system to be *easy to operate* once it is installed. Many central computer rooms have been shifted to a lights-out environment and have organized their operations to reduce operator interactions. MIS connection to central processors has grown simpler, but many users have perceived their interconnection with central processing to be more complex. Many users have selected PCs or workstation alternatives to simplify their daily operations and avoid the perceived bureaucracy of the

MIS group. Desktop computers were used to mask problems with the interaction to the mainframe by embedding many of the procedures directly.

As servers augmented the workstations and mainframes, operations again grew complex. Additional software and larger databases have created more complexity for the user, as data and software updates require handling. Active users in corporations must connect to central systems and to servers, while also maintaining the code on their individual desktops. Although variations exist, much of this operation begins to assume a complexity that the desktop was intended to relieve. The power exists within the processors to mask this complexity.

Even simple service tasks require an increasing knowledge of system operations and connection procedures. The users must remember different interfaces simply to perform their daily jobs. Although common interfaces enable users to move around the organization, the operational complexities still pose a problem for the average user. Further simplification of these interfaces can be found by locating the information in expert systems resident in the network. The task of operating the system can be greatly simplified with tailored screens and menus.

Many companies have operations abroad that can benefit from a well-designed interoperable network. The system should assume a capability that permits expansion of language fonts within the network. Complexities of languages such as Japanese and Chinese make open systems support problems more complex, but open systems also provide unique solution alternatives.

Workstations can improve individual performance more than traditional mainframes can. The increasing performance can lead to complexity problems, unless the additional power is allocated to ease the user interfaces. Problems of interactions with multiple vertical applications and complex data structures have made the user at the workstation the equivalent of early processor users. Tools designated for this purpose remain primitive by standards usually employed for mainframe processors, but there is hope in sight.

Simplification of user interaction with programs and data involves creation of tools that can use the power of the server to provide backup or file distribution on an automated basis. Equally important is the problem of massive amounts of data shifting between the server and the desktop computer. The desktop must be able to handle this powerful movement of information.

The third requirement is *ease of use* for inexperienced end users. Many users of open systems have never completed education above high school and must perform complex tasks on the system. As the labor pool continues to shift, companies will continually encounter a situation that increasingly exposes untrained individuals to the complexities of open systems. Simplification in the architecture will aid them in understanding their tasks and performing them well. Actions taken by end users must become simple and reversible. Feedback loops permit the system to perform in increasingly intelligent fashion, but most of the feedback should be handled directly by the computer. Nothing can be more frustrating than beginning an action on a display screen and not receiving any positive reaction that the program has been initiated.

Placing end user-sensitive designers in the design team for open applications helps make final products sensitive to the needs of the users. Usability begins with the design process and continues through the development and testing process. In production situations, a few extra dollars spent designing for the inexperienced user will have significant payback. Limiting access to complete intelligence also eliminates the possibility that users will create some system-threatening code. Many interactive systems have selected X terminals to avoid such occurrences.

Although there is wide use of packaged applications, there is also a demand for specially designed programs that reflect the needs of the business. Internally developed or contracted applications must reflect the same or better quality as those found on the open market. Interface consistency is an initial step in reaching ease of use. In an open environment, fixes must be applied in an operational environment. In this environment, it is expected that fixes will be applied with a minimum of disruption to the running operation. Suppose you have an open systems network with thousands of clients who need to have their changes synchronized. Simple calculation will demonstrate that serial update can take an excessive amount of time and may actually disrupt production operations.

The fourth consideration for interoperability is *easy changability* or modification of the system. A valid question will address the probability of failure of the hardware and software elements in the system. The hardware—especially the processor chips—is very reliable, but there can be significant failures in the software components. Automated systems must define distribution techniques that verify the levels in the different systems, determine error points, and provide access to updated system facilities. Ease of correction becomes a significant factor as the size of the system continues to grow.

An ideal condition for an open systems configuration is end users who are unaware of the changes and modifications. Modifications should be transparent to the end user. Troubleshooting is performed remotely with the system performing the necessary updates. Some redundant systems place orders directly for express messengers to deliver parts for an update. You can imagine the surprise of the people involved in the process when a messenger arrives with a special package that can simply be plugged into a slot with a blinking red light. Repair in this system is simple enough for most users to effect the change and keep the system running.

An open system must use the power of the system to reduce the learning cycle. Many tasks require long learning cycles to enable users to connect to the different databases and application programs necessary to complete a task. Learning can be reduced by including information in the system or removing the need for the end user to be involved in certain decisions. Measures of success are reduced training periods and increased productivity for quality results.

The modern open system can serve as a training vehicle for the users connected to it. Desktop computers can receive video information directly from the servers. The end user has access to a complete body of system information that will be continually updated. The user can be on a production line and benefit from direct interaction with engineers, who send the assembler precise video instructions about the techniques used to create a specific part or parts. Beyond the production floor, interactive video on clients can be used by users in the financial community to access training information in periods when telephone systems are idle.

Open systems learning can be passive or active. Using a system until a familiarity grows is a way to achieve passive learning. The end user eventually learns the nuances of the commands and menu structure and eventually becomes proficient with the system. Sufficient prompts embedded in the application code will assist users in passive learning (Carroll and Mack, 1984). GUI applications are an ideal example of a passive learning system that requires a minimum of interaction with training systems. Applications with GUI interfaces benefit from access to common menus, icons, and even data structures. It is simple for even novice users to access applications on the system without ever using the manuals.

Many active education programs benefit from the usability features found in modern desktop computers. Typically, active education programs for open systems follow four phases of activity. Although it is assumed the entire organization will need education, the first phase begins with designers, who must make the system perform well. An examination of the four phases will demonstrate the directions of companies that have made the transition.

The fifth consideration listed by end-user managers is *sufficient function* to improve the overall flow of the jobs within operations. The users are looking for growth capability that meets the other four requirements. Functional extensibility assures a smooth transition into additional functions with the ability to remain competitive and responsive to the needs of the business.

11.2 BUILDING THE KNOWLEDGE BASE

Many companies begin with little knowledge of open systems, design, or even the basic building blocks found in the system. A four-phase program helps introduce the key people in the company to open systems.

Phase one is an introductory set of courses that provides a basis for explaining the building blocks of open systems. It is assumed that many people in the company have already been introduced to the PC. As the introduction proceeds, questions of interconnection, data flow, operating systems, and unique features of open systems will be covered. Standards are important, since they provide the glue for many open systems configurations. The intent of phase one is to introduce the company to the terms and equipment used in building open systems. Since there are many doubters, accelerated education will define the relative benefits of different choices and change some minds.

Phase two introduces the concept of new tools to design and develop the system. This phase begins with the potential languages and extends into new paradigms of creating applications in distributed systems. An understanding of the tools will serve as a first step in introducing techniques to perfect existing code and make it better. Since the network is the system, new design challenges will exist in defining a network across multiple systems with different interfaces. Variant data structures are also handled in this stage of the training process.

Phase three will introduce new applications to end users. This phase will originate within the company and benefit from experience with the previous two phases. The end user will learn the interaction with new computing paradigms and, more importantly, the way business cycles change based on the development of new techniques of system design. This phase will also address questions of installation, operation, and repair, as the systems are beginning to be installed into active networks. In many ways, this level of education is an end product of the development cycle. During the code development, course designers will outline the necessary ingredients of a well-structured course in operations. Phase three will consider open systems as a productivity tool. System shortcuts will change but continue to exist in an open systems environment. The feedback mechanism will permit these changes, as the open design becomes a comfortable tool for the company.

As mentioned above, it is assumed that open systems will continue to change and grow. This will reflect the requirements of the business and the ever-changing technology. *Phase four* provides developers and managers with the necessary tools to adjust to change. Although this phase examines some features, it is important to pass along the information about change points in the system. Feedback is intended to improve the system and to make the process a living and changing environment.

The education process is a necessary step in reaching full interoperability. Complexity can be reduced by careful design, but there is little likelihood the reduction will be total. Education helps in understanding the remaining levels of complexity in the system and enables both the developers and the end users to cope with the changes.

11.3 THE ARCHITECTURE

Frank Lloyd Wright introduced a school of architecture emphasizing open systems while creating enduring buildings. A visit to Wright's center at Taliesin West in Scottsdale, Arizona, serves as an inspiration to the open systems' architect. Wright believed architecture emanated from the ground and represented a natural integration into the surrounding environment. He believed in building using basic materials, while creating an open structure that complemented and blended with the surrounding environment and also met the user's requirements (Pfeiffer and Nordland, 1988).

The open systems architect can learn from Wright's design principles. The design of an open system should complement the business but also present it with an enduring open structure that serves as an inspiration. The architecture begins with basic building materials: the hardware, software, and standards that are molded into an open structure to blend with the surrounding system and meet the user's needs.

In computing history, we find early system architects of such systems as the IBM System/360 and the Digital's VAX systems preoccupied with the question of identifying the location for the system control point as well as the time frame for binding resources to program execution. In open systems, which depend on distributed capability, separate control points reside at the network nodes—each with an autonomy that provides personal productivity control. The distributed system control point is a virtual point contained within the system architecture and is the definition point for control and binding. Conformity to enterprise standards represents the actual control point for distributed processing. Within the framework of standards, individual nodes retain their local autonomy, while the enterprise exercises overall network control.

The processing and memory growth introduce an indeterminism that places additional burdens on the system architect. It is no longer possible to assume there is a simple connection that will provide communications between the different nodes of the system. Open systems require well-structured designs, which depend on the skills of trained professionals in system architecture. Examination of distributed systems will find them constantly changing and perhaps creating a replacement system. Study of selective systems can show us a way to consider the workings of distributed systems (Pagels, 1989).

Some design problems can be answered by acceptance of standards that provide frameworks for installing open solutions from alternative companies. Many standards have been completed and now form the base for processing paradigms that are different from those many information managers are accustomed to. The UNIX operating system has become the base for open solutions, as companies adopted it as a base for software development. UNIX has become as popular on Wall Street as it has been in engineering laboratories. Even IBM, Digital Equipment Corporation, and nearly every other remaining mainframe and minicomputer vendor have adapted UNIX to their major workstation and server offerings and enhanced the legitimacy of the system. Although it is true that UNIX is not a required element for open systems solutions, it does represent the broadest accepted base.

Adopting a standard architecture facilitates systemwide access to distributed services. Advances in designs have permitted access to multiple processing levels within the network. As the architecture progresses, it is important to understand that users will want to access information at different nodes in a transparent fashion. A system must be created that reflects capabilities at different nodes.

A number of considerations are important in designing an interoperable system architecture. Simple guidelines that determine selection criteria will aid the company in selecting different network alternatives and vendors to assist in the implementations. Combinations of hardware, software, and documentation will affect the actual implementation of interoperability.

Six major components are required to complete an interoperable open architecture. Applications are at the heart of a well-executed business system. Many system functions are needed to support a viable distributed application environment. Robust communications and secure databases provide the basis to create a system capable of supporting ongoing operations. Since distributed processing represents a unique application environment, tools must be acquired that facilitate effective use of graphics presentation services. Distributed processing increases the complexity of managing multiple active nodes and creates a need for modern management tools. User interfaces in a distributed system require that functions across the system be shared commonly on different systems. The final step is to create a system that appears as a single unit. The architecture must reflect commonness of design.

The first component in an interoperable system is communications, which is the basis for other support services. Communications connects different parts of the open system in a manner that ensures transparency between users of long-distance and local nodes. Adoption of communications standards facilitates the move to interoperability. The adoption of a standard is very important. The best standard would be an industry standard to assure the capability of attaching multiple vendors. The alternative is to adopt a widely used vendor standard.

Questions concerning the correct location of protocol converters should be raised at this point in the design process. Should the conversion occur at each PC or workstation, or should servers be focal points for conversion? We have examined in detail specific parts of the communications question, but we should investigate a process that resolves the combinations of different communications protocols.

Interoperability is a level above the simple connection or integration of systems. The second component for system interoperability is data access across different multiple network nodes. Heterogeneous database connections require a method that connects to different data types with the necessary data and protocol conversions. Different database protocols are used to access and update data from different storage systems, which must be transparently connected in interoperable systems. Many server database vendors have introduced products that provide an automatic connection between other database facilities in the network. Interoperability assumes these connections function well to ensure high-level connection.

The complexity of distributed open systems raises significant questions about techniques to develop application interoperability. Simple tools used for mainframe computing must be replaced with development tools that can span the different computers found in the system. Many development tools have been created for individual environments, but few that permit the creation of truly networked applications have been built. Such tools will provide functioning partitioned applications across different system components. Separate tools will initially provide the capability to produce single-node applications as well. The third element is, therefore, network tools that provide transparency across multiple applications.

The fourth architectural element is those management tools that provide information about the network components. Individual nodes within an interoperable network are rich in capability and susceptible to significant problems. Managing an interoperable open network requires balancing status information collected at individual nodes with systemwide analysis tools. A great deal of information was collected and synergized in central systems that controlled all the elements in the network. When the system spans multiple processors, problems can be spread to remote nodes. Management tools must recognize the capability of individual nodes while providing central coalescing of the open node data.

The fifth element of the architecture is a common user interface that permits easy access to facilities found across the interoperable network. Since some clients may support only character screens and others support full business or scientific graphics, common definitions may be more difficult. Eventually, all interfaces will adopt graphics interfaces that will greatly extend the end-user capability. Both application development packages and industry standards have advanced to the point where they can be adopted by using system architects. Although there are multiple user interfaces (such as Motif and Microsoft Windows) that can be used, there is a good deal of commonalty between the different alternatives in the GUI space (in general, more commonality than there had been on older terminal-based command interfaces to applications and systems).

The sixth element of interoperability is the traditional system functions, which appear to act as a single entity. Included in these global system items are elements such as reliability, maintainability, availability, and security. These system elements represent the biggest challenge to the system architect. Each system element depends on cooperation of the computing nodes attached to the system. Since powerful processors reside at each node with their own design for these system elements, the collection of these elements is often inadequate for completely reliable interoperable open systems. Each element of the system must be designed to meet the needs for reliability, availability, and maintainability. Finally, network security must reflect the sum of capability in individual nodes. All these elements must be defined in the completed architecture.

These six elements are combined in a comprehensive architecture that will work well for the different users in the systems. Desire for seamless integration drives users to expect a constant and steady state of change based on robust designs. In the era of central processing, the architect for the system was a vendor architect that could supply the solution using one brand of hardware and software. Since open solutions are heterogeneous, the architecture shifts to the using companies or their agents.

If you visit any of the great buildings designed by Frank Lloyd Wright or his students, you will be impressed by an open architecture that blends into the natural surroundings. These buildings meet the needs of the users with lovely rooms and startling views, which build on the strengths of the surroundings. An open computer architecture blends into the natural surroundings of the company and provides powerful business tools for the future.

11.4 INSTALLATION

Once the architecture is completed and the initial development is underway, the team must consider the installation process. New open systems are added to existing networks, demanding commonality between technology areas of the different parts. An understanding of the installation process aids later modification but must first be resolved for the complete system to function well.

Stage one, or the pilot phase, is the initial installation of open systems solutions. Since fitting into the network is an essential element of success, it is not sufficient for computers and communications equipment to arrive on the loading dock with a set of directions. Initial installments require a plan and a stepped process. Select a pilot application and begin with the limited scope a pilot delivers. After the system elements are running, the next step is to develop downsized applications.

Understanding the environment is pivotal for completion of the job. Building on old system roadmaps, it is important to understand special wiring or cooling requirements. Special hardware devices, such as performance monitors, may improve the process and ensure rapid access to the network. Installation processes should be reviewed with an understanding of the skills of the local team. It may be necessary to hire special employees who understand the open systems components.

Stage two moves the installation from the pilot to a limited production environment. Additional operational systems are added and brought into operation. Complex systems will often require the generation of central code, which corresponds to the connected elements of the system. Separate code generation may be necessary at each level to ensure connection. Most modern designs are built in a way that permits the addition of network nodes without bringing the total system down.

Stage three brings the limited production systems into full production. Additional users are added, often in remote locations. As the additional systems are added, sufficient control and management routines are included, which permit access to servicing and management information from remote sites.

Stage four shifts the limited production system into full production with a wider spectrum of users. Ongoing maintenance will be added without disrupting the continual flow of the system. The system design is built in a way that permits the continuous addition of new functions and features. The interoperable system becomes the new base for future growth. It is from this base that subsequent designs are built.

11.5 NETWORK MANAGEMENT

As discussed previously, the growth in the network causes new strain on the ability of management tools to keep pace with the developments at the workstations. Many companies moving to open systems find they are heavily committed to central management tools that keep track of the operations of the network. In an interoperable network, these tools must be modified to reflect the needs of open systems.

This, too, can be accomplished in a step process. Since workstations and servers possess significantly higher levels of intelligence than terminals, the system must be built to use this increased intelligence. Interconnected LANs can perform many of the tasks allocated to central network management routines. Previously, networks could be managed assuming each terminal had little intelligence. A few experts located in a central place could determine what problems were occurring in the specific nodes and exercise remedies from remote control rooms.

In the generation of client/servers, both the workstations and the servers have high intelligence and high local performance. This intelligence can be allocated to the intelligent network problem. Early network management tools have specialized in detecting and diagnosing errors across the network. Complex networks make detecting these errors even more difficult, but the network manager must provide this service. Preventative network management requires a knowledge of when the network is beginning to deteriorate in either its response characteristics or its overall health.

Equally important is the dissemination of code to the different processors within the network. It is necessary to retain the information about the version levels of the code and data that is transferred to the system. The best network management tools are tailored for the specific needs of the company. It is often possible to assume common network management tools that are available across the industry, but these tools must be tailored to meet the specific needs of the individual companies.

11.6 CONSIDERATIONS

Interoperability refers to the ability to connect and understand information from different computers in an open systems network. It goes beyond simple connection and provides information that can be interpreted in the light of specific problems.

The architect for interoperable networks begins the process with a basic business and computing environment representing the culture of the company. Like Frank Lloyd Wright, the architect blends an open design into an existing environment in a way that meets the needs of the users and provides for future growth.

Architecture for an open system presents new challenges beyond those found in a fixed system environment. Communications becomes the first step in interoperability. Robust management tools that provide the connection protocols sought for open systems do not exist.

Careful consideration must be made not to ruin existing applications while introducing new protocols. Roadmaps of both old and new systems are required to make the process function well. The next step in understanding this process is to examine the life cycle used to build open systems.

11.7 REFERENCES

Carroll, James M., and Robert L. Mack. "Learning to Use a Word Processor: By Doing, by Thinking, and by Knowing." In *Human Factors in Computer Systems,* edited by John C. Thomas and Michael L. Schneider. Norwood, NJ: Ablex Publishing Co., 1984, pp. 13–51.

Pagels, Heinz R. *The Dreams of Reason: The Computer and the Rise of the Sciences of Complexity.* New York: Bantam Books, 1989, pp. 45–46. (Pagels discusses how reason can help us understand the changes in computer systems. In this section, he discusses the linkage between complex computer systems and evolution.)

Pfeiffer, Bruce Brooks, and Gerald Nordland. *Frank Lloyd Wright: In the Realm of Ideas.* Carbondale and Edwardsville, IL: Southern Illinois University Press, 1988.

12

The Open Systems Life Cycle

Imagine beginning from scratch and putting together all the pieces that create an operational open system. This chapter develops a perspective of an open systems project, starting with the initial selling and commitment. The open systems life cycle covers the steps and processes necessary for successful commitment, design, implementation, and operation of a new open systems solution. The chapter discusses problems encountered in the world of implementation of new ideas. Some of these problems involve changes to existing systems, including management, culture, philosophy, and existing technical solutions.

Managing information technology has always been a challenge, but the adoption of open distributed systems has complicated the understanding and commitment process. Processing power once confined to central computer centers has shifted to individual desktops and even to portable computers. Evidence points to continued growth in performance and capability for individual workers and departments. Open systems challenge management to understand the underlying culture and philosophy of their organization and to build a process using information technology as a competitive leverage.

A view of the life cycle enables us to examine techniques that have helped companies adopt open systems without greatly disrupting normal operations. In examining the life cycle, we examine the foundations and characteristics of open systems that determine directions. Techniques are discussed that facilitate open designs, using the new solutions in conjunction with existing solutions. We will examine approaches to development and how the process differs from those used for standard central computing. Once development is completed, it is necessary to integrate the system into operations.

Developing open distributed solutions requires tools that facilitate new approaches to traditional application creation. Equally important, the allocation of resources across multiple nodes increases the need for management tools that can provide an understanding of problem areas. Understanding the life cycle can also identify techniques for creating an environment that facilitates change and permits the addition of solutions that provide for smooth daily operations and facilitate growth.

The process of switching from existing technology to open solutions involves commitment from different organizations within a company. Internal political considerations often are weighed and affect the acceptance of new information technology. Dominant vendors have achieved account control, which guarantees their levels of revenue, and these vendors will work hard to retain the status quo in the face of strong logic for movement to an open systems design.

Within the company, there is a natural resistance to change that affects employees at all levels. Some resist change that diminishes their responsibilities or makes their jobs more complex. This group will deny the value of the proposed change to the system and work to delay or avoid it. Others will resist change that modifies comfortable working environments or jeopardizes their customary procedures. This group is content with the status quo and resists the change to avoid disruption of the business. Many resist change because they are honestly confused about the correct approach and opt not to make a decision. The challenge for management is to bring all these groups to a clear understanding about open systems and the advantages that can come from its use.

Education can assist at all levels of resistance and potentially allay honest fears. Understanding real benefits can alter the resistance of many within a company and help them understand the critical nature of using competitive approaches. This will be especially difficult if the resisters determine that open systems solutions are threatening their jobs, so a positive retraining program should be included with any move to open systems solutions. Most important is a recognition that the shift to new approaches is a commitment of the company or the operating division. This commitment begins with top management, who must communicate to the rest of the organization the need to adopt the change.

A first step in the commitment process is understanding the real benefits of open technology and its implications to the business. Expectations often exceed the organization's ability to implement the solution in a timely manner. It is therefore important that the true size of the transition be understood. Expectations must be realistically stated and managed.

Personal computers enabled workers at many levels to raise their working knowledge of computing. This increased awareness and brought many executives, previously unskilled in computing, to a conversational base with technology. This awareness has resulted in PCs being adopted by many businesses. The PC has also facilitated a move to open systems. This experience has partially tapped the full potential of individual productivity and has only begun to introduce the idea of group productivity based on distributed open systems.

Examining the life cycle of open systems enables us to understand both the technology directions and the techniques used to manage these directions. It helps create a level of understanding that can facilitate change by using realistic techniques for affecting the change. By reviewing an open systems life cycle, we can demonstrate how a management vision gains the largest payback from transformed business approaches. Transformation in management approaches may be the best way to gain the highest payback from open systems. Through the introduction of open systems, it is assumed enterprise operations must continue, as newer technology continually improves the process. Successful companies have spent time understanding and adjusting management systems to aid the decision, design, development, integration, production, and operations and growth phases. These are shown as a continuous cycle in Figure 12.1.

Changes are expected to occur in an evolutionary fashion to operations, but management must be capable of completing some revolutionary changes in an evolutionary way. Evolution often involves consensus across many different levels of management but can frequently be completed without total consensus. New environments can be designed to bring together evolutionary processes while the management team itself is undergoing a transformation.

Culture and personalities affect the migration to open systems. The culture may have become ingrained in a single solution, which does not easily convert to the new technology. Personalities will support or resist the pro-

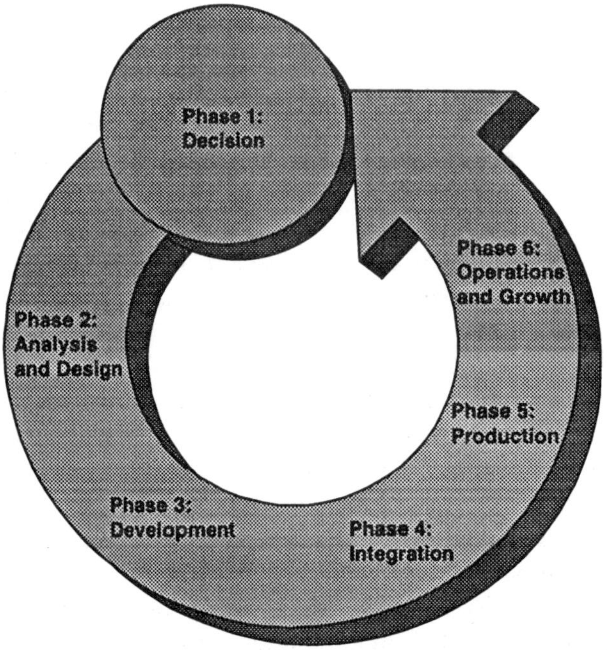

Figure 12.1 Phases to consider when introducing open systems

posed changes as a direct measure of the effects on their way of working. There is inherent opposition to change, and this is exaggerated in an environment of clear opposition.

12.1 DESCRIPTION OF LIFE CYCLE

The six life-cycle steps or phases begin with commitment and track successive steps of development to operations. Each step will be considered, as we examine important elements of open systems. A shift to open systems extends beyond technology paradigms to an examination of the work process within the company. Reengineering or transformation of the work process interacts with technology to produce the optimal solution for the using companies. Effective transformation augments the value of technology, and ineffective transformation reduces the value. Transformation will be explored in more depth in Chapter 13.

The cycle begins with the decision phase, which determines the direction for development of specific solutions. During the decision phase, there is a need to assess the capability, provide the overall vision, and make the necessary commitments that will result in the completed work. Many alternatives that can respond to the requirements are possible. Weighing the value of each alternative, along with its financial implications, will set the direction and commit the resources. Understanding the elements of open systems aids the decision process and creates an impetus for commitment. The decision process determines the depth of commitment and can affect successful completion of subsequent phases. A strong and forceful commitment by the company will compel participation; a weak commitment can cause foot-dragging.

The second step in the process is the design and analysis phase. The design phase refines information known before the decision. Companies that have introduced open systems have discovered unique challenges in defining open distributed solutions across many different working environments. The elements for the design of the basic building blocks found in open systems include clients, servers, and the network. The system becomes the network and is tailored to specific requirements. Many companies have been successful in creating open designs, but they often adopt organizational and architectural approaches that are different from the single-system designs.

The third step is the development phase. A number of key moves must be made during this phase, which includes the organization and resource allocation. There is debate as to whether open systems implementations should be folded into existing development operations or be a separate group. The argument for the separate group emphasizes the ability to allocate resources that are familiar with open systems and the tools needed to produce the applications. Whichever direction is selected, a development team must be created that is sensitive to the requirements of open systems. The team must be able to apply development methodology to producing applications.

Another important aspect of the development stage is the development of open systems programs. Tools that either can be acquired or built for the multiple processor area will be needed. Testing techniques that reflect the need to provide a unique open environment will be defined. Advances in languages have aided the development process, but there remains a challenge to retrain existing development teams in modern tools and development processes.

The fourth step is the integration phase, which identifies how and where to connect the new solutions into the system. This process blends the new solutions into existing processes. Integration provides coherence between different parts of the system. One of the largest challenges for open systems is to connect smoothly with existing processes in a nondisruptive or seamless fashion.

From integration, there is a movement to limited production, which is the fifth step. The integrated open solution is merged with existing environments, and viable prototypes are shifted into place. Prototype systems will be introduced to the production environment after they are tested successfully against predetermined success criteria. Limited production tests the system in real environments and discovers unique problems.

The final step in the process is the operational phase. New developments must fit the ongoing process that drives the business. As open systems are applied, the plan must reflect the operational needs of the day-to-day business. Prototypes will be extended beyond the simple single solution to include many workers. The completed applications and other software packages will bring together an operational process that enhances the business and changes the normal techniques for doing business. Realistic measurement plans will enable management to assess the relative success or failure of the new solutions.

It should be noted that a skunkworks or accelerated prototype effort can jump-start the life cycle and shorten the time to completion. Try a joint development project with an open systems vendor.

12.2 DECISION PHASE

Figure 12.2 maps the different parameters found in the decision phase. Existing systems have achieved a high degree of equilibrium with time. The decision to change begins by unfreezing the equilibrium of the current system and proposing necessary changes that will create a system that can adopt to an ever-changing environment of technology. Professor Schein at MIT Sloan School has addressed the various aspects of these changes.

The unfreezing process creates motivation to change and often involves changing the minds of individuals who have resisted the necessary changes. Schein, in his work at MIT, points to the need to identify the force field, which identifies individuals who drive and resist change. Often motivated by positive motivation, some individuals resist change to achieve stability in the company. Others find the company running well within the constraints of current technology and are reluctant to change to another environment. Unfreezing begins by convincing key individuals that progress and change

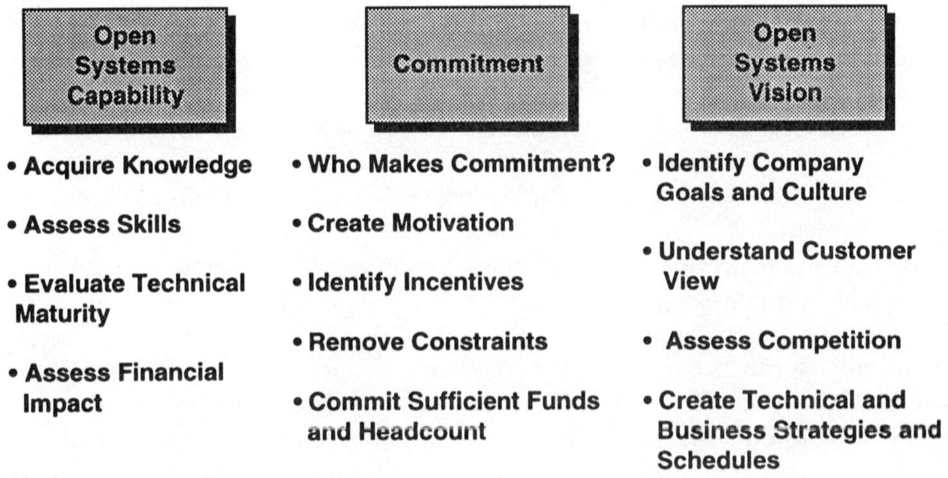

Figure 12.2 Decision-phase parameters

are in the best interest of the corporation and even in the best interest of the individuals within the organization who support change. A number of techniques are used to accelerate the unfreezing process. An example is demonstrating that current processes have become overly costly and ineffective in rapidly responding to the needs of customers. Demonstrating change will provide competitive or cost leverage, which can convince many doubters.

Study how the organization benefits from switching from current systems to the more dynamic open systems. If change is executed without major disruption of the operation, an advantage will accrue to people willing to change. Often, executives have read about the success of other organizations that have switched technology from existing paradigms to open paradigms. This knowledge base helps to persuade executives that the direction could be beneficial for their company. In other words, do organization standards reflect a commitment to bring in multiple vendors, or are the standards still slanted toward a specific vendor?

Determine the levels of management committed to open systems. If the chairman of the corporation has made a specific deal with one vendor, then all the commitment at lower levels will become meaningless. Is the corporate business management team behind the selection of open systems? Do the technology groups oppose the introduction of open systems? Divisional department management and users must also welcome the support.

Independent knowledge is important in deciding a technology shift. Obtain outside experts, who can explain advances in open systems and describe methods used to resolve problems in other companies. Do not depend on vendors to make important open systems decisions. It is important to build a knowledge base internally that can provide insight and leadership for open systems. Management's understanding of technology must be at a level sufficient to commit to further investigation or to implement changes. Presentations must focus on practical expectations that reflect potential problems and benefits.

Along with education for upper management, it is also important that the technical and advisory community be briefed on the technology. These briefings should be more in-depth and should cover the design, development, and deployment tools. Sufficient time should be spent to ensure that the staff can provide intelligent input to the decision-making process. Entrenched old-line thinkers will want to make pronouncements based on inadequate knowledge. It is important to ensure that both they and new-wave thinkers have sufficient knowledge to understand the pros and cons of any open decision. A company that understands the technology and alternative implementations is better able to make a clear decision as to when and how to implement open systems.

Technical skills within a company may need reinforcement or fresh people to facilitate the shift to open systems. Mainframe programmers have to be trained and refocused for the new environment. A team of skilled individuals must be allocated to completing the implementation of open systems. Modern equipment requires skilled people who can design, develop, and use these new solutions. Open systems raise the threshold of skills required within the development organizations by requiring development versus simple coding capability. People trained in older paradigms of computing must be introduced to modern tools that can compete effectively.

The widespread use of open computing will introduce many unskilled end users to computers for the first time. The power of the computer system must be tailored to shield the novice worker from too many learning requirements. Many earlier tools are limiting the capability of companies to make the shift to new computing paradigms. To help this, a company must assess the capabilities of today's workforce and determine the needs for tomorrow. Necessary training courses will have to be put in place for those who can make the shift. Separation will probably be a course of action for those in the computer business who are unwilling or unable to make the shift to new technology.

Vision begins with a realistic understanding of company goals and how these goals map into the company's culture. Culture is difficult to change, but it is often necessary to modify the culture to reflect the changed environment. Is the company undergoing a transformation in the business direction or simply using technology to augment existing techniques for doing business? A vision can be articulated in technical and business strategies that detail techniques and schedules for meeting new goals. In creating the strategy, a view of customer needs and their ability to adjust to and use new systems is required.

Customer requirements change almost as fast as technology. A new vision for processing reflects customer needs and the company goals for improvement and acceptance. Each item can affect the process that will be adopted. To reach an intelligent decision, the organization must have sufficient maturity to understand new technology and be able to adopt it. True commitment exists in an organization that shares a vision and can adjust the culture sufficiently to make the necessary changes.

A number of factors will lead to an acceptance of open systems. Some of the driving forces are:

- The acceptance of new technology by mature management within the organization.
- A knowledge level that understands the relationship of open systems to the existing environment and a way to move from current processes to open solutions.
- A cadre of professionals who are familiar with workstations and understand techniques for implementing change.
- An identification of meaningful tools that can be employed to produce the new applications and meld them within the existing compute environment.

As companies examine techniques to justify open systems, they will find lower-cost alternatives to mainframe processing, which represent a powerful argument to commit to implementation. Open systems will facilitate both the decision and implementation of new solutions, since costs will be lower and within the control of local management. Users will welcome open systems to reach a level of empowerment directly tied to the control available on individual desktop computers.

Resisting forces to change include arguments that the current systems work well and provide levels of control necessary to ensure continued productivity of the business. The cost of change is an important argument, since it is usually estimated too low and gets higher as implementation progresses.

Personnel barriers are also quite real, as examination of skills versus needs will quickly reveal. Many managers become frustrated with the ramp-up costs for newly trained personnel in distributed processing, but these costs are necessary to incorporate new technology.

Opposition will come from the central groups, which will view the new technology as a major problem in maintaining their control points. Jobs will change, and many older workers and managers will resist change. Fear of any change exists, and a radical switch from mainframe computing to distributed computing will create a problem for many organizations.

Control of a distributed network represents a significant challenge. Many enterprise networks have come to terms with the complexity of system control. In like manner, the lack of clear management control tools will represent either a deterrent or challenge to the management teams. The reward systems within a company often appear to deter acceptance of new technology. This is especially true in open systems, where more of the work flows to the local environment. Empire building becomes a problem when individual departments gain a higher level of control of local computing. Once the change is accepted, it is a good idea to create a process that continues to build on technology knowledge. Open technology is changing rapidly, so periodic updates will be necessary to keep all parties up to speed on changes.

The concept of click time identifies the point at which commitment actually takes place. Direction is given by the proper levels of management, and the necessary resources are authorized. Once commitment is made, incentives must be established to ensure that all major operations within the company provide sufficient support to ensure success. Positive motivators must be defined to overcome inherent resistance. Internal mutiny can eventually sink a major project, unless the culture provides a way to handle the mutiny. At this point, a strong manager must be appointed to be responsible for the open systems process. The manager must have sufficient leverage to form a strong team and remove obstacles.

12.3 ANALYSIS AND DESIGN PHASE

The next critical stage in developing open systems is to create a design that provides flexibility and a growth path for the different solution paradigms while using mainline standards. The objective of this stage is to create a design that begins at the open system interfaces and correctly interacts with the existing system. A number of design approaches have been used that can prove beneficial in considering the system approach.

The creation of the new system design begins by understanding the control and data flow of existing systems. This is a roadmap of existing systems, which is aimed at understanding important elements found in the network. The roadmap describes how processes and data elements interconnect. The focus will be on three major items: communications, data flow, and user control flow through the system. Specifically, the user control and data flow of the existing network can identify connect points for new networks. Data flow enables designers to understand different approaches to the system and create techniques to modify these for open systems. Control flow enables designers to identify necessary control points and potential modifications.

A second roadmap will define the new design for an open systems network. This map will benefit from understanding the defined standards within the company and may use existing standards to provide the first level of support. It represents a guideline for integrating designs into the current base and provides a basis for future growth. Older systems required a regeneration of each node of the system. Each system level reflects correct interconnect protocols, which may need to be changed by new technology.

Figure 12.3 illustrates the contents of legacy systems representing the historical and operational base of a company's system design. Legacy systems include components found in the operational systems of the enterprise—items such as the basic hardware and operating system environments, databases, communications protocols, networks, and procedures used in the system. Legacy systems include the applications development environment and skills of different programmers and designers. Legacy systems are also driven by culture and management.

A third step in design is to create a strong team that can work together to create new designs. A quandary often experienced in assigning the team for open systems is how to organize it to ensure a successful design and development process. Successful companies have tried alternate approaches to organization questions. Some have integrated the open systems team directly into the existing development group, while others have created a special team to handle open systems technology. A successful strategy is to adopt separate teams for open systems and additional ones to maintain legacy systems. Each team contends for vital resources, but the open systems team will benefit from new hires who are knowledgeable in modern programming techniques. At the same time, long-time mainframe programmers charged

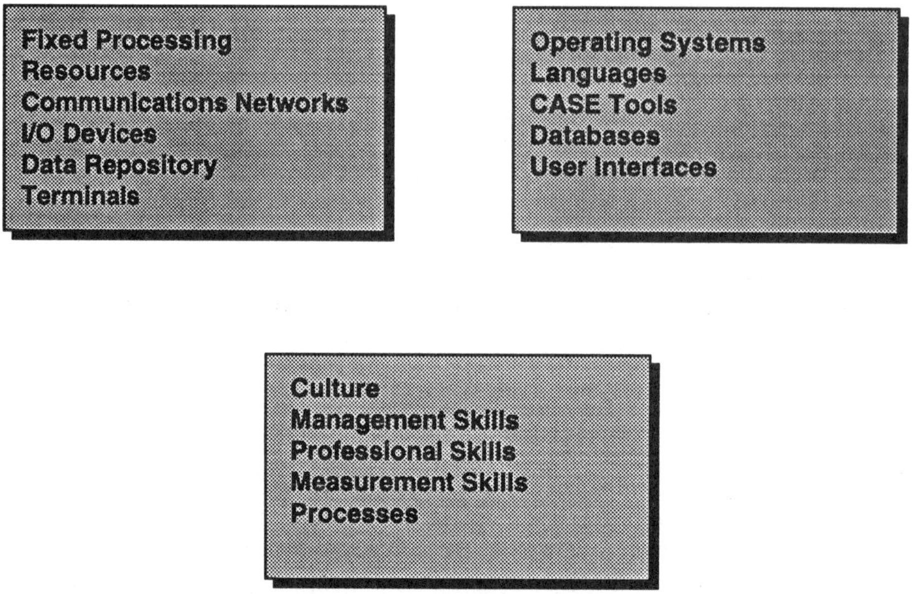

Figure 12.3 Contents of legacy systems

with maintaining the legacy system won't be forced to learn new technologies and products if they don't wish to do so. Such a strategy, though, must be done in a way so that those working on the legacy systems won't be considered "second-class citizens" within the organization and move on elsewhere, resulting in damaging losses from the personnel resource base.

A well-designed system leads to a development stage that uses the design in a completed project plan. Project plans for distributed systems differ from those used for central processing. Discovery and allocation of critical tools are important in completing the plan for open systems implementation. Resources must be balanced correctly to get the open systems work completed.

12.4 DEVELOPMENT PHASE

Development of open systems solutions requires tools that either can be bought or built to support distributed development (as seen in Figure 12.4). It is possible to use mainframe development tools, but testing assumes the ability to have multiple processors working together. Although more tools are emerging on the market for open systems, there is not yet a robust set of tools that meets the needs of open systems developers. Sufficient tools exist

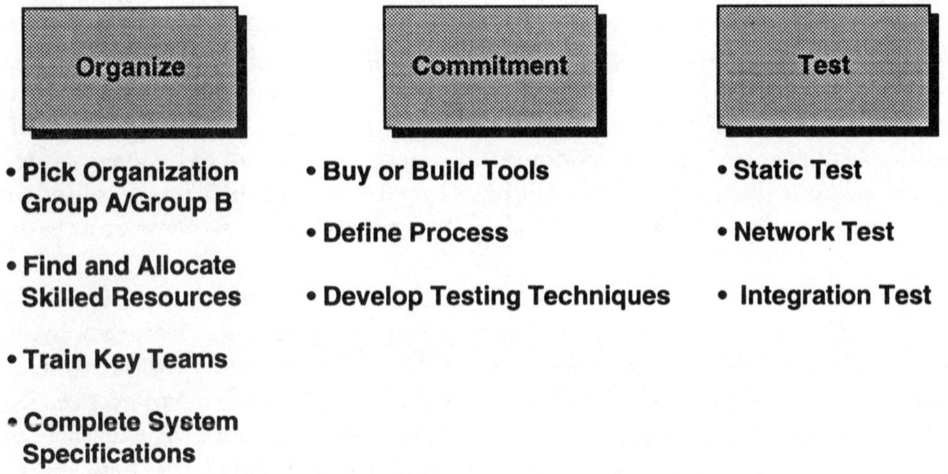

Figure 12.4 Development of open systems solutions

to create prototypes and define preliminary implementations. Complete life-cycle tools are being developed by software vendors. Additional in-house tools can augment those found on the market.

New development processes should delineate development directions and define access points to the system. In a distributed environment, development can occur rapidly at different locations around the world. Many engineering groups have adopted global development tools. Once the tools are in place, a process that considers the complexity of building an open systems implementation should be defined. The process will determine how the specific code is built for the first release of the new support, but it also should address how updates and fixes can be transmitted to operational systems.

Open systems implementations typically involve large numbers of workstations and servers. Distribution and testing must realistically reflect the larger numbers. Once the code is created, it must be synchronized in libraries and then distributed to large numbers of workstations and servers. Synchronization is mandatory in many companies to ensure smooth operations. The network becomes the distribution tool, and synchronization is allocated to management processes, which must monitor and record the status of different shipped modules. Since companies have a need to have all their people operational at the same time, distribution through floppy disks is inadequate. Simple calculation of minimal connect time will demonstrate the need for approaches that use the power of the network and servers.

Testing multiple-node networks has always been a problem. When the author managed the telecommunications testing for IBM, it became necessary to create hardware to simulate the interaction of multiple terminals on the network. The problem is made more complex with the introduction of multiple clients on a single system. Automated scripts need to be assigned to networks to test the system thoroughly. Once the testing technique is identified, a method must also be established to record and track the results of testing.

As open systems are implemented, company MIS groups face new challenges of support. Often, the first surge of open solutions increases activity on central databases, since more successful applications can now be applied against the data. MIS must contend with the increased workload as a result of this increased access. Additional use of cooperative processing will place a new strain on existing resources and accelerate the search for new skills. These skills will prove valuable in defining group solutions, placing additional reliance on MIS. During the design stage, close involvement between the MIS and open systems design groups is mandatory. Creative managers have contributed significantly to successful open systems implementations.

Many constraints develop in organizations that inhibit successful implementation of open systems. MIS groups can represent a constraint if they must sign for all development. There is a balance that must be determined between the need to keep the group involved and inhibiting actions. Constraints to success should be removed. These constraining forces include barriers to successful implementation. Simple barriers can include inaccessibility to sufficient test or development equipment to complete the task.

Successful development will lead to the creation of the first operational system or prototype. This prototype will test not only the local code in the client/server environment but must also exercise the connection points to the existing network. The prototype will use actual operational data—if only for testing processes. It will also test the interconnection techniques.

Once a prototype is created, there is a need to roll the solution to multiple locations. Deployment through the operational system represents a challenge.

12.5 INTEGRATION PHASE

Deployment demands an integration of the solution into the system used by the company. During integration, installation and massive testing are completed on a limited basis. By the end of testing, the completed project can be integrated into the company's operation. From prototypes defined in the previous section, subsequent locations duplicate the defined configuration and facilitate subsequent installation. Packaging the solution so it can be brought into new locations easily is a critical factor in replicating an existing prototype throughout a large system. Throughout the process, monitoring occurs to determine the success of each stage. As each stage of deployment is completed and brought on line, the new system will interact with the network to produce operational output.

Integration becomes pivotal during the deployment stage. The first stage of integration begins at the LANs. Each network must work well, as clients interact with servers and larger sources of data. The next integration stage is the blending of multiple LANs and the final blend of open solutions into an enterprise network. The connection protocols are important at each point in this process. Melding a new system into the complexity of operational systems can require close involvement with the identified connection points. Achieving full interoperability is the goal of this stage.

Integration can be one of the more challenging steps of the deployment stage. Complex contact points affect the smooth integration points. For instance, if the LAN uses TCP/IP protocols and the enterprise network is a backbone network, convergent points must be identified and used to insure smooth operations. Careful staging will help ensure the successful implementation of open systems in the enterprise.

There is increasing use of a concept called surround, which helps stage the integration in complex systems. Legacy code is protected from change by having the open systems solutions use existing paradigms. First, a simple connection to the mainframe is used to capture terminal interfaces such as an IBM 3270. As this interface is brought to a working condition, the next stage is to move to a peer-driven protocol. Finally, clear object connections will improve the overall flow through the system. These steps prevent distortion of existing systems and reduce the cost of implementation.

12.6 PRODUCTION PHASE

The shift from simple integration of a single prototype will introduce multiple workers to the open solutions or move to the production phase. Once the prototype is operational and can be rolled into multiple sites, the size and scope of the problem increase. Additional problems will arise during the production stage, as the simple prototype is shifted from a single system to multiple users. As the numbers increase, the potential problems will also increase. Production is the first step in a shift to operations.

12.7 OPERATIONAL AND GROWTH PHASE

Once the integration process is complete, control of the system is turned over to operations. Operations must be sure that the new system meets the continuing needs of the company while providing a framework for adding changes to the open solution. As new users are added, the operation's system must be able to ensure this growth without disruption. Equally important, sufficient control techniques must exist to permit an ongoing understanding of the system status. Automatic input to both the network management system and to the servicing system seem mandatory for any system design in this age.

The shift from a central to an open systems environment causes unique challenges for support organizations. Central processing imposed its form of control on company operations. In a central operation, system events flow through a single control point, which makes it possible to define problems early in the operation. The single control point facilitates detection and correction of problems and provides a common point for effective updates to the system.

During the sailing of the America's Cup, the race committee continues to assess progress against the expected results. The race demonstrates weaknesses in the design of the ship specifications or the ground rules for the race. Managing an open system is similar. Each installation is an educational experience that demonstrates how the process can be improved. Data paths and communications linkages can always be enhanced. The process must be designed in an open way to access these different paths.

In distributed open processing, new operational challenges emerge, which change the detection of problems and the application of corrections to the system. Network computing takes the openness of the personal computer a step further. Vertical applications have been adopted to meet the needs of the business. These applications are often the operational heart of the company and require specific attention when the system design is completed.

Operations begins with the large-scale installation of the completed products in the processing line of the business. Installation is approached in stages to ensure nondisruptive operation of proprietary applications. New software packages tend to be unstable and require additional attention as they are applied within a working environment. Older applications and hardware are often retained as a parallel effort to ensure that the completed new application is operational before full production is achieved. The step process aids the installation in creating an ongoing operation.

Many installations have hundreds, if not thousands, of these intelligent processors. The large numbers of clients and servers represent a challenge of synchronization. Changes to workstation software must be coordinated across multiple processors, since changes to one often affect others. Change control systems must reflect the network and the need to synchronize different subsystems. Increasing capability in server software enables some of this synchronization to be shifted to the servers. Coordination of neighboring peers requires sufficient control to insure functions approximating mainframe management routines. A number of techniques have been adopted to permit an orderly synchronization.

Another challenge is to define a verification process for new releases. Testing an open distributed system becomes more complex as additional processors are added. Multiple processors must be connected into the entire network in a way that ensures efficient operation. Test cases must simulate the operation of large networks of systems that have a high degree of change.

The next challenge is to define a maintenance system that coordinates across the operational systems without causing additional disruption. Since the distributed open nodes are often as powerful as the central processors, verification of the fixes can occur on individual processors and be transmitted to central management routines. The same degree of power also causes a higher degree of complexity in the specific software components. Each component has the original capability of large mainframes. The debugging mechanisms must recognize that the interaction between multiple software packages and the network makes isolation of errors difficult.

Training is another difficult challenge for the distributed environment. Training courses built on technology provide unique learning environments. The workstation can be used as an independent training center with interactive video connected to the workstation. Central training locations serve as pivot points for information for many workers. Video tapes present subjects in a distributed environment in which different workers can access information from different workstations. The concept of distribution applies to the process of educating tomorrow's workers.

An important challenge in distributed systems is the ability to monitor system activities from control operations. Increased power in the open systems model has provided an additional opportunity for local monitoring.

Autonomy must be balanced with the need to predict system performance in the operational area. Measures of productivity will be provided to management to test the health of the company. Instant problems in on-line programs can greatly affect the predictability of success.

In many installations, open systems are placed in critical applications that require accuracy and correctness. Consider the use of open systems technology in an intensive care unit (ICU) of a hospital. Patient well-being depends on the system being up and accurate and therefore requires that the system maintain high standards of performance and operation. Comparable examples exist in manufacturing, where open systems solutions are being applied to processes that simply cannot fail. Failure in many of these processes could have catastrophic results on lives and property.

Monitoring open systems requires unique tools, which measure and determine the status of the network at any point in time. Elements of this support include fault analysis, performance monitoring, tracking the various fixes, and corrections to the system. Tools that were once prevalent in mainframe environments usually will not work well in distributed environments.

The process determines the system's ability to be dynamic in the addition of new and advanced solutions. This dynamism affects the response to changing technology and management environments. A well-structured process can enable rapid response, which retains competitive leverage. Thus, as we witness an acceleration of technology, we can also witness a response to the changes that guarantees a consistent and ordered result.

Exclusive contracts, which lock into a single proprietary relationship, violate the advantages of open systems. In the long run, such agreements are a disservice to stockholders from the using company. It is very difficult, if not impossible, to reach the necessary gains by engaging in such processes.

In the early days of central processors, the correct detection of problems and application of fixes became a significant problem. It was often necessary to bring operations to a halt while new fixes were applied to the system. Significant fixes could reduce production over longer periods of time. Tools were eventually introduced that facilitated the addition of new corrections to the system. Systems could be repaired while they were still functioning.

Operation is an ongoing process vital to the running of a business. Eventual success or failure of an open solution will be measured as it is applied to the 24-hour-a-day support reflecting the needs of customers. Many operations cannot be halted for extended periods, because the company will lose revenue. Changes and modifications to systems are assumed to occur dynamically. Many companies are increasingly turning to nonstop systems that ensure responsiveness. An open system's operational phase must contain processes that guarantee continuous system operation.

Many companies have connected operations directly into management information systems. Sensitive operations will automatically alert management concerning system failure or even a softening in the response time. Open systems management routines will meet their challenge in supporting on-line operations that must inform management about changes in status of the system. Direct connections to *Executive Information Systems* (EIS) have been achieved through mainframe-based applications. This same support must exist in the open systems solution and must be able to blend with the needs of individual departments.

Critical data must be gathered automatically to avoid having individual workers provide special input. Fortunately, the trigger system found in server software makes this process much easier. A natural flow, which permits management to understand the flow of data across the system, can be identified. Like other aspects of open systems, the ongoing process should meld into the existing culture to continue and enhance existing information system bases.

Adoption of new technology such as open systems is only a first step. Technology is changing rapidly. We can expect 100 percent improvement on the desktop in less than two years. Supporting technologies are also on schedules that guarantee an ongoing period of modification. Any new process must be built to accept a dynamism of change in the 1990s. Figure 12.5 illustrates some major consideration points for the operational phase of open systems.

Not only is technology changing, but there are also modifications in the process to reflect improvements. These process changes must be factored into an ongoing running of a business. The phase must have techniques to introduce new technology without upsetting existing operations.

Open systems provide extensive power at the individual nodes. This power, when combined with the reporting systems of EIS, can enable management to dynamically adjust compute flow through a system and stage power to the nodes that need it. In most businesses, this capability can provide predictive recovery techniques, which forecast production downturns and enable management to adjust the system accordingly.

Operational systems provide the base for running the company. Frequent troubleshooting and updating processes are designed to retain full opera-

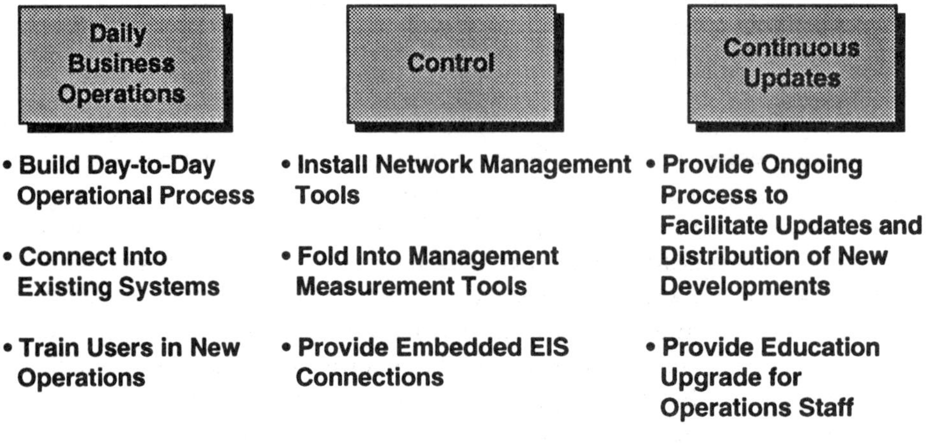

Figure 12.5 Considertion points for the operational phase of open systems

tional support while providing for continual improvement in the systems. Maintenance is made more complex in distributed systems, since large numbers of dispersed systems must be simultaneously updated to reflect the latest information.

Many examples exist of systems that have thousands of workstations that must have the same change introduced at a given time. These changes reflect critical operational information or new development of technology. The system must permit this interactive real-time modification.

We have examined how open systems affect the life cycle. Six separate steps, which represent the challenge in open systems, have been addressed. In step one, we began unfreezing the old processes to define new approaches to business, creating a decision. In step two, we examined techniques used in the design and analysis processes. Step three explored the new development environment, which uses open systems tools to create new solutions. Step four investigated the process of integration. Step five discussed how we move from integration to deployment and finally shift to step six, or operations. The completion of the plan that handles open systems across these six steps assumes we will refreeze the new process, which reflects the capability to grow as new technology is available. The refreezing process stabilizes changes and integrates them into the organization to facilitate future growth.

12.8 CONSIDERATIONS

Just as technology is changing, management techniques for effectively working within the framework of open systems are also changing how to deploy and introduce open systems. These changes extend to the philosophy of management as well as the way people interact.

A strong executive commitment is necessary to ensure the success of a change to open systems. This commitment for complex systems must begin with the top management in the company and be communicated to the correct levels of management. Support people must be aware of the direction, and their full commitment must be ensured to avoid in-place opposition and delay tactics. It is important to have managers who embrace open systems lead the effort to ensure the correct level of support.

A company vision is born from a view of the present and a feel for the future. The vision builds on the culture but must be willing to adjust to reflect changes in the competitive environment and the technology. The vision must be widely shared to ensure that it is a key ingredient in the process adopted to make it work.

Five stages are important in completing a well-balanced open systems life cycle. The decision phase defines the thrust and brings management together to commit to a common direction. The design phase lays out the necessary first step to install the new solution. The design stage may identify a step migration to full open systems implementation beginning with existing design techniques. The development stage completes the design, develops the solution, and then tests the product. The final product of the development stage is a prototype system, which conforms to the design. The deployment stage spreads the solution across the entire network. The operational stage provides the framework for the day-to-day operations of the system.

Deployment of the system will find the solutions operational on multiple locations. The system will normally be carried through a multiple-step process to reduce the possibility of total system collapse. The step of surrounding existing code reduces the need to have too heavy a dependency on existing code changes.

Operational systems are critical to the success of the company. Built into many operational systems are management reporting mechanisms that automatically alert Executive Information Systems.

13

Integration

Integration of new applications represented a challenge in centralized mainframes. Techniques were eventually defined to connect different programs together in complex networks, which were often global. The integration challenge has been made more complex with the introduction of powerful processors linked in open systems. The lack of clearly defined control points helps to make this process complex. Although the challenge is large, it is necessary for corporations to experience the full benefits of open systems. Integration is also one of the fastest-growing computer business opportunities.

In a wider sense, the introduction and integration of new technology affects the broader culture of society and the acceptance of new processes. In this sense, integrators bring together different pieces to be melded into a complete system (Toffler, 1980) and encounter both resistance and acceptance. Integration is based on the company vision applied across the different technical solutions.

Beyond local integration, there is growing interest in the question of enterprise integration. Figure 13.1 shows the concept of focal firms, which are central to a process or a business community. As an example, General Motors is a focal firm to many suppliers and service companies. Focal corporations extend their internal connections to suppliers and marketing companies vital to their business. Obviously, a clean enterprise integration must

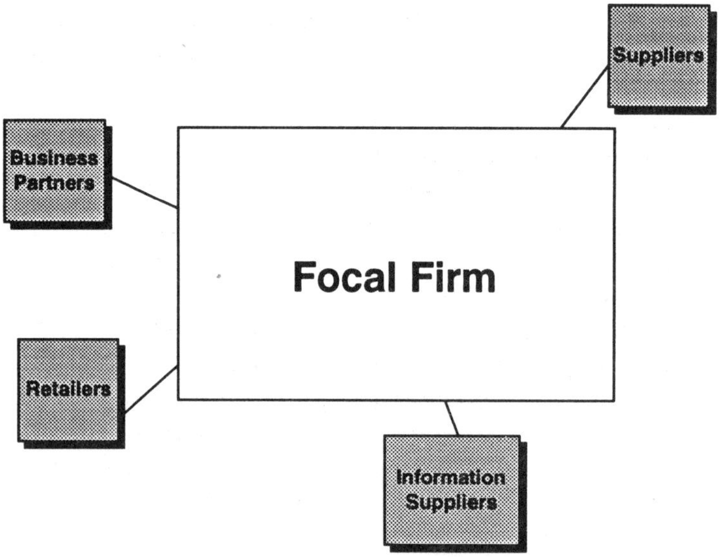

Figure 13.1 The concept of focal firms

begin with the focal firm first. General Motors' systems must work well before they are extended to support companies.

Consider kaleidoscopes as representative of the complexity of integration and the variability across different companies. The integration process reflects the complexity found in the individual components and also reflects the complexity of business structures, which view the process in light of their immediate requirements. Solution flexibility, using a well-balanced approach, which can be shifted to reflect changing requirements and unforeseeable results, is necessary.

Effective integration depends on a future vision balanced with an understanding of which legacy products affect the eventual completion of the vision. An integration roadmap determines how new products can be introduced and used with legacy products. Company standards help ensure a consistent direction. Integration must consider legacy code and hardware. A large amount of the installed equipment can be retained through a well-executed integration process.

The goals of integration vary from organization to organization. Some groups simply want to add systems as they come on line while retaining mainframe systems as the primary vehicles for corporate computing. Others want to retain a combination of both systems. Still others want to completely unplug the old systems and revolutionize their operations on open systems. The common goal is to identify connections to existing systems that can ease the transition.

The task is enormous. Estimates range above $1 trillion of applications written on proprietary systems. Of the $30 to $40 billion being spent on new technology, only $500 million is being spent on standards. The General Accounting Office, which oversees 53,000 government computer systems, reports few successes and many costly failures in its attempts to modernize. If an organization that can spend $20 billion annually to effect change experiences problems, what hope is there for the rest of us (GAO, 1990)?

There are successes among companies that have followed a simple step approach to integration. These companies recognize that software is the glue of the integration process. An advantage falls to the company that can hook various pieces together with well-developed software. Like much of open systems, integration depends on finding and developing the necessary people skills within the organization. Formal and informal organizations contribute to the success of the integration process. There is a unique vision required from system integrators that is different from other working areas. True integration skill is in an early stage of creation and therefore is a challenge to find.

In a single control point system, integration appeared relatively simple. As aggregate power shifted to departments and workstations, the problems grew in complexity. Desktop computers communicate as peers and have created their own peer control points. The logical control point for the system becomes the integration point of the network. Companies that have been effective in achieving smooth integration have adopted multiple approaches to integration.

The integration process must solve the need for shared resources that include different computers. New tools can facilitate integration, but many of these tools remain in development or planning stages. An integration process must meet the specific needs of each company. In many senses, system integration involves the identification of complex applications shared across multiple levels of hardware and software.

13.1 MODELS OF INTEGRATION

Two distinct models of integration have been applied within businesses. The first is a top-down model, which is driven by the needs of the business and is applied from the top of the business. Top-down is generated from the MIS groups within the company and often begins with a definition of the needs of the central data processing components. The central definition of integration protocols is applied across the company, as local implementations are expected to conform to the central approach. This model of integration works most effectively when the authority of the central control group is accepted throughout the organization. The central group must be sufficiently perceptive to recognize the power of new computing paradigms and fold them into the defined protocols. Top-down assumes strong central control that can define and enforce standards for the purchase and installation of computer hardware and software.

Top-down simplifies the job of the integrator and vendors. There is a clear definition of accepted interfaces and a knowledge of the users, which will not deviate from this pattern. Vendors can respond with products that conform to the published interfaces, and using departments know which vendors comply with the ground rules for the company. Top-down standard approaches permit the company to obtain leverage from purchasing multiple copies of the same solution.

The second model is bottoms-up, which begins with a specific department implementing an open solution. The department solution is connected to the existing network. Eventually a repertoire of accepted applications is integrated into the network. There are many examples of companies that have successfully achieved integration by one organization adopting open solutions and spreading it to other groups within the company.

Dramatic tales exist of engineering departments that transformed their environment by introducing PCs. Initially introduced as stand-alone processors, these simple workstations were then lashed together across local area networks. The networks were eventually connected into existing corporate computer systems using existing protocols. Much of this connection is achieved through local agreements between departments that want to share data. Simple programs were built to connect to existing databases, and the solution was propagated across many departments. Corporate MIS became involved after the fact.

Organizations achieve a bottoms-up solution when individuals have sufficient freedom in selecting hardware and software that meets their immediate needs. Adoption and integration are left up to individual managers, who are measured on their production costs and schedules. Since the costs for simple open solutions are within the purview of managers, they can create systems that meet their measured needs. The cost of long-term support is usually missing from these bottoms-up approaches.

Vendors find autonomous bottoms-up organizations more difficult to understand, since there can be many different definitions used within the company. However, competition is open, since local decisions can be made to work and be accepted within the company. Often, teams of vendor personnel can be applied to help individual departments create a reference implementation, which can then be applied to a broader population.

The needs of the larger organization will eventually impose standards on the bottoms-up approach. This will initially cause havoc within the company, as a degree of freedom must be sacrificed to meet the corporate goals. The definition of standards should be based on existing implementations that can meet the desired new directions. Once the strategy and standards are defined, it becomes possible to create an active framework for integration. The integration schedule uses the framework to determine how individual groups are brought into compliance with the strategy.

13.2 CONTROL POINTS

Much of the integration problem resolves around understanding system control and integration points. As noted earlier in this book, control points represent the convergent points for new software. As the network becomes the system, new control point designs have been identified that combine lessons learned from the design of mainframes, workstations, and LANs. This complex mix requires the identification of a logical system control point that can be used to manage the different elements of open systems. Treating the network as a system demands a control point that spans the different entities within the network.

Enterprise control points represent the combination of multiple control points within the network. These control points are really an architecture in which each computer in the system participates. The architecture builds on the legacy of older systems while expanding to support a broader system view. Each component has its own domain control point, which is local to that particular system. For example, participating PCs retain their local autonomy but must participate in the broader architecture design to obtain the services across the network. New local area systems have a domain and control point that can be included in a wider definition for the enterprise.

The enterprise control point identifies logical functions that reside virtually in the network. These functions represent the minimal definition of adherence to rules, which each member connecting to the network must reflect. Although there can be a single regulator residing in a server or administrative workstation, conformity to the architecture is the real control point and integration point for the network. Physically, the control point is shifted to the location of the highest network activity. This control point resides at the virtual center of the network. Although virtual and architectural, the control point provides supervisory control over system resources. An example is the virtual control point contained in IBM's Logical Unit 6.2. Since open systems can be a mix of heterogeneous hardware and software, the virtual control point depends on the adoption of a single architecture that refines the flow between different processors.

Traditional local functions are migrated to the enterprise control point. In central computers, the master scheduler balanced resources to support requirements for multiple users. These resources included primary and secondary memory, as well as time slices of processing power. The enterprise control point serves as the entropic control point for multiple use resources for the entire system. It balances requests across multiple parallel resources while assuring the integrity and security of the entire system.

Open systems rely on aggregate compute power, which begins at user desktops. Workstations connected to servers and central processors, which are managed and controlled through a central complex environment, are included in the enterprise. Balancing the system involves many different technical components but certainly includes the different compute and data resources available through the network. Many examples exist where multiple resources are placed on line with an open system and depend on the balancing across different granularities of computer power.

Central computer systems depended on single computer power to support multiple users. With open systems, each user has a shared power capability. Although shared resources are a part of the total support equation, they represent only a small portion of the complete environment. Changes in the integrated system must be balanced through a network of systems that include central processors. Synchronization of these changes is part of the control point concept.

The practical challenge involves creating software that manages the distribution of complex software across multiple processors. Components include storage and data management, timing synchronization, and more pragmatic considerations for understanding the software resident on each workstation.

A simple first step is to access varying applications through an interface that appears common. Application tools provide productivity and quality benefits to specific groups in the company, but there is generally a software license that must be policed and tracked by the system software. The integration process further provides a clear direction point for users within the departments.

13.3 THE INTEGRATED HIERARCHY

The design of an integrated system begins with a definition of an operational vision for new and old systems running together with a common appearance. The integrator must identify the major strengths of the legacy system and elements in that system that can serve as points for introducing new technology. The broad set of alternatives found in open systems results in mixing different computers and software to meet the application needs of the company. Solutions from different vendors are combined, providing the integrator with the challenge of connecting different hardware and software approaches. Integration has created its own confusion for the users, as incompatible hardware and software must work together. The eventual acceptance of standards will help the implementation, but the reality of the moment is a world with only partial implementation of standards and the need to achieve fast connections.

A systematic approach will identify where we are today and the eventual goal. This is usually expressed as a roadmap that shows the control and data flow through the old system and identifies the locations where new technology will require change. Understanding this roadmap will result in the identification of an integration hierarchy which, at the highest level, gives the appearance of an integrated system. At the implementation level, it provides connectability.

Integration hierarchies represent locations of synergy that can give the appearance of a single system. Although there is often an active mapping occurring below the surface, the end user experiences a seamless system. Connection points are identified that enhance the system flow. A number of pivotal solutions are important in defining the points of commonalty.

The first level in the hierarchy creates the appearance of a single system. Diversity is masked by interfaces to the users, which hide real system complexities. This level involves the definition of user interfaces and processes that appears to be a common system. In this model, reality is mapped by a layer that accepts and converts different protocols to a single image. Can a user interface that is shared across old and new applications be defined? Can the user interface mask complexity of connections below the surface of the system? Adoption of an accepted user interface creates the first step toward an apparently seamless system and gives at least an illusion of oneness.

The appearance is also mapped by processes that operate on top of divergent systems. A good example is the use of a single data image to all users, when the actual implementation is performed on a diversity of subsystems. Processes are also identically mapped across the system with apparently identical results. Results must often be corrected to reflect different system underpinnings. Whether the system is the executive information system or the processes used by financial experts, the results should appear common when run on the system.

The second level of the hierarchy defines a subsystem interface that connects to different systems and maps the differences. A system interface module that permits code to be migrated across different hardware and software architectures is developed. This technique has been widely used by different software firms that must migrate across different systems. The complexity of system interconnect is concentrated in a handful of modules that support the integration process. Acceptance of new protocols will require the acceptance of connections to older protocols. Mapping processes will facilitate the real connection between different processors. This is the point where the gateways, routers, and bridges discussed earlier will make a difference in the integration and will involve locating the necessary people who can introduce new technology in a transparent fashion. The integrated system will benefit from advances in technology.

The third level of the hierarchy is the adoption of common protocols across all systems in the enterprise. These common technologies would be adopted by the different software packages throughout the enterprise. The next section will discuss examples of the common technologies.

13.4 INTEGRATION TECHNOLOGIES

A number of specific technical areas should be addressed in an integration plan. These technologies identify connection points in legacy systems and are important in creating any detailed integration plan. As each implementation is brought into conformity with the legacy system, connection becomes possible and eventual integration is achieved.

An early consideration is to determine the level of system conformity required to reach sufficient integration to create an operational system. In earlier integration processes, it was necessary to reach commonalty between platform environments, which include hardware, operating systems, support code, and languages. With the introduction of standards, this level of integration is no longer necessary, but it does reduce the cost of integration in complex environments. Standardization once depended on platform commonalty, but today's interfaces, which conform to operating system standards, can be met without common hardware. The standards have actually moved further with conformity to the interfaces sufficient to achieve the necessary level of integration.

Reducing the operating system alternatives helps the integration process. It is possible to have many operating systems in an integrated environment, but the reduction helps control the code alternatives and the eventual difficulty in meeting the full integration requirements. The UNIX operating system has been selected as the operating system of choice by many open systems vendors. Conformity to the standard definition of UNIX interfaces has been committed to by other vendors. The adoption of a common operating system interface enables users to select from a larger repertoire of internal and external packages.

Solutions to core technical problems are required in addition to base operating system solutions. These core technologies reflect the system philosophies of designers and should match the needs of the installation. Core support is usually defined as a company strategy but is implemented in the different parts of the network. Examples of core technologies which affect the day-to-day operations are reliability, availability, and serviceability (RAS) alternatives. RAS enables the using departments to identify and correct problems that occur on the different system components of the hardware and software. In a more sophisticated system, RAS provides information to network managers that will enable them to debug the entire network. Security is another important cross-system consideration. As the integrated system progresses, it is a good idea to define the techniques that will ensure that the security direction of the company can be shifted to the new designs.

Applications are pivotal to the success of integration processes. A number of techniques have been identified to facilitate the movement of application code to different processors. The transition from central to open applications is an important step in the overall shift to an integrated system.

Another software consideration is definition of common languages or generation tools to create applications. Legacy codes have been replaced by modern open systems support languages, such as C and C++. Some companies have benefited from conversion programs that transform legacy applications to modern software languages. More advanced languages, which can reduce the problem of creating common applications across an open system, are also available. Much of the integration burden can be shifted to development tools based on modern languages. This enables programmers to reengineer older applications on the open network without the extensive difficulties in managing implementation differences.

As the shift in applications occurs for the integration process, it is important to remember that long-term objectives call for improved features, such as portability and scalability, in applications. Portability provides the flexibility to shift applications across different levels of granular hardware and operating systems. Portability is an asset in implementing long-term integration goals. Scalability permits the use of identical applications across different-size computers in the network.

Communications, a pivotal technology to successful integration, is the heart of open network connections. Communications standards have been defined with clean layers, which permit mapping between existing protocols and standard approaches. The lowest layers define hardware connections between workstations and other processors attached to the network. It is possible to use the same hardware connections for many different software protocols. It is also possible to retain the same physical attachment cards while shifting to integrated systems.

Each layer in the communications system brings a higher level of system integration and the ability to reach complete interaction between programs. Middle layers assure the connection between similar levels of the network. At the highest or application layer, peer-to-peer communications is achieved, which permits operational programs to communicate on the network. Large amounts of data can be shipped across the network.

Another important element in the complete integration process is the database. Local and remote data must be integrated into the existing networks. Since open databases are complex combinations of compound data, this integration process will begin with the simple connection between textual systems. Legacy databases often do not support compound information. The integration scenarios define connections between databases on different-size computers. As discussed in Chapter 7, many software packages available on modern servers provide code that enables easier connections between different elements of the network.

Database conversion often begins with the simple mapping of data between different systems. This can involve the transformation of data where there is a mismatch between different data formats. More importantly, modern relational data may have to communicate with older hierarchical or network database systems. Conversion packages, which perform both high-level protocol and data translations, are available for most open systems. Simple file transfer can be achieved on most open systems with a minimum of effort. File transfer programs move the data from applications on local servers to archive files in large mainframes. Simplified access is possible as the transfers are completed.

Another basic element that must be considered in the integration process is usability packages. Sufficient advances are occurring in the human interaction code with the system to guarantee that an open systems approach will be different from the customary approaches to end users. Features such as ease of learning facilitate the shift to open systems solutions. The use of commands, menus, and icons has increased the flexibility of shifting people to multiple processors within the network. Advances in user interfaces that use 3-D graphics will change the support equations for the network.

The effective integration of the new system in the management control network for the system is an area of interest in many companies. As functional capability is expanded in the open systems definition, the integrated subsystems must provide sufficient management control code to facilitate embedding the pieces within the system. Network management protocols support the monitoring and recording of events that affect systems performance and reliability. Autonomous collectors augment the collection process, as remote nodes are blended into a complete system management process.

The identified technical areas represent the basic support level needed to achieve integration with the existing system. Legacy code represents a valuable asset, which must be included in the long-term plans for open systems introductions. Legacy code also represents a challenge to implementors, since new systems, which conform to standards, must be connected to this older code. A number of approaches have proved successful in making the transition to open systems by modifying the above technical control points. Each of these points provides increasing levels of integration.

Although there are increasing numbers of products that aid in moving to open systems, the user will still find a challenge in determining which tools are most effective for a specific installation. Products are defined to work well with specific software systems to standard interfaces. The increasing firmness of the standards is an incentive for other vendors to produce meaningful application products to assist integration.

A careful plan, which includes the technologies discussed above, will facilitate integration. These plans depend on an understanding of and definition for attachment of system functions, user interfaces, communications, and data routines. Integration will depend on the effective movement of these technologies.

A definition of the technical direction for future work assists the integrators by predefining the potential problem areas. Integration teams benefit by considering future directions into the total roadmap for the system development. The step functions defined in this section will facilitate the actual implementation of a complete system.

13.5 MAKING INTEGRATION WORK

Once an integration strategy and architecture are completed, a working integration plan should be prepared. This plan reflects the technical direction and the available people resources that can be applied to the process. Companies are pursuing active search programs for individuals with experience in integration skills. Talented programmers, who can span both open systems and the existing environments, will be necessary to complete the integration process. The author was able to create an effective integration team from highly skilled and motivated field engineering personnel. This group could react to problems as well as build scaffold software, which replaced missing functions.

It is possible to find external integration specialists, who understand open systems well enough to assist in both the planning and execution of an integrated solution. Many companies that have been successful in integration have extended the work scope of their internal groups to accept outside contracts. Traditional consulting companies have recognized the value of integration as a business and have established their own specialists to aid in the planning and execution of integration efforts. Computer vendors have also created their own specialists to define the detail bridges between their specialized hardware and software and existing systems.

A tactical plan, which details the integration steps, should be prepared. The tactical plan outlines the steps necessary to complete the proposed integration. The plan details the actual ordering of necessary wiring and attachment devices. It lays out the step functions necessary for integrating software and the order of integration. Tactical plans include manpower assignments as well as timelines for the completion of different work items. The tactical plan will define the details of special software, which must be written to provide the glue for the system. Some code can be purchased, but a good deal of the code may have to be prepared within the organization doing the integration process. Connection software will require in-depth knowledge of the connected parts—both the base system and the new open system that will be linked with the base system.

As integration progresses, specific pieces of the system are brought into execution as prototype systems. These systems are tested and verified and then released for broader system support. The tested products provide the base on which to build the rest of the system.

Successful integration begins with a connection strategy for existing systems into the open systems environment. Adoption of bridges or routers to help perform the connections will assist the total effort in completing the integration. Connections will be built between different parts of the system in a way that makes the system appear as a single entity. At the highest level, the system dialogs will be connected, giving the user community an appearance of a singular system. Interfaces will work across multiple processes.

Automation must be thoroughly tested before it can be brought into final production. Testing begins with individual units and proceeds to the integrated whole. As each new software program is connected, it must be checked against existing support already on the system. The physical integration process usually starts with a kernel of important functions and expands to less important functions over time.

The final test of integration is performed using a completed automation product set. In this model, product parts for testing would be designed on individual personal workstations. The integration test would measure interactions between different workstations during design. At stage two, the parts are integrated into a complete product on the department computer. Stage two tests the integration process. At stage three, there is a prototype test correlated to earlier simulation runs through the computer. The final test will check information flow to corporate computers representing product status as well as archived databases.

During the execution phase, it is necessary to reassess progress and assure the organization that there is no breaking of the traditional stress points. Constant monitoring should be done on the operation systems to ensure that they are continuing to function without major disruption.

13.6 CONSIDERATIONS

Many companies introducing open systems have experienced the frustration of integrating the system with their current environment. Retaining the value of their legacy systems while introducing new systems represents a challenge. Each is trying integration approaches that combine the best cases in the literature with the systems that meet their needs. Many vendors claim "integrated" solutions, but few have created processes that can guarantee effective integration for multiple companies.

An integration approach should adopt a holistic strategy. Mapping the total environment will enable the system integrator to identify major areas of problems. The integration map gives management a perspective on the levels of progress that have been made.

Horizontal organizational structures will be helpful, as coordinating units become involved in defining different pieces of the integration puzzle. Informal organization helps, but it will be necessary to establish formal procedures, which include goal-setting and recognition, for the accomplishment of specific tasks.

Open systems integration will depend on the use of skilled people. Systems thinking is an inherent characteristic of the team that is put together to perform the integration. This system thinking should consider business as well as technical implications of the new support. Full recognition of payback will come, as open systems are folded closely into the business environment.

The organization is rebuilding itself, as a new major function such as open systems is introduced. Although there is a high expectation of cost savings, it should be recognized that there is an initial surge of new costs to handle conversions and connections to the new systems. Since we are looking for a modernization of the organization, there will be management costs as well.

Many traditional vendors that have specialized in hardware development will have an increasingly difficult time adjusting to an environment in which the users are looking for assistance with complex systems. Many companies will not manage the transition and will suffer a loss of business.

Other companies will acquire integration companies to assist in their move to the new world of computing. The large number of mergers, consolidations, and joint ventures within the telecommunications, entertainment, and information systems industries—all under the umbrella of "getting ready for the Information Superhighway"—is indicative of the realization that stagnation is likely to produce disastrous results.

A fully integrated system can only be verified by the end users. The correctly integrated system will combine the older system with a clearly running open systems environment. External consultants have helped in a number of integration efforts, but the consultant must have an understanding of the specific needs of the business.

13.7 REFERENCES

General Accounting Office. *Meeting The Government's Technology Challenge.* Washington, DC: February 1990, GAO/IMTEC-9-23, p. 4.

Simon, Alan. *Network Re-engineering: Foundations of Enterprise Computing.* Boston: AP Professional, 1994.

Toffler, Alvin. *The Third Wave.* New York: William Morrow and Company, 1980, pp. 76–80.

14

Building for Continual Improvement

The past 40+ years of computing have proven to be dramatic in their ongoing change. Yet, many companies have been able to stabilize operations using either mainframe or minicomputer technology, with software based on these computers. We have seen how technology advances have provided the foundations to build new open systems solutions that can augment existing systems. Many legacy systems will eventually be replaced by open systems, as users understand the computing alternatives that provide the highest benefit to the business. The selection of new alternatives creates unique opportunities and challenges for those implementing the new solutions.

The acceptance of open computing ensures increasing power on desktop computers, which is further augmented by access to servers. Servers provide expanded function, data, and I/O services at a local level. All these computing units are melded into systems that can include remote units connected through radio or telephone links to the system. Advances in technology promise further progress to anywhere and anytime computing.

Based on developments in laboratories, we can expect accelerating change in hardware technology during the next decade. There will be an acceptance of modular systems, which use the same building blocks to create multiple system configurations. This modularity will extend beyond the use of electronic chips and disks to include other parts used in operational systems. Plans for open systems should reflect the continued growth in granularity and the widespread use of desktop solutions, which can interact with large-capacity servers. As companies build open systems, increased attention must be paid to creating an environment conducive to positive change. This environment will provide growth platforms for creative employees.

Open systems acceptance challenges the development of people skills to create a team adaptable to change. Many tasks, which were customarily driven by information systems groups, will shift to using departments or automated programs. IS people will learn new skills, as key employees recognize the need of acquiring marketable skills. People communications will be just as important, as traditional technical management must participate in the groupware environment.

IS managers must develop closer relationships with the user departments to reflect the shifting emphasis on computing control. Old motivational skills will be replaced with new skills, which recognize the power of individual workers to effect change in open systems. Creativity must be fostered, or creative people will move to working environments that challenge their minds. The shifting groupware emphasis will provide challenges to the designers to define effective connection techniques that promote people interactions. Knowledge of older systems can be very valuable in integrating these new technologies.

Once established, teams must be provided with tools that facilitate their active participation with the systems supporting them. Workstations and open systems are important development and operational tools for the team members. The team should be augmented by an organization that accepts open systems and a user community that can use the new tools. Subsequent change for the management and user community should be transparent, as the system protects the user from too much involvement with system functions.

Although small changes can happen rapidly, complex changes, such as full implementation of open systems, will probably occur more slowly than projected by the enthusiasts. Computer history has demonstrated that many complex solutions have taken decades to reach full acceptance. Object programming, for instance, was well known to system designers in 1970, but it is just now beginning to achieve a wide level of acceptance, as the hardware performance reaches a point to fully support it. Relational databases took about 15 years to move from their initial introduction to implementation across a wide range of processors. IBM's System Network Architecture was introduced in the early 1970s and did not achieve wide acceptance until the early 1980s. We can expect many complex solutions to await sufficient tools before they are fully accepted. Open systems, client/server computing, enterprise computing . . . all of these areas have had their respective share of problems during the past four to five years, yet all are valid "movements," which will continue to grow in significance.

The demand for industry standards has been very strong, but in the final analysis, standards are determined by the products that are accepted for full use. Standards groups and consortia guide the standards, but user acceptance is the ultimate criterion of support. Standards groups have a number of advanced standards efforts underway to match the advances in technology. These include the definitions of distributed computing, which address the needs of client/server implementors, users, and administrators. Objects are being accepted as essential to the growth of future systems. The goals of this standard are to support the use and maintenance of technologies that facilitate simplified communications between programs.

Shifts are occurring in the technology and business environments that guarantee constant change in the solutions applied to run a business. Market forces are also shifting the major suppliers of computing and communications technology from traditional vendors to fast-moving companies. Even traditional management thinking is changing, reflecting a shift in business and competitive positioning around the world.

14.1 BUILDING FOR FUTURE GROWTH

The daily operation and administration of large complex networks spanning global enterprises require unique capabilities not typically found on central processors. Synchronization of updates and the interaction between updates and existing code cause a strain on operations. Preferably, new tools can provide cross-system coordination between different parts of the open system and simplify the entire operations process.

Unscheduled events often affect global operations. The robust open system will be designed to handle potential failures in the system or in the political structure at the heart of the business. Additional checks within the network will balance the system across processors. Scheduled events must be synchronized across distributed open systems. An automated technique, which would permit the system to reflect different versions of hardware and software, must be identified.

Technology provides the capability of building modern systems with hooks for growth. By accepting and using open standards across the enterprise, a platform can be established to create new developments. Fortunately, most standards groups have been sensitive to the needs of innovation and have shifted definitions to reflect growing technology breakthroughs. It is possible to create an open system design that provides for significant growth.

14.2 TECHNOLOGY DIRECTIONS

Discontinuities in technology will continue to test management skills. At a high level, certain technologies will appear beneficial to the corporation, but closer study will question their value to the integrated system. An examination of trends can help balance probable technology breakthroughs from others that are more hype than reality. New technologies often cause restructuring in existing applications to interact with new support, and the integration factor must be part of the total equation. Old technologies have a threshold that makes their retention more expensive than adopting a newer approach.

UNIX is popular and important in open systems. It has served as the base on which to build and define open systems applications, and it is the only system that has a span of hardware platforms. UNIX also has limitations—a fact that has caused many to look for its successor. A number of candidates that capture the concepts and interfaces of the original system, while expanding them to reflect modern computing paradigms, have been proposed. Many features included in advanced system design can be introduced in these alternative directions.

Modern operating systems must run legacy code that supports existing applications. These systems must demonstrate a clear growth path from existing designs to future technology. Advances in distributed systems, parallelism, object programming, and advanced microkernels will support future open systems. Developers have been searching for alternative designs that support advanced computing algorithms while retaining older interfaces.

A number of post-UNIX experimental designs were created to provide a base for the advances in hardware and software (Cook, 1991). Advanced microkernels, which are stripped-down kernels with only primary services, have been incorporated into many new systems. The microkernel is modular; it is different from the original kernel, which has grown very large. These experimental designs include MACH, which was funded by the *Defense Advanced Research Projects Agency* (DARPA) at Carnegie Mellon University. MACH was developed at Carnegie Mellon under contract from DARPA. It is a part of the OSF/1 definition. Although the system uses many UNIX paradigms, it is not strictly UNIX. It has three advantages over UNIX: multithreading, interprocess communications, and virtual memory. Interprocess communications and windowing systems are ideally suited for client/server systems. Work will continue in this realm, as well as throughout the industry and university research communities, and, given the emphasis on open systems, it is inevitable that most results will have an "open flavor" to a large degree.

Further advances in software technology are changing the characteristics of open systems. Increasingly, the layers above the operating system are as important to the definitions of the new environments as the operating system. Growing emphasis on providing access to different services from simpler user interfaces has opened the door to advances in user technology.

At the beginning of the 1990s, the prevalent philosophy was that this would be a decade that would enable the increased power of the networks to be used fully. Partially due to economy-induced factors, such as budget cutting and personnel downsizing during this past recession, many corporate efforts to implement open systems technology were "back-burnered" for a while. Increases in capital spending, as the U.S. economic recovery gathered steam through 1993 and into 1994, however, have brought about a rebirth of many of these efforts to widely implement network computing for mission-critical applications.

Advances in graphical user interfaces are being seen throughout the open systems community. It is expected that the initial uses of visualization for scientific and engineering applications will be expanded to provide widespread use of enhanced 3-D imaging for commercial applications.

With hardware performance continuing to improve, we can expect that additional user interfaces will use parallel computing and high-powered computing using new protocols. Artificial reality will become more common, as the performance of workstations and their attached servers exceeds the capability of people to interact effectively with the computer. Parallel computing has created a new challenge for the designers of open systems. Few languages available today provide a sufficient base for the end user to feel comfortable with the system. Advances in organizations such as MCC in Austin, Texas, give hope that there will be development of languages that will facilitate access to these important processors.

14.3 WORKPLACE DIRECTIONS

Many promised changes in the workplace have been disappointing. Some reports have questioned the productive value of information technology, but many companies would not be able to complete their business without computers. Some companies have built their business around information technology and have benefited greatly from the constant use of this technology.

The largest measured benefit can be derived by companies that have reassessed their business to reflect the changes in technology. Additional demands will be to replace existing processes with those that affect the value of the company. Transformation and reengineering are significant steps management must take to gain full advantage from open technology.

In the early 1980s, there were expectations that work would shift to electronic cottages and telecommuting (Toffler, 1980). Many executives interviewed by Toffler were quoted as believing that technology existed in 1980 to reach electronic cottage computing. The belief was that large corporations would increasingly shift work away from central processing environments to cottages, where families could be together during the workday. Certainly, sufficient technology existed in 1980 and subsequent years to shift away from centralized locations for work, but the expected transformations have not occurred in large numbers. There has been some adoption of electronic cottages by entrepreneurs and small companies. The majority of large businesses still rely on systems in central working environments, where people can assist in the installation and support processes. Even workers who require little face-to-face contacts are still focused in large offices.

Since 1980, further advances in technology have aided the movement toward electronic cottages. The introduction of open systems provides a new base of optimism. Many problems that were not completely solved in the 1980s have been corrected through open design. Modern user interfaces are run directly on workstations, and the systems can be remotely serviced across existing networks. Installation of systems is simpler in a distributed environment with greater software capability. Additional capability in database and communications permit a wider acceptance of working off premises. Most important, sufficient advances have been made in security to permit remote computing.

Many companies have benefited from pluggable solutions, which can be applied in different geographic areas. Flexibility is achieved when different vendor hardware can be applied to an application and brought into production in a relatively short time frame. Access to application rightsizing will assist the different companies in defining solutions that can work in different-size offices and different geographic locations.

Crumbling cities, heavy traffic, and the desire for quality of life will continue to drive workers to seek alternatives to commuting. The reduction in skilled employees will serve as an incentive for business to retain the best skills, if only for a few hours of working remotely. The cottage industry that works today for some professions will broaden if business and government leaders can reach a consensus about its value to individuals and to business.

14.4 SHIFTING MARKET FORCES

Rapidly shifting market forces have affected the way computers are sold, installed, and used. Open systems provide a powerful tool to reshape markets that depend on technical currency for leadership. Design can be accomplished on simple open systems configurations, including workstations and servers. This simplicity of offerings provides a rapid response capability to market forces and a technique for introducing products faster and of higher quality. The decreased time to market for new products is an advantage. Integrated order, design, and manufacturing systems provide a capability to respond rapidly to shifting needs of customers.

The introduction rates of technology also affect the acceptance rates of open systems. As costs have tumbled relative to other forms of computing, open systems are a more attractive alternative to central processing solutions. The introduction of cellular processing, which enables people to connect to a network from any location, has provided a new tool to field personnel. Sales or service staff can connect to central design or marketing databases to determine the latest product information. Pen-based computing enables sales people to transmit the order directly across the radio connection and provide timely deliveries.

Secure mainframe markets are eroding, as companies recognize the value of alternative approaches to data processing. Increasing use of servers has provided a basis for applications that are independent of traditional mainframe approaches. Technology advances challenge each level of computing to adapt or go out of business. Today's workstations and servers will be challenged by new generations of devices, which use parallel processing or create an object environment for end users.

The sale of open systems is made more complex by the requirement to integrate the solution into the existing network environment. Simple computer stores must find people skilled in integration or face the possibility of lost business opportunities. Return on investment will make the competitive posture more difficult, as margins have continued to fall and retailers must depend on value-added services.

Open systems have created changes in the sales force. They are no longer limited to offering only one company's hardware but provide mixed-vendor solutions.

Companies can begin to use an entire repertoire of different hardware solutions to meet the customer's needs. The best hardware can interact with the best software, depending on the specific needs of the end users. This has resulted in strange alliances, which can bring together the talents of former competitors to complete an open systems solution.

14.5 WORLD BUSINESS FORCES

Business forces affecting open systems have shifted from a domestic to a global environment (Davis and Davidson, 1991). Vendors and users alike are finding that competition is a worldwide phenomenon, as suppliers are emerging in many countries. Product designers are interacting directly with manufacturers to create new businesses in emerging countries. The entry cost into some aspects of the computer business is relatively low, which has an appeal to countries with limited treasuries. Skills to implement effective open systems on a moderate scale can be created in most countries, making the acceptance of the technology appealing as a national strategy.

Acceptance for the components of open systems has been almost universal, as different countries have begun building their solutions on open hardware and software. Local workstations have been adopted to UNIX interfaces as more companies are becoming competitive in the marketplace. Wide acceptance of such common chips as the SPARC has made solutions more universal.

User interface advances have contributed to the ability to have developers and users reside in different countries. Advances in input devices have been driven partially by the complexities of languages. Recognition devices are strong in countries where typical keyboards represent a complex input medium. Output devices capable of accurately representing complex languages are also excellent at reproducing images. The introduction of rapid communications has made interaction with other countries simpler and relatively free from error. Using standard interfaces, it is as simple to communicate across the ocean as it is across the continent.

Reduction in technology costs permits low-cost introduction of open systems in new countries, without the overhead of legacy systems. Increasingly, companies in emerging countries gain a leverage from the lack of an overhead from established systems. The continued decline in technology costs will provide an incentive for developing countries to compete favorably with companies in established markets. Open systems solutions provide unique ability in a global market to provide support for specific national requirements. Language and currency support are the first priorities.

14.6 ADVANTAGES OF OPEN SYSTEMS

A growing number of major corporations have already accepted implementations using open systems. Companies with critical applications, such as process monitoring and intensive care units, have shifted to open systems. Other companies are sending executives and technical personnel to learn more about the benefits and to adopt an open direction over the next few years. There will be a product and skill mismatch between the vision and reality of implementations until massive training is completed. Much of this mismatch will be found in the lack of a clear technique in existing processes to integrate the system. Integration skill will be an important asset during the next decade.

Open systems will be the place of work for many people by the end of the decade. Leading-edge companies have already begun to regard the network as the control point for their companies (Malone and Rockart, 1991), and other companies will shortly follow their lead. Although open systems installations will happen more slowly than enthusiasts believe, they will become important working environments for many working professionals.

A number of companies have identified significant gains by introducing open systems. The first gain is the choice of multiple vendors, which helps reach the best solution at the lowest costs. The flexibility and scalability enable simple designs to be propagated throughout the enterprise. Many companies find alternatives remove the need to provide badly needed overhauls for existing systems. Since the technology brings the solutions close to the source of the problem, there is a direct gain in achieving this proximity to the problem location. Compute power resides throughout the network, providing a natural redundancy and fault tolerance. Central failure no longer stops the organizations, since local operations can continue unchanged.

14.7 CONSIDERATIONS

Some of today's legacy software will eventually be supplanted with code developed for client/server environments—how much is still uncertain and is subject to factors such as the maturity of standards and technology, corporate and organizational commitments to open technology, and so on. Until legacy software is replaced in any organization, open systems must communicate with existing systems and use the rich legacy code . . . the principles of enterprise integration (Simon, 1994).

Clients will use familiar operating systems, but these will gradually be replaced with modern systems that use objects, networks, and advanced graphics. These same operating systems will expand distributed functions using 64-bit addressing on newer hardware. Increased balancing will be performed through the use of expert systems, which can provide embedded rules for open systems operations. Advanced designs, such as the knowledge navigator, will depend on rules-based searches to find data.

Modern competition will stimulate further introductions in the technology, which will provide business leverage. Initial steps will continue to use evolutionary steps to the new technology, but leading businesses will transform their mode of doing business to further capitalize on the technology. These companies will gain the highest leverage in competitive situations. An identification of mature technology will stimulate growth in the effective use of open systems.

In spite of these shortcomings, we can expect technology to improve in price and performance through the next decade. Faster development of modern chip technology will stimulate unexpected applications of hardware and software and raise challenges for companies to remain competitive. The microprocessor will remain the largest influence in computing throughout the strategic period, as it is used as a building block for workstations, servers, and even multiple parallel processors.

Client/server technology will continue to grow in acceptance, resulting in a modification of traditional models of successful business computing. Reduced cost of computing and communications will shift computing away from shared logic environments to a shared and cascading resource. By the middle of the decade, client/server computing will be installed in major companies. Companies will adopt powerful parallel processors as alternate storage units. Control issues will focus on the enterprise networks.

Communications technology has been pivotal to the development of open systems. Continued advances in this technology will enhance the capability of anyplace, anytime computing. Advances in communications technology promise further use of optical alternatives, such as FDDI LANs. Additional breakthroughs are expected in SONET, *Asynchronous Transfer Mode* (ATM), *Switched Multi-megabit Data Service* (SMDS), and Gigabit Networking.

Although some precision can be reached in predicting the growth and application of existing technology, there is no guarantee when new products will revolutionize open systems further. The PC was not predicted to be the phenomenon it was in the early 1980s, yet it is inarguable that the PC has revolutionized not only the information systems realm but business in general.

Product life cycles have been significantly reduced through the use of technology. It does not take very long for a competitor to reengineer the business we have developed and produce a quality product. Each manager must learn to use the technology to ensure a competitive posture in a dynamic market. An aging cycle is also apparent for existing paradigms, which have been the primary vehicles in developing open systems. Systems such as UNIX can be replaced, as new solutions overcome the difficulties in the use and support of the total system. It is well to refreeze a process that provides access to open solutions. The full use of open systems technology can result in significant transformation of business processes. Global competition is moving to the adoption of this technology. With a combination of a technology push and a competitive pull, we can expect a continuous shift from central processing to open systems. Open systems are also affordable in all the countries of the world; proven solutions that permit language adaptability can be shifted to emerging societies, which can benefit from this technology. The use of widespread technology can presage a shift in government paradigms.

For a long time, futurists have been discussing the advent of the technology cottage or electronic work from the home. The introduction of anywhere, anytime, anyplace attachments to open systems moves us closer to the reality of this work environment. The technical pieces, which can facilitate this working environment, are in place. The cultural acceptance by business should be advanced by the transformation process.

Industry standards groups must continually consider the future to ensure that they are providing state-of-the-art definitions. Solving last year's problems will not help the advance of computing. Companies are already experimenting with leading-edge technology, which will affect their overall directions of the business, and leading companies will implement those technologies in order to retain their competitive edge.

Like the yachts in the America's Cup races, the definitions will determine the rules for the race. The winners will be those companies that can transform their business and use technology to continually lead the other racers.

14.8 REFERENCES

Cook, Rick. "An Operating System Mores." *CommUNIXations*, 1991, pp. 15–20.

Davis, Stan, and Bill Davidson. *2020 Vision: Transform Your Business Today to Succeed in Tomorrow's Economy*. New York: Simon and Schuster, 1991.

Malone, Thomas W., and John F. Rockart. "Computers, Networks, and the Corporation." *Scientific American*, vol. 265, no. 3, September 1991, pp. 128–136.

Simon, Alan. *Network Re-engineering: Foundations of Enterprise Computing*. Boston: AP Professional, 1994.

Toffler, Alvin. *The Third Wave*. New York: William Morrow and Company, 1980, pp. 210–223.

Index